# HARMONIZING FOREIGN POLICY

*To my son, M. Tarık*

# Harmonizing Foreign Policy
## Turkey, the EU and the Middle East

MESUT ÖZCAN
*Istanbul Commerce University, Turkey*

ASHGATE

Published by
Ashgate Publishing Limited
Gower House
Croft Road
Aldershot
Hampshire GU11 3HR
England

Ashgate Publishing Company
Suite 420
101 Cherry Street
Burlington, VT 05401-4405
USA

Ashgate website: http://www.ashgate.com

**British Library Cataloguing in Publication Data**
Ozcan, Mesut
  Harmonizing foreign policy : Turkey, the EU and the Middle
  East
  1. European Union - Turkey 2. Turkey - Foreign relations -
  21st century 3. Turkey - Foreign relations - Middle East
  4. Turkey - Foreign relations - European Union countries
  5. Middle East - Foreign relations - Turkey 6. European
  Union countries - Foreign relations - Turkey
  I. Title
  327.5'61'056

**Library of Congress Cataloging-in-Publication Data**
Ozcan, Mesut
  Harmonizing foreign policy : Turkey, the EU and the Middle East / by Mesut Ozcan.
    p. cm.
  Includes bibliographical references and index.
  ISBN 978-0-7546-7370-5
  1.  Turkey--Foreign relations--21st century. 2.  Turkey--Foreign relations--Middle East. 3. Middle East--Foreign relations--Turkey.  I. Title.

DR477.O93 2008
327.561056--dc22
                                                                2007046436

ISBN: 978 0 7546 7370 5

Printed and bound in Great Britain by TJ International Ltd, Padstow, Cornwall.

90 0899978 7

# Contents

*Preface*                                                                      *vii*
*Acknowledgements*                                                              *xi*
*List of Abbreviations*                                                         *xiii*

**Introduction**                                                               **1**

1   **Theories of Integration**                                                **3**
    The Need to Theorize                                                       3
    Federalism                                                                 5
    Neo-functionalism                                                          7
    Intergovernmentalism                                                       10
    New Approaches in Integration                                              12

2   **Europeanization of the Foreign Policy**                                  **21**
    Definition of the Concept of Europeanization                              21
    A New Analytical Framework of Foreign Policy                              25
    Increasing Cooperation among the Member States                            27
    Europeanization in Candidate Countries                                    29
    The Results of the Europeanization                                        32

3   **European Integration and the CFSP**                                      **43**
    The Development of the CFSP                                               44
    Success-Failure of the CFSP                                               51
    The Effects of Global Conditions on the CFSP                             55

4   **The Middle East Policy of the European Union**                           **59**
    The EU's Interest in the Middle East                                      60
    The Palestinian-Israeli Peace Process and the European Union             62
    Mediterranean Partnership                                                 65
    The Second Intifada                                                       67
    9/11 and its Aftermath                                                    68
    Relations with the Gulf Countries                                        69
    The EU's Policy on Iraq and Changing Priorities of the
    Member States                                                             71
    Harmony between the Policies of Turkey and the EU                         75

5    **The Making of Turkish Foreign Policy**                                    **81**
     Basic Factors and Formation of the Foreign Policy                           81
     Identity in Turkish Foreign Policy                                          84
     Periodization of Turkish Foreign Policy According to
     Influential Factors                                                         91

6    **Turkish Foreign Policy towards the Middle East until the end**
     **of the Cold War**                                                         **107**
     The Cold War and Security-Based Foreign Policy: 1945–1964                   108
     Diversification of Foreign Policy: 1964–1980                                111
     Economic Factors and the Search for a Balanced Policy:1980–1990             112
     The End of the Cold War and Shifts in Foreign Policy                        114

7    **Turkish Foreign Policy towards the Middle East since the**
     **Cold War Era**                                                            **115**
     TFP towards the Middle East in the 1990s                                    115
     Relations with Syria                                                        116
     Relations with Iran                                                         118
     Relations with Israel and Palestine                                         119
     Relations with Iraq                                                         130

8    **The Europeanization of Turkish Foreign Policy**                           **147**
     Foreign Policy Change                                                       147
     The Foreign Policy Process                                                  153
     Foreign Policy Actions                                                      157
     Other Schemes of Europeanization and Turkish Foreign Policy                 161
     Europeanization in Candidate Countries                                      162

**Conclusion**                                                                   **165**

*Bibliography*                                                                   *179*
*Index*                                                                          *191*

# Preface

This book analyzes Turkish foreign policy towards the Middle East and the changes in this policy as a result of the European Union (EU) candidature and the harmony and/or disharmony between the policies of Turkey and the EU towards the region. The change in the foreign policy of Turkey towards the Middle East in the post-Cold War era is a highly debated issue in academic circles. I believe that the year 1999 represents a turning point in the post-Cold War era for the Turkish foreign policy towards the region. There is a change in the foreign policy of Turkey towards the Middle East after that year and I look at the impact of the EU candidature on the changes in the policy towards the region. I argue that the decrease in security threats against Turkey and the candidature of the country to the EU resulted in a change in the foreign policy towards the region and the cases of Iraq and Palestinian-Israeli conflicts are two important issues with which this change can be grasped. The changes in this period made the policies of Turkey and the EU towards these two cases closer to each other.

Turkey's candidature to the EU and the decline of the security threats against the country coincided with the increasing efforts on the side of the EU to have a more common foreign policy. And the Middle East as a neighbouring region to the Union has always been on the agenda of the EU in these attempts. Beside the changes in the Turkish foreign policy towards the Middle East, I also investigate the place of Turkey in the Middle East policy of the EU since this issue is highly debated in terms of the candidature of the country to the EU and the positive and negative sides of the possible membership of Turkey.

I limit my analysis of the changes in the foreign policy towards the Middle East after the EU candidature and the place of Turkey in the EU's Middle East policy to two cases: The Palestinian-Israeli conflict and Iraq. The reason for this choice is two-fold: Both of these cases are dynamic issues of conflict in the region and are high on the agenda of Turkey in terms of its policies towards the region. Second, it is more realistic to analyze the policy of the EU towards the region with these two cases, with similarities and differences.

In order to analyze this title in detail, I focus on the one hand on issues related with the EU integration and formation of a common foreign policy in general and a common policy towards the Middle East in particular. On the other hand, I examine the decision making in the Turkish foreign policy and the foreign policy of Turkey towards the Middle East in a historical perspective before and after the EU candidature. In relation to that, this dissertation is organized into two main sections.

After an introduction, the first part focuses on the side of the EU with chapters on the theories of integration and international relations, the concept of Europeanization and the changes in the foreign policies of member states and candidates, the development of the Common Foreign and Security Policy (CFSP) of the EU and the European Union's Middle East Policy. In the first chapter, first I will give a theoretical framework for the analysis of European integration. Here the explanatory capacities of different theoretical approaches are analyzed along with the developments in the direction of European integration. I think that this theoretical framework is necessary to explain the course and direction of the European integration as well as to understand what kind of an institution the EU is. I approach these theories from the point of analysis of European foreign policy in addition to understanding the nature of the EU.

Chapter 2 is about the concept of Europeanization, the changes in the member states and candidates of the EU, especially in terms of foreign policy, as a result of the EU agenda. This part provides a theoretical analysis of the changes in the making and implementation of foreign policy in EU members and candidates. Several theoretical approaches and different examples from European countries are covered in this part. Within different definitions of the term, in this chapter, instead of dealing with the institutionalization at the EU level, I focus on the changes in the member states and candidates. My analysis is confined to the changes in the area of foreign policy, including decision making, and the content of the policy and policy actions. These two chapters constitute the base for the analysis of the changes in the Turkish foreign policy as a result of EU candidature.

Chapter 3 is about the developments in the formation of a common foreign and security policy within the EU. In this part, I briefly cover the transformation of the European Union from its establishment until today and the emergence of the need to construct a common foreign and security policy. In this respect, my greatest attention is given to the post-Cold War era. Without giving the historical background on this issue, it would be difficult to understand changes in the foreign policies of the member states and candidates and also to analyze the common foreign policy of the EU on some specific areas like that of the Middle East. After providing some basic historical information about the development of the European integration and construction of the CFSP, this chapter discusses the institutionalization of the CFSP. The second part of this chapter analyzes the success and failures of the CFSP from different points of criteria, like the functions of the institutions, the issue of a common identity, financing the common operations, and also the effects of global conditions on the CFSP.

The last chapter of this part on the Middle East policy of the EU discusses the reasons for the interest of the EU in the region, the important aspects of this policy and the successes and failures of the EU's Middle East policy. The Middle East as a region outside Europe has strategic importance for the EU and the first attempts to have a common approach among the member states emerged in relation to the Middle East. The European policy towards the Middle East and especially towards the Palestinian-Israeli conflict constitutes an ideal case for the analysis of the EU's ability to form a common foreign policy. When the EU's or the EU's member countries' policies regarding the Middle East are analyzed, it is seen that the Palestinian-Israeli problem and the developments in Iraq after the Gulf War have been the two most important issues for the foreign policy considerations.

As mentioned, the first part of the study deals with Europe and the EU. After providing a theoretical framework for the analysis of European integration, the developments in this direction, the impact of the EU candidature on the foreign policies of nation states, the need to have a common foreign and security policy is covered within different chapters. At the end of this part, the policy of the EU on the Middle East is analyzed as an example of the common foreign policy of the EU.

The second part of the study deals with Turkey and Turkish foreign policy. This part begins with Chapter 5 on the making of Turkish foreign policy. This chapter presents the theoretical framework and the background in which the foreign policy is made. After discussing the basic factors and historical development of the making of the policy, the impact of the EU candidature on these factors are also investigated at the end of this chapter. In doing this I touch upon the major turning points in the general direction of Turkish foreign policy.

Chapter 5 is followed by a short chapter on the foreign policy of Turkey towards the Middle East, from the establishment of the republic until the end of the Cold War in order to provide a historical background for the analysis of the Turkish foreign policy towards the Middle East. After providing historical background, this chapter goes on with the different periods of Turkish foreign policy towards the region. In this chapter, as in the others, my focus is on Turkish policy towards issues of the Palestinian-Israeli problem and Iraq. This part is useful since it helps to locate the reasons for the differences between several periods in Turkey's policy towards the region and also the peculiarities of the post-Cold War period.

Chapter 7 is on the Turkish foreign policy towards the Middle East since the post-Cold War era until 1999 and changes in this policy after 1999 as a result of the EU candidature of Turkey. After discussing basic changes in the Turkish foreign policy towards the region, this chapter gives a quick overview of Turkish policy towards Syria and Iran as two neighbours of Turkey. Then it discusses Turkish policy on two main issues, the focal points of the work: The Palestinian-Israeli conflict and Iraq. In both cases, namely the Palestinian-Israeli conflict and Iraq, I begin by discussing the impact of the Gulf War on Turkish foreign policy on these two issues. The developments in the post-Cold War era and Turkish activism in the region in this period are followed by the changes in the policy of Turkey on these two issues after the EU candidature.

The last chapter is about the application of the theoretical framework of Europeanization, and the impact of EU candidature on the Turkish foreign policy towards the Middle East. After reviewing the different theoretical approaches about Europeanization and the impact of EU candidature and membership on the foreign policies of the countries, I analyze the developments in Turkish foreign policy within several theoretical frameworks. In this respect, the changes in the perceptions of the decision makers in foreign policy, the changes is the process of policy making and the changes in the policy actions are analyzed. Due care is paid to the unique condition of the CFSP within the European integration and to the special case of the candidate countries. I discuss several theoretical approaches and conclude some aspects of these theoretical discussions are valid for Turkey but some others are not. Some of the factors in different theories have more relevance for Turkey but some others have less. By giving several examples in each of the points of analysis, I make some comparisons between other cases of Europeanization and the case of Turkey. These comparisons are made according to several factors like geographical location, the size of the country, the cultural characteristics, and the political and economic background of the country and the tradition of foreign policy.

Mesut Özcan

# Acknowledgements

First of all I would like to thank Prof. Aydın Babuna, from Boğaziçi University, for his continuous support and help during the process of writing this book. Dr. Philip Robins, from University of Oxford, has read and commented on the chapters on Turkish foreign policy. The Social Sciences Library and the Library of St. Antony's College, University of Oxford, provided invaluable materials for me about the theoretical parts on the European integration. I also would like to thank Prof. Ahmet Davutoğlu for his encouragement to work on this topic and his insightful criticisms about the general framework of the book.

Last but not least, I would like to thank my wife Sevinç, for her patience, encouragement and support during the process of writing this book.

# List of Abbreviations

| | |
|---|---|
| ABGS | General Secretariat for the European Union |
| AKP | Justice and Development Party |
| ASAM | Eurasia Strategic Research Centre |
| CFSP | Common Foreign and Security Policy |
| CHP | Republican People's Party |
| CJF | Combined Joint Forces |
| DP | Democrat Party |
| EC | European Community |
| ECO | Economic Cooperation Organization |
| EPC | European Political Cooperation |
| EPRI | Economic Policies Research Institute |
| ESDI | European Security and Defense Identity |
| ESDP | European Security and Defense Policy |
| EU | European Union |
| EUPM | European Union Police Mission |
| FDI | Foreign Direct Investment |
| GAP | Southeast Anatolia Project |
| GCC | Gulf Cooperation Council |
| ISAF | International Security Assistance Force in Afghanistan |
| İKV | Foundation for Economic Development |
| KDP | Kurdistan Democratic Party |
| MFA | Ministry of Foreign Affairs |
| MSP | National Salvation Party |
| MÜSİAD | Association of Independent Businessmen and Industrialists |
| NATO | North Atlantic Treaty Organization |
| NGO | Non-governmental Organization |
| OIC | Organization of Islamic Conference |
| OMC | Open Method of Coordination |
| OSCE | Organization for Security and Cooperation in Europe |
| PLO | Palestinian Liberation Organization |
| PUK | Patriotic Union of Kurdistan |
| SETA | Foundation for Political, Economic and Social Researches |
| TASAM | Turk-Asia Strategic Research Centre |
| TESEV | Turkish Economic and Social Studies Foundation |
| TEU | Treaty on European Union |
| TFP | Turkish Foreign Policy |
| TIKA | Turkish Agency for Cooperation and Development |
| TOBB | Union of Chambers and Commodity Exchanges of Turkey |

| TÜSİAD | Association of Turkish Businessmen and Industrialists |
| UK | United Kingdom |
| UN | United Nations |
| UNIFIL | United Nations Implementation Force in Lebanon |
| USA | United States of America |
| USAK | International Strategic Research Institution |
| USSR | Union of Soviet Socialist Republics |
| WEU | West European Union |
| WMD | Weapons of Mass Destruction |

# Introduction

The changes in foreign and domestic politics, in the domain of jurisdiction and in other parts of the life as a result of the EU candidature are lively topics of debate in Turkey. The domestic support for the candidature of the country to the Union was high when Turkey is declared as candidate in 1999. After several years, however, the public opinion seems divided on this issue. The developments related with Turkish foreign policy and the impact of the EU here were topics of contention. In relation to the EU candidature, the changes in Turkish foreign policy towards Iraq and Cyprus caused a division among the public opinion and also within the academic circles.

The EU candidature of Turkey, however, is not only an issue of domestic debate. This issue is widely discussed in public as well as in academic and bureaucratic circles in Europe and also elsewhere in the world. Arguments in support of the membership of Turkey and against it rose in the Middle East and in the USA also. The developments after 9/11 and the revival of arguments about the clash of civilizations have their repercussions for Turkey's EU candidature and possible membership. The rise of xenophobia and fear of Islam made the place of Turkey in the world politics crucial. The arguments for and against the membership of Turkey to the EU are raised in this atmosphere. Turkey's membership to the Union is presented by some politicians and academics as an answer to the arguments of clash of civilizations in Turkey and abroad. Some conservative circles in Europe, however, opposed to Turkey's membership deriving from the arguments of incompatibility of different cultures and argue that Turkey belongs to another culture. The arguments for and against the membership of Turkey to the EU also contributed to my interest in this topic.

Another reason behind my choice for this topic is to understand the extent of the influence of the EU candidature on the change of Turkish foreign policy towards the Middle East. In several academic researches, the Middle East is mentioned as the region in which Turkey is actively involved in the post-Cold War era. Security concerns dominated Turkey's interest in the region in the 1990s. Turkish foreign policy towards the region changed dramatically after 1999. Two important developments in that year contributed to the change: the decrease of terrorist threat against Turkey after the capture of Öcalan, head of PKK, and the declaration of Turkey as a candidate to the EU. In order to analyze this change within the framework of Europeanization, I reviewed the existing literature on this issue. The EU candidature is a new development for Turkey and the analysis of the changes in foreign policy after this development requires academic interest.

The changes in the Middle East policy of Turkey are recognized by some scholars but I tried to approach this issue from the perspective of the EU candidature. I evaluated the changes not only in TFP but also the developments on the side of the EU to have a common foreign policy and tried to show that Turkish candidature increased the harmony between the foreign policies of Turkey and the EU. In order to do this, I reviewed the theoretical discussions on the integration and international relations theories and the emergence and development of common foreign policy of the EU in general and the EU's Middle East policy in particular. Beside the changes in the TFP towards the Middle East, I investigate also the place of Turkey in the Middle East policy of the EU since this issue is highly debated in terms of the candidature of the country to the EU and the positive and negative sides of the possible membership of Turkey.

   I examined the theoretical frameworks developed to analyze the changes in the foreign policies of the countries after the EU candidature and membership. By comparing the changes in Turkish foreign policy with the changes with some other European countries, I tried to figure out the similarities and differences between Turkey and other countries. I believe that analysis of the changes in TFP in general and towards the Middle East in particular after the EU candidature with such a theoretical framework will contribute to the academic research on this issue in Turkey.

# Chapter 1

# Theories of Integration

## The Need to Theorize

This section analyzes European integration and its effects on the foreign policies of the member countries and the latest enlargement of the European Union in respect to theories of integration. The European integration process has attracted a great deal of attention in the field of international relations. Various theories and conceptual approaches have been applied to the European integration process and to the politics of the European Union. By theorizing, the conditions and structure of the European Union are studied systematically and some predictions about the Union or the constituent parts are made. Chryssochoou argues that the efforts of theorizing about the structure and dynamics, forms and functions of European integration have created a situation in which little remains to be said.[1] According to the same author, this should not lead to theoretical inaction; rather it should result in seeking for the refinement of the old attempts to explain the current and future conditions.

The new theorizing efforts on the European Union are very much dependent on the classical theories of integration. In describing the position of the European integration theories within the social sciences, Puchala argues that integration theory will amount to a rather long but not very prominent footnote in the intellectual history of twentieth century social science.[2]

Manners and Whitman summarize the attempts of theorizing about the EU by different theoretical tools as follows:

> International relations theory is thought of as the domain for thinking about the EU primarily as a form of co-operation among sovereign states where intergovernmental relations remain the most important arena for understanding both the EU and its place in global politics. Comparative politics theory is thought of as the domain for thinking about the EU primarily as a form of political system in which member states participate and where theories of comparative politics have become most important way of understanding both the EU and its place in the global politics. Integration theory was the domain for thinking about the EU as lying somewhere between these two domains of international relations and comparative politics where the process of deepening integration (becoming

---

1   Dimitris N. Chryssochoou, *Theorizing European Integration* (London: Sage, 2001), p. 9.

2   Donald. J. Puchala, "The Integration Theorists and the Study of International Relations," in *The Global Agenda: Issues and Perspectives,* edited by Charles W. Kegley and Eugene R. Wittkopf (New York: Random House, 1984), p. 198.

more like a form of state) and widening integration (to include more members) need to be thought about in dynamic terms.[3]

The existence of different theories about the Union is related very much to the problems with the definition of the nature of the European Union. The EU is neither an international institution nor an ordinary state in conventional terms. In general terms, theories of European integration investigate the changing relationship between the Union's multiple arenas of governance. The nature of sovereignty within the European Union is one of the most contested areas of discussion in the integration theory debate.

These discussions about the nature of sovereignty within the Union also are related very much to the perception of the nature of the Union and the theory applied to explain it. The discussions on the nature of the EU and the sovereignty in it have been criticized by some scholars by narrowly focusing on the formal structures. It is argued that much of the theorizing efforts on European integration have been trapped in the supranational-intergovernmental dichotomy and this has resulted in an "unhelpful focus on the formal characteristics of the actors at the expense of the processes which characterize their interactions."[4] Much of the contemporary theories of integration try to avoid this dilemma and focus on other aspects of the integration.

The continuously changing nature of the EU also makes theorizing difficult and incomplete. The EU is not a full fledged state and may not become one in the future. But it already possesses some state-like characteristics in the conventional sense, such as a common currency, an independent central bank, a single market and an evolving common foreign and security policy. The EU has been conceived by some scholars "as a political system with a network rather than hierarchy of decision making, an expanding membership and agenda, and degrees of boundedness rather than clear cut boundaries."[5] Instead of deciding whether the EU is supranational or international governance, the same authors propose the term "hybrid polity" to define it.[6] Defining the Union as a federal state, confederation of states, a quasi-state, a political community, a partial polity or a partly formed political system is seen as a remedy to finding the most suitable word for the EU. In order to overcome this problem of definition, labelling the European Union as a *sui generis* political phenomenon and offering new conceptual paradigms or *ad hoc* theoretical interpretations is one of the methods employed often. However, this way of scholarly work is criticized by some authors as carrying the risk of complying with undisciplined and often ill-founded formulations.[7] Such a definition may result in perpetuation of the in-between position

---

3   Ian Manners and Richard G. Whitman, "The 'Difference Engine': Constructing and Representing the International Identity of the European Union," *European Journal of Public Policy* 10, no. 3 (June 2003), pp. 392–393.

4   Ann P. Branch and Jacob C. Ohrgaard, "Trapped in the supranational-intergovernmental dichotomy: a response to Stone Sweet and Sandholtz," *Journal of European Public Policy* 6, no. 1 (March 1999), p. 124.

5   Ian Manners and Richard G. Whitman, "The 'Difference Engine': Constructing and Representing the International Identity of the European Union," p. 384.

6   Ibid.

7   Chryssochoou, p. 16.

of the EU in international politics. There is no conceptual consensus among scholars about the ontological conundrum of the EU. The reason for this failure derives from the existence of different polity ideas, different visions of regional political order and contending orientations for the European polity about the conceptualization of the European political entity.[8] In order to make theorizing about the EU easy, it is argued that instead of focusing on the peculiarities of the Union, it might be more profitable to examine those aspects of the EU that are familiar to the existing forms of polity and models of government.[9]

The most common theories applied to the European integration are neo-functionalism and intergovernmentalism. In addition to these, federalism and new theoretical approaches, like multi-level governance and constructivism also are used in the analysis of European integration. The use and explanation capacity of several theories are related directly to the course of European integration and discussions in the field of international relations theory. Different phases in the history of the Union and subsequent theoretical discussions devoted to explain this situation lead to the assumption that the distinct nature of the European Union resembles an asymmetrical and analytically incongruent synthesis of academic disciplines.[10] This ambiguous nature of the EU has provoked various theoretical approaches to analyze several aspects of the European integration process.

In the early years of European integration, neo-functionalist theory was the first to be studied by students of the European Union.[11] From the mid-1960s to the present day, however, intergovernmentalism has been situated at the heart of European integration theory. With the transformation of the European Community into the European Union, there has been a return to neo-functionalism and also to the study of other theoretical approaches, especially reflectivist and structuralist, in explaining the integration process.

## Federalism

The terms federalism and federation and federalism as a theory of government have often been used in describing the European Union. Although different definitions of federalism exist to explain different federal structures in the world, it generally refers to the co-existence of distinct but constitutive units. In a federation sovereignty is divided and shared between a central (federal) government and the constituent (member states) governments and federations are more representative in comparison to the unitary states. The term "federal Europe" broadly refers to the constantly changing EU, but which has its core of basic principles. The practical definition of federal Europe is given as the combination of centralist and decentralist imperatives

---

8   Ibid., p. 23.

9   Dimitris N. Chryssochoou, Michael J. Tsinisizelis, Stelios Stavridis and Kostad Ifantis, *Theory and Reform in the European Union* (Manchester: Manchester University Press, 2003), pp. 5–6.

10   Ibid., p. 7.

11   Carsten Stroby Jensen, "Neo-functionalism", in *European Union Politics*, edited by Michelle Cini (Oxford: Oxford University Press, 2003), p. 80.

that facilitate common solutions to the common problems of the member states and their citizens.[12] Other simple axioms used to define federal Europe are "unity in diversity" and "self rule plus shared rule."

Jean Monnet, one of the founders of the EU, is also considered one of the main advocates of the federalist approach for European integration. He wanted to remove the causes of war from the European scene and to persuade Europeans to channel their conflicts into a form of cooperation that would enable them to achieve their goals by seeking out their common interest. The shocks of nationalism and the terrible effects of the interwar period played an important role in this understanding. Federalism was seen as a remedy for illnesses of the continent. He underlined the interaction between politics and economics as the driving force behind integration. It is argued that Monnet's approach to the building of a federal Europe meant gradually internalizing what were previously the externalities of the state.[13] In this way, the consolidation of the all of the power at the hands of the nation states might be prevented.

Concepts like participation, democracy and liberty also provided an important stimulus effect to federalist theorizing. Federalists argued that the inability of states to provide new means of popular participation and the unprecedented legitimacy crisis had shaken the foundation of their structures and people should look above the nation-states to resolve the acute legitimacy problems.[14] Federalists stressed the representative character of the central institutions in order to convince the European peoples to the merits of federalism as a means of safeguarding their cultural and political traditions.[15]

The essence of Monnet's method for European integration was piecemeal, cumulative integration whereby "political" Europe would be the culminating point of a gradual process and at the end there would be a qualitative change in the constitutional and political relations between states and peoples.[16] He believed that this change would occur when it came to seem natural in the eyes of Europeans. Monnet ignored the realities of organized political power and the fact that the building of a political Europe based on economic performance criteria did not necessarily follow.

The role of the political leadership in furthering the integration has been decisive in the history of the EU. Federalism has been portrayed by its proponents as the only alternative to eliminate the possibility of great wars on the continent of Europe. However, the difficulty lays in convincing the people that they, rather than their governments, must create a political federation.[17] The federalists have been criticized with the argument that they are consciously undermining the necessary gradual nature of integration in order to achieve a rigid constitutional setting.[18] The current

---

12 Michael Burgess, "Federalism and Federation", in *European Union Politics,* edited by Michelle Cini (Oxford: Oxford University Press, 2003), p. 66.

13 Ibid., p. 73.

14 Chryssochoou, pp. 45–6.

15 Ibid.

16 Burgess, p. 74.

17 Chryssochoou, p. 47.

18 Ibid., p. 48.

state of the EU shows that federalism's ultimate goal is not the primary goal for many Europeans and those national governments and their elites are not persuaded by the arguments of federalism.

From a federalist perspective, there should be a balance between the centre and the constituent units. However, the EU still remains at the mercy of intergovernmental bargaining and the current institutional structure within the EU represents an imbalance in favour of the national governments.[19] The EU remains confederal and intergovernmental than federal and the failure of the constitutional treaty process constitutes a setback for a move towards a more federal Europe.

## Neo-functionalism

Neo-functionalism was the first attempt at theorizing a new form of regional integration. The well known theorist of neo-functionalist integration, Ernst Haas, defined integration as a process "whereby political actors in several, distinct national settings are persuaded to shift their loyalties, expectations and political activities to a new centre, whose institutions process and demand jurisdiction over the pre-existing national states."[20] This is a very broad definition and includes several elements like social and political processes. Neo-functionalism focuses on the internal dynamics of a "self regulated pluralistic society" of organized interests, multiple spillovers and patterns of elite socialization.[21] The end product of the integration in the neo-functionalist approach remains open-ended. From the beginning, neo-functionalist writings have argued that the incompleteness of their European integration project would create the need for new central arrangements for a directly elected regional parliament to ensure democratic control over the European political community.[22]

The neo-functionalist theory stresses the role of non-state actors like supranational organizations, interest groups and political parties in the regional integration efforts. The neo-functionalist theory has been pro-integration from the outset and mainly concerned with the process of integration instead of the end results. This theory benefits from three theses in explaining the neo-functionalist integration, namely the spillover thesis, the elite socialization thesis and the supranational interest group thesis.[23] Haas's theory was based on the assumption that cooperation in one policy area would create pressures in a neighbouring area, placing it on the policy agenda and leading to further integration. Another basic characteristic of this theory is its reliance on the role of the societal groups in the process of integration. Although it places importance on groups in the integration process, integration tends to be driven by functional and technocratic needs and consequently this theory often is labelled as

---

19  Burgess, p. 76.

20  Ernst Haas, *The Uniting of Europe: Political, Economic and Social Forces 1950–1957* (Stanford, CA: Stanford University Press, 1958), p. 16, quoted in Antje Wiener and Thomas Diez, *European Integration Theory* (Oxford: Oxford University Press, 2004), p. 2.

21  Chryssochoou, p. 27.

22  Ibid., p. 55.

23  Jensen, p. 81.

an elitist approach.[24] This approach is very popular in Brussels since its technocratic elitism appeals to the EU officials, who naturally see extensive theorizing about the workings of the Community as a confirmation of their historic role as the guardians of integration process.[25] According to this theory, the Commission's role is to act "as the motor of the integration, the source of integrative initiatives and centre for technical expertise for joint projects of supranational character."[26]

As the first theory of European integration, neo-functionalism had wide support in academic circles until end of 1970s. The reasons for the disappearance of the theory from that time onwards were the lack of a solid base for its observations and the stagnation of the European integration and the failure of the predictions for the incremental political integration.[27] The revival of the integration process in the Europe after 1990s led to a revival of neo-functionalist interpretations.

Neo-functionalism's best known concept spillover refers to a process "where political cooperation conducted with a specific goal in mind leads to the formulation of new goals in order to assure the achievement of the original goals."[28] The type of spillover can be analyzed under three headings, namely functional spillover, political spillover and cultivated spillover. Functional spillover generally refers to the increasing integration in the area of economics and common market regulations. Political spillover represents situations where the issues are linked together not because they are functionally related, but for political or ideological reasons. This might be a result of the bargaining process among the members to protect their interests in different policy areas. Cultivated spillover refers the situations in which supranational actors like the Commission try to push forward some policy proposals.

Another thesis of the neo-functionalist theory in explaining the integration is related to elite socialization. The thesis here is that "over time people involved on a regular basis in the supranational policy making will tend to develop European loyalties and preferences."[29] This might be especially true for the Commission officials, since they are expected to uphold the common benefit of the Union instead of their country of origin. The Commission occupies a central position in the scheme of neo-functionalism in the European policy change.

Supranational interest groups also play an important role in the integration process in the neo-functionalist scheme. According to this understanding, organized interest groups are expected to become more European in their outlook and formulate their own interest with the supranational institutions. Neo-functionalists believe that interest groups pressure governments to speed up the integration process.[30] These interest groups may ally themselves with supranational institutions like the European Commission in pursuing their agendas.

---

24  Ibid., p. 82.
25  Chryssochoou, p. 54.
26  Chryssochoou et al, p. 23.
27  Jensen, p. 83.
28  Ibid., p. 84.
29  Ibid., p. 86.
30  Ibid., p. 87.

With the slow pace of integration in Europe in the 1970s and early 1980s, several criticisms against neo-functionalist theory emerged in the area of integration theory. Even theoreticians like Hass criticized some aspects of the neo-functionalist approach. The criticisms against this approach are grouped under three main headings: Elite socialization and supranational loyalties did not occur, the prediction of incremental integration by spillover was not the case in European integration, and the role played by the nation states in European integration were much more important than the role of the supranational organizations.[31] The criticisms against the supranational loyalties of the bureaucrats were based on the argument that interests of civil servants did not become European; they pursued the national interests of different governments. The criticisms against the incremental integration by spillover pointed out the growing interdependence among the nation states in the world and the global context in which the European integration is taking place. These criticisms pay attention to the global conditions that are causing similar effects not only in Europe but also in different parts of the world. The third criticism stressed the importance of the autonomy of national leaders in the regional integration schemes and pointed out the central role of the nation states in understanding international relations. The elitist and technocratic nature of the integration proposed by the neo-functionalist theory was also a source of criticism from the perspective of the democratic deficit.

The neo-functionalist approach's assumption of the mutual reinforcement of the scope and the level of integration was also a point of criticism. It is argued that the scope of integration has not altered the nature of the system to be closer to a supranational community as seen in the reforms of the TEU, which did not alter in any fundamental sense the locus of sovereignty from national governments to common institutions.[32]

With the late 1980s and early 1990s, there was a revival in the neo-functionalist theory of integration. This was very much related with the positive developments in European integration like the Single European Act and later on the Treaty on Europe. This time, however, along with the developments in the social sciences in terms of a post-modern turn, the neo-functionalist theory is used as a partial theory.[33] Post-modern approaches in the social sciences led to the replacement of meta or grand theories by partial, middle range explanations. Some of the new theoretical approaches introduced transaction-based theory instead of spillover and some others referred to the example of the European Court of Justice in order to show the autonomy of the EU's supranational institutions.

As the first theory aimed to explain the European integration process, the ups and downs of neo-functionalism very much reflect the developments in the actual integration taking place. It is still a reference point in theorizing about European integration. Despite the failure of some its overrated predictions about the integration process, neo-functionalism has performed an important duty in integration theory.

---

31  Ibid., pp. 88–9.
32  Chryssochoou, p. 57.
33  Jensen, p. 90.

Neo-functionalist school has encouraged theorizing to avoid state centricity and power politics and to focus on other types of units of analysis.[34]

The slowing down of integration caused questioning of the validity of neo-functionalism and rise of other explanations for European integration. The return to this theory in the 1990s was very much different and middle range explanations replaced the meta-narratives (i.e. Marxism, liberalism) of the post-World War II period. Currently, intergovernmentalism represents the main stream in integration theory.

## Intergovernmentalism

Intergovernmentalists define integration on a narrower base and focus on political process and political integration.[35] Even the name of the theory provides the clue that this approach has realist underpinnings and is state centric. This theory privileges the role of the national governments in the European integration process and argues that integration is driven by the interests and actions of nation states.[36] With its state centric approach, intergovernmentalism has its roots in the realist tradition of international relations theories. This approach accepts states as unitary and rational actors, pursuing their own interests in a hostile environment for their survival as the key actors in international affairs.

Intergovernmentalists believe that there are costs and benefits of cooperation (instead of the term integration, they prefer cooperation) and participation in this cooperation is the result of calculation for the member states. They argue that cooperation has nothing to do with ideology or idealism, but is founded on the rational calculations of the nation states within the context of global politics.[37] For intergovernmentalists, the sovereignty of the nation state is important and European cooperation implies at most a pooling or sharing of sovereignty rather than any transfer of sovereignty from the national to the supranational level.[38] Such a definition leaves limited place to the role of the supranational organizations in the European integration. The role of the institutions within the European Union is not autonomous or independent from the will of the member state. According to this theory, these institutions are in the service of the national governments.

Despite the earlier optimism about the integration process in Europe, the actual integration in the mid 1960s faced difficulties. The appeal of neo-functionalism in explaining the integration decreased and intergovernmentalism became the dominant paradigm used in this area. Stanley Hoffman's criticisms of neo-functionalist theory laid the foundations for intergovernmentalism.[39] Hoffman argued that neo-functionalists focused on the process of integration and had forgotten the context

---

34 Chryssochoou, p. 58.

35 Wiener and Diez, p. 2.

36 Michelle Cini, "Intergovernmentalism," in *European Union Politics* (edited by Michelle Cini), (Oxford: Oxford University Press, 2003), p. 94.

37 Ibid., p. 95.

38 Ibid., p. 96.

39 Ibid., p. 97.

within which it took place.[40] Since intergovernmentalism placed the driving force for integration on the side of the nation states, it also opposed to the unintended integration as a result of the spillover. The challenges against the sovereignty of state were real according to the intergovernmentalists, but nation states were not superseded by other actors in international politics. They argued that despite the real challenges state governments remained powerful for two reasons: first, because they held the legal sovereignty over their own territory, and second because they possessed political legitimacy, as they were democratically elected.[41]

Hoffman's intergovernmentalism focused on a political integration instead of the technocratic integration of neo-functionalist understanding. His type of intergovernmentalism made a distinction between high and low politics and argued that there were clear boundaries between the economic sphere in which integration may occur and the political sphere in which integration would not occur.[42] Hoffman's clear distinction between high and low politics and ignorance of the increasing interdependence among the states in the global world were main points of criticism, with the actual developments in the European integration process.[43] Despite these criticisms, his approach has been influential in the study of European integration process.

This intergovernmentalist approach has been supplemented with some other approaches like liberal intergovernmentalism, confederalism, domestic politics approach and the locking of the states approach. Confederal approaches point out the institutionalized nature of the European integration and recognize, unlike intergovernmentalism, its distinctiveness.[44] The domestic politics approach argued that it is impossible to understand the integration process without taking domestic politics into consideration and by benefiting from the term of Europeanization; this theory demonstrates how the intergovernmentalists fail to look in any coherent way within the member states when analyzing the European integration process.[45] The locking in of the states tried to show that how states have become locked into the European integration process by emphasizing institutional factors.[46]

Beside these approaches, the liberal intergovernmentalism of Moravscik has attracted a great deal of attention in integration theory. Drawing on earlier intergovernmentalist accounts and incorporating the realist and neo-realist elements of international relations, this theory deals with the interface of domestic and international politics.[47] This theory is based on the assumptions of the rational actor model and emphasizes the preferences and the power of the states in the integration. Moravscik's main conclusions about European integration process are summarized as follows:[48] First, the major choices made in favour of European integration

---

40 Ben Rosamond, *Theories of European Integration* (Basingstoke: Macmillan, 2000), p. 76.
41 Cini, p. 98.
42 Ibid.
43 Ibid., p. 99.
44 Ibid., p. 100.
45 Ibid., p. 101.
46 Ibid.
47 Ibid., p. 103.
48 Ibid., p. 105.

are a reflection of the preferences of national governments not of supranational organizations. Second, these national preferences reflect a balance of domestic economic interests rather than any political bias of politicians or national strategic security concerns. Third, the outcomes of negotiations among the members reflect the relative bargaining power of the states, and the delegation of decision making authority to supranational institutions reflect the wishes of the governments to ensure that the commitments are honoured.

It is argued that this approach offers a range of intellectual opportunities by integrating three important sub-disciplines of international relations theory: regime analysis, negotiation theory and intergovernmentalism.[49] This theory also makes another contribution by linking the domestic political orders and economic agendas of the governments to joint decision making and to coalition formation in the Council.[50]

The criticisms against liberal intergovernmentalist approach are as follows:[51] This theory may apply to history making decisions but has little to say about the day-to-day politics of the EU. Beside this, it is simplistic since it focuses solely on economic and geopolitical concerns. This theory also fails to see that although supranational institutions (like the Commission) tend to operate within the limits determined by the member state preferences, these institutions benefit from the differences among the members in pursuing their own agendas.

Similar to the neo-functionalist approach, intergovernmentalism provides important insights into the analysis of European integration. As can be seen from the examples given above, several theories base their arguments on the basic assumptions of intergovernmentalism. Despite the deepening of integration in the EU after the 1990s, intergovernmentalism became flexible enough to adapt to new conditions and remains an important reference point in integration theories.

**New Approaches in Integration**

Although neo-functionalism and intergovernmentalism remain the basic approaches in the integration field, new explanations for the changes in the European integration, most of the time building their arguments upon the classical approaches, have appeared in academic circles. The emergence of new theories not only relates to the changes in the European context, but also to the developments in the social sciences. The criticisms of the new approaches of the old debate between the two big approaches focus on three points: "its alleged inability to capture the reality of integration and the EU, its supposed entrapment in the disciplinary wilderness of international relations and its so called scientific limitations."[52]

From the 1980s onwards, there has been a new dynamism in the European integration process and reflections of this dynamism in integration theory. The attempts to increase integration have resulted in revisiting the old theories and the

---

49 Chryssochoou et al, p. 46.

50 Ibid.

51 Cini, pp. 106–107.

52 Ben Rosamond, "New Theories of European Integration," in *European Union Politics,* edited by Michelle Cini (Oxford: Oxford University Press, 2003), p. 111.

emergence of new ones. Neo-functionalist explanations re-emerged along with the increasing integration. However, it should be made clear that the role of the governments of nation states have been crucial in the direction of integration. For example, supranationalism has been championed in areas where states want to see increasing integration like the single market program. However, the demand for increasing integration has been limited and intergovernmentalism has prevailed in areas in which national interests seem to be at stake, like European Political Cooperation.[53] So, the dynamism for integration is not deterministic and not drives from neo-functionalist spillover, but from the convergence of interests among the governing elite in several countries who are also sensitive to the sovereignty of states. The three pillar structure of the TEU and limitation of the Community approach to one pillar is an example of this approach. States were insisting on protecting their sovereignty and without a consensus at the elite level, nothing can be achieved in terms of further integration. Below, we will look at several new approaches that have emerged in the integration field. Some of them are the products of the post-1980s when a new optimism for further integration in Europe emerged, but some of them appeared earlier. The post-modern turn in the social sciences had its reflections in the theories of integration and most of the new theories are middle range ones.

*Regime Theory and Interdependence Theory*

In the late 1970s, two approaches of international relations, namely regime theory and interdependence theory, were among the most prominent approaches to explain international relations and also European integration. Regime theory brought "the question of whether institutions really mattered in the process of internationalized governance – in the case of Community, capable of producing publicly binding decisions – and interdependence theory portrayed a dynamic system of increased interconnectedness, which set the pace and the depth of regional management arrangements."[54] Regimes are defined by Stephen Krasner as "sets of explicit and implicit principles, norms, rules and decision making procedures around which actors' expectations converge in a given area of international relations."[55] Regime theory focuses on the norms that regularize the behaviour of actors and guide their choices. And norms constitute standards of behaviour defined in terms of rights and obligations.[56] Here the basic question that regime theory tries to answer is whether norms can transcend possible sources of tension among regime actors stemming from the self-interestedness of governments?[57]

In examining several crises in the history of European integration, it is accepted that dissenting state have not seriously contemplated the possibility of withdrawing from

---

53  Chryssochoou et al, p. 41.

54  Ibid., p. 25.

55  Stephen D. Krasner, "Structural Causes and Regime Consequences: Regimes as Intervening Variables," in *International Regimes*, edited by Stephen D. Krasner (Ithaca, London: Cornell University Press, 1983), p. 2.

56  Ibid.

57  Chryssochoou et al, p. 26.

the common regional system and this is an indication that regime analysis remains an important part of integration theory.[58] The position of the British government during the second half of 2005 about the incoming budget of the EU also might be seen as an example here. Despite the earlier opposition to a cut in the tax rebate that Britain receives from the EU, the British government could not continue the opposition and had to compromise. Regime theory is criticized for failing to undermine the impact of the Community's legal order on shaping the national patterns of behaviour and also criticized it for failing to differentiate the specific conditions of cooperation within the fragmented system of Community.[59]

The interdependence approach was useful in analyzing the EU integration especially after the stalemate in the late 1960s. Contrary to the expectations of the neo-functionalist theoreticians, the nation states continued to play the leading role in the integration process. Interdependence theory differs from neo-functionalist approach by pointing out the loss of control on the side of the governments in the complex economic integrations and reactions of the governments to the process to safeguard the welfare of their electorates.[60] It is more realistic since it deals with the questions arising from the changing conditions of the economy. It is helpful in analyzing the relations between nation states and other actors within the European level. Although the interdependence approach has been criticized for failing to address the explicit political choices of the political elites' involvement in joint cooperative schemes, it is a helpful tool since it diverts attentions from the structured analysis of hierarchical conceptions to a wider pluralist perspective of post-industrial relations.[61]

*The Concordance System*

Donald Puchala critically analyzed several conventional theories of integration with an article published in 1972 in which he established similarities between the efforts of the conceptualization of international integration with the story of the elephant and the blind men. He argued that, similar to the efforts of blind men to discover what kind of an animal the elephant is, in the theorization of the international integration several scholars looked at the different parts, dimensions and manifestations of the problem.[62] He argued that the phenomenon, which is to be described by the observers, is changing over time and the normative preferences of the observers are influencing the nature of the phenomenon. He claimed that most of the efforts to theorize international integration discussed it in terms of "what it should be and what it should be leading toward" and argued that his analysis about international integration was in terms of what it really was and was actually leading toward.[63]

---

58  Ibid.
59  Ibid., p. 27.
60  Ibid., p. 28.
61  Ibid., p. 30.
62  Donald J. Puchala, "Of Blind Men, Elephants and International Integration," *Journal of Common Market Studies* 11, no. 2 (December 1972), p. 267.
63  Ibid., p. 268.

Puchala argued that the developments in the field of international integration after World War II were essentially new and peculiar at this period. For this reason, analyzing this phenomenon with "more familiar and time tested patterns" and asking wrong questions about the nature of this new development were the mistakes committed by the conventional analytical models.[64] He described the weaknesses of several theories like federalism, functionalism, nationalism and realism in conceptualizing the international integration. His criticisms of the conventional models of analysis reflected the state of theorizing of integration in the early 1970s, when intergovernmentalism seemed more suitable to explain the working system of the Community.[65]

Since no model described international integration with complete accuracy and the combination of several conventional models yielded artificial results, Puchala claimed that a new framework needed to be developed which reflected and raised questions about what international integration was.[66] He argued that "contemporary international integration can best be thought of as a set of processes that produce and sustain a Concordance System at the international level."[67] Concordance mean harmony or peaceful relations among nations and nation states were among the major component units of his system and governments remained central actors in integration. Beside states, the institutions of the larger system possessed their own organizational and operational logic. Puchala described his Concordance System as a system of relations not exclusively government to government relations, but as relations among sovereign states and separate peoples. This system was a new kind of international system created by the Europeans to meet the European needs of the post-World War II period.[68] The destruction caused by the war and the weak condition of Europe in world politics after war induced the countries of the continent to cooperate on several issue areas. The atmosphere in which such a system could operate needed the following characteristics: Pragmatism is the prevailing political doctrine of the Concordance system, this system is supported by the perceptions of international interdependence, common programs are formulated and decided upon with mutual sensitivity and responsiveness and the Concordance system includes people.[69]

The tools of the Concordance system capture the structural and procedural aspects of international integration and also leave the normative, hypothetical and ideological interpretations of the integration aside. This approach proposed a new angle for integration theory exploring the possibilities of consensus, responsiveness and pragmatism. This theory is an important contribution to the European integration theory.

---

64  Ibid., p. 269.
65  Chryssochoou et al, p. 31.
66  Puchala, "Of Blind Men, Elephants and International Integration", pp. 276–7.
67  Ibid.
68  Ibid., p. 278.
69  Ibid., pp. 281–2.

*New Institutionalists*

In considering the distinctive institutionalized nature of the EU among other regional integration schemes, the new institutionalists stressed the role of the institutions within the EU. This new institutionalist approach was not a single theoretical perspective, but consisted of several accounts like rational choice institutionalists, historical institutionalists and sociological institutionalists. The focuses of these approaches are summarized by Ben Rosamond as follows:[70]

> Rational choice institutionalists are interested in how the relative power of actors shifts in accordance with changes in institutional roles. Historical institutionalists deal with the long term implications of institutional choices made at the specific points in time and sociological institutionalists pay attention to the culture of institutions and the ways in which patterns of communication and persuasion operate in institutional settings.

Beside these institutionalist approaches, other new approaches emerged with the argument that policy making in the EU was so complex that it could not be captured by state centric models. With the assumption that the boundaries between national policy making and European policy making was so blurred, the multi-level governance approach emerged to analyze different tiers of authority in the EU policy process (the European, the national and the supranational).[71] This approach is in direct opposition to the two-level game of the liberal intergovernmentalist approach of Moravcsik. The multi-level governance approach opposes the idea that there can be a single all-encompassing theory and argues that the authority is dispersed among a variety of actors and policy making in the EU is complex, uneven and variable.[72]

*Constructivism*

Social constructivism brought fresh ideas to the debates in international relations (IR) theories and EU integration. Constructivism questioned the legitimacy of the ontological grounds of the rationalist theories with the argument that interest are socially constructed, rather then pre-given. The Constructivist approach stressed the "intersubjectivity" and "social context" on the continuing process of European integration and it is argued by some scholars that "finding the tools to analyze the impact of intersubjectivity and social context enhances our capacity to answer why and how European integration arrived at its current stage."[73] The conventional theories of European integration describe the integration process as a strategic exchange between autonomous political agents with fixed interests. In contrast to them, constructivism deals with the neglected dynamics of social learning, socialization and normative diffusion which addresses the identity and interest of

---

70  Rosamond, "New theories of integration," p. 117.

71  Ibid., p. 120.

72  Ibid., pp. 120–21.

73  Thomas Christiansen, Knud Erik Jorgensen and Antje Wiener, "The Social Construction of Europe," *Journal of European Public Policy* 6, no. 4 (1999), p. 529.

the agents in the integration process.[74] Social learning is described as a "process whereby actors, through interaction with broader institutional context, acquire new interests and preferences."[75] Here interaction between different actors during the integration process plays the crucial role. Constructivists focus on questions like how collective understandings emerge and how institutions constitute the interests and the identities of actors. It is argued that constructivism claims to offer a middle way in IR theories between rationalism and reflectivist theories (post-modernism, feminism, critical theory).[76]

The most important contribution of the constructivist approach to the EU integration is in regards to European identities, especially the inclusion into the analysis of the impact of norms and ideas on the construction of identities and behaviour. The EU is not based exclusively on the original set of political and legal organs, but also includes shared norms, commonly accepted rules and decision making procedures. Constructivists study European integration as a process and focus on social institutions. As a process, European integration has had transformative effect on the European state system and its constituent units. European integration itself has changed over the years and it is argued that the integration process led to a change in the identities, interests and behaviours of the agents.[77] Here we might see some kind of similarities between the arguments of neo-functionalism and constructivism in terms of the emergence of a new kind of identity. However, we should identify some basic differences. The conventional theorizing efforts, like neo-functionalism, are substantive theories aiming to explain every aspect of integration, whereas constructivism is a middle range theory with modest aspirations. Another difference between neo-functionalism and constructivism is about the stance towards the identity to emerge as a result of integration. Here neo-functionalism believes that there will be a greater common identity and interest, whereas constructivism is "agnostic whether the endpoint of social integration is greater common interest and identity."[78] Beside this, the neo-functionalist approach has an agent-centred view of social interaction and has a strong element of rational choice for the formation of common identity. Different from the neo-functionalists, the constructivist thinking stresses communicative action in the formation of a common identity.[79] Constructivism is still marginal in integration theory in comparison with neo-functionalism, since it is ill-suited to explain the problems in the transnationalization of the state. Consequently, it is argued that this approach is corrective to neo-functionalism, instead of being an alternative.[80]

Beside the neo-functionalists critique of the constructivist approach, liberal intergovernmentalist theoretician Moravcsik also criticizes the constructivists. He argues that the constructivist scholars are unwilling to test their claims

74 Jeffrey T. Checkel, "Social construction and integration," *Journal of European Public Policy* 6, no. 4 (1999), p. 545.

75 Ibid., p. 548.

76 Rosamond, "New theories of integration," p. 121.

77 Christiansen et al, p. 529.

78 Checkel, p. 557.

79 Ibid.

80 Gerard Delanty and Chris Rumford, *Rethinking Europe: Social Theory and the Implications of Europeanization* (London: Routledge, 2005), pp.13–14.

against empirical data.[81] Moravcsik also argues that the approach proposed by the constructivist is not the solution but the problem, since "philosophical speculation is being employed not to refine or sharpen concrete concepts, hypotheses, and methods, but to shield empirical conjectures from empirical testing."[82]

A theory failing to problematize the changing ontologies in the integration process will be a limited tool at hand. Here constructivism plays an important role by focusing its research on the relationship between individuals and the emerging polity, both in terms of development of the institution of the Union citizenship and in terms of reconstructing identities through the practice of socialization.[83] The focus of the constructivists on identity formation can be grouped into three subcategories: research on the nature of a potential European identity, research into the construction of national identities under the influence of the integration process and the question of the plurality of national identities and cultures and to what extent a European political identity can be founded upon such difference.[84] The issue of the existence of a common European identity along with the existence of diverse national identities is an issue of contention.

Another criticism of the constructivist approach towards the conventional theories in relation to the identity issue is about the perception of the nature of the national and European identity. The conventional theories perceive the identity as "essentially fixed, usually categorical and that the nation state social model is the norm."[85] As a result of this, the evaluation of the success or the failure of the EU very much depends on the construction of a supranational identity. However, constructivists emphasize the complex, multiple and relational construction of identity.[86]

The general question posed by the constructivist theory in the EU integration is to what extent and in which ways a new polity is constructed in Europe. The principle aim of here is to problematize the changing social ontologies of European polity formation.[87] Instead of accepting the emergence of ideas of "European economy, European security community, European citizenship" as a response of the actors within the EU to the changes like globalization and the end of the Cold War, the constructivists argue these identities are constructed through the use of language, the deployment of ideas and the establishment of norms.[88] The contribution of constructivism to the European integration theories is especially valid with reference to the issues of polity and democracy, since the means and ends of the Union's social legitimating are becoming objects of analysis.[89] The issues of democracy, legitimacy and the participation of the European public in the discussions related

---

81 Andrew Moravcsik, "Is something rotten in the state of Denmark? Constructivism and European integration," *Journal of European Public Policy* 6, no. 4 (1999), p. 670.

82 Ibid., p. 678.

83 Christiansen et al, p. 540.

84 Ibid.

85 Ian Manners and Richard G. Whitman, "The 'Difference Engine': Constructing and Representing the International Identity of the European Union," p. 395.

86 Ibid.

87 Chryssochoou et al, p. 57.

88 Rosamond, "New theories of integration," p. 122.

89 Chryssochoou et al, p. 57.

to integration are hot topics of the discussion related with the EU. It is claimed that the constructivist approach is examining the transformatory process of integration critically by focusing its efforts on the nature of the change taking place in Europe and that this style will be moving the study of European integration forward.[90] The contribution of constructivism to this ongoing debate provides a theoretical background to the discussions.

After reviewing the different approaches in the field of theory to explain the European integration process we can summarize the arguments in this chapter. Intergovernmentalism and neo-functionalism have been the two main competing approaches in explaining the European integration since the 1960s. Both intergovernmentalism and neo-functionalism focus on integration as a process. However, some of the other theories of integration, like federalism, also are concerned about the outcome or end product of the integration process. The issues of European integration theories are related directly to the developments in Europe and to the field of international relations. For example, the expectations of the earlier neo-functionalist or federalist perspectives for increasing integration on the road to a federal Europe have not come true. The deterioration of global economic conditions and the return to the idea of the maintenance of a degree of autonomy in internal affairs have played their roles here.

A review of European integration demonstrates an ongoing debate in the integration literature. Several theories were influential for some periods and helped to understand the European integration. Thomas Diez and Antje Wiener argue that there are three broad phases in integration theory in the history of European integration:[91] From the 1960s to the 1980s integration theories focused on explaining integration and tried to answer the outcomes of integration and why European integration takes place. From the 1980s onwards integration theory focused on analyzing governance and aimed to answer the questions like what kind of a political system the EU is and how the political processes in the EU can be explained. The post-Cold War years represented a new era in the European integration process and the EU became an institutionalized body. The most important questions of these years for integration theory were what the social and political consequences of integration theory are and how integration and governance can be conceptualized.

Different phases in the history of the European integration and the attempts at theorizing have assumed that the formation of European polity is distinct from the making of a new regional state or of a classical confederal union and consequently resembles an asymmetrical and often analytically incongruent synthesis of academic disciplines.[92]

Several traditions of international relations theory (like pluralist paradigms of interstate behaviour or the neorealist interpretation of state centric preferences and power) and several middle range theories were part of the effort to explain European integration and it is argued that they have exhausted the analytical spectrum.[93] The

---

90  Christiansen et al, p. 537.
91  Wiener and Diez, pp. 6–7.
92  Chryssochoou, p. 29.
93  Ibid., pp. 25–6.

revival of theory in the integration studies in the 1990s was related to the developments in the EU integration process and also to the emergence of new theoretical approaches in the social science in general and IR theory in particular. With the questioning of modernist and rationalist approaches in the social sciences, reflectivist and constructivist approaches introduced new questions and answers. The application of these new approaches to integration theory enriched the theoretical discussions on the EU. The new theories in the social sciences opposed the meta-narratives of the rationalist and positivist approaches and focused on partial explanations instead of big theoretical frameworks. The nearly "unidentifiable" nature of the EU sometimes creates confusion and it is difficult to produce a theoretical scheme to explain all aspects of it. The current vibrant atmosphere of theoretical discussions on integration will ease the job of explanation.

The two big theories of integration have dominated the discussions related with the EU. The neo-functionalists argue that the process of integration is driven by functional spillover and describe it in a deterministic way, whereas the intergovernmentalists argue that the integration process is driven by international bargains. Consequently, "neo-functionalists focus on the role of the Commission and examine its role in the EC's external relations, whereas the intergovernmentalists focus on the role of the member states and examine their role in the EU's CFSP."[94]

Chryssochoou argues that intergovernmentalism has survived the tides of supranationalism and regional centralization.[95] In considering the arguments of Manners and Whitman, I share the argument of Chryssochoou about the longevity of intergovernmentalism since the EU has not created a new base of sovereignty and the Council has influential powers in the decision making within it. The EU has not taken us beyond nation the state and some of the state qualities are reserved despite the participation of the members to the integration process. Despite the explanatory capacity of the new approaches in several aspects of the EU, intergovernmentalism remains as a base for different middle range theories and also provides a general explanation for the functioning of the EU. The explanation capacity of intergovernmentalism as a theory of European integration is especially true for my analysis, since my focus is on the Common Foreign and Security Policy of the EU. Although I generally prefer Intergovernmentalism for the explanation of the European integration given the role of the Council, theories like neo-functionalism is also helpful in the analysis of the role of the Commission. The CFSP is structured in the Treaty on European Union within the second pillar and out of the community method. Since governments are sensitive about sharing their sovereignty with other states on issues like foreign policy, the common foreign policy of the EU basically remains intergovernmental. Consequently, intergovernmentalism is the suitable approach to analyze the general picture of the CFSP. My focus on the CFSP and the impact of EU membership and candidature on the foreign policies of the state in this work makes me closer to the intergovernmentalist approach.

---

94 Ian Manners and Richard G. Whitman, "The 'Difference Engine': Constructing and Representing the International Identity of the European Union," p. 393.

95 Chryssochoou, p. 26.

# Chapter 2

# Europeanization of the Foreign Policy

## Definition of the Concept of Europeanization

In this part, the impact of European Union membership on nation states will be examined. It is a fact that EU exerts influence on its member states. Within the concept of European foreign policy, the foreign policies of the member states have been changed by participation in policy making at the European level. Several years of cooperation have transformed the making of national foreign policies within all member states. Each crisis and each failure leads to modest but cumulative improvements in commitment of the member states and the procedure to have a common policy. This development counterbalanced the existence of national foreign policies.[1] EU membership or even prospects of it causes drastic domestic changes. This process is referred to as the "Europeanization" of national foreign policies.[2]

There are also other definitions of the Europeanization process. A broad definition of Europeanization "consists of processes of construction, diffusion and institutionalization of formal and informal rules, procedures, policy paradigms, styles, ways of doing things, and shared beliefs and norms which are first defined and consolidated in the EU policy process and then incorporated in the logic of domestic (national and sub-national) discourse, identities, political structures and public policies".[3] Today, despite several usages of the term, Europeanization most often is associated with domestic adaptation to the pressures emanating directly or indirectly from EU membership.[4] The constructivist approach advocates another definition of the concept of Europeanization, which focuses on society beyond nation states. Unlike conventional accounts of European integration, the constructivist definition tries to go beyond national governments and "highlights the multiple ways social reality is continuously created in processes that cannot be reduced to either agency

---

1   Christopher Hill, "Actors and Actions," in *The Actors in Europe's Foreign Policy*, edited by Christopher Hill (London: Routledge, 1996), p. 13.

2   Brian White, *Understanding European Foreign Policy* (London: Palgrave, 2001), p. 118.

3   Heather Grabbe, "Europeanization Goes East: Power and Uncertainty in the EU Accession Process," in *The Politics of Europeanization,* edited by Kevin Featherstone and Claudio M. Radaelli (Oxford: Oxford University Press, 2003), p. 309.

4   Kevin Featherstone, "In The Name of Europe," in *The Politics of Europeanization,* edited by Kevin Featherstone and Claudio M. Radaelli (Oxford: Oxford University Press, 2003), p. 7.

or structures."[5] This approach puts particular emphasis on globalization and the historical process of modernity in which Europeanization operates. This description of Europeanization accepts it as a process of social construction and points out the importance of cultural dynamics in this process.[6] In these respects, it differs from other definitions, which are generally framed within IR theories. The key dynamics of Europeanization by the same authors are: Europeanization as societal interpenetration, the transformation of the state is central to Europeanization, Europeanization as discursive and socio-cognitive transformation and Europeanization as transformation of modernity.[7] In sum, this definition of Europeanization stresses the impact of globalization as the wider context in which Europeanization occurs and focuses on the diverse logics of construction of Europe.

The Europeanization process is confined not only to the EU member states and the several dimensions of the term explain changes in different actors. According to the definition of Featherstone and Kazamias, Europeanization has three key dimensions: the increase and expansion of institutionalization at the EU level, the relevant adjustment at the level of the member states and other similar adjustment in non-member states.[8] The last two dimensions of this definition of Europeanization are more suitable for my analysis. In this chapter, instead of dealing with the institutionalization at the EU level, I will focus on the changes in the member states and candidates. My analysis will be confined to the changes in the area of foreign policy, including decision making, content of the policy and policy actions. So, the Europeanization process is related not only to the issue of foreign policy, but also to candidature and the membership of the EU greatly affects the domestic politics of the countries.

The relations between the EU and the member states are defined as a two level process that have bottom-up and top-down dimensions. Although this relation is described as a two way process, the research on this issue initially focused specifically on national adaptation to the Europe. The bottom-up concept emphasizes the evolution of European institutions as a set of norms, rules and practices. Top-down refers to the impact of these new institutions on the political structures and processes of the member states.[9] Since this is a two way process, the member state governments both shape the European policy and also adapt to them. It is argued that the governments strive to minimize the costs which the implementation of European norms and rules may impose on their home constituencies. Consequently, the member states compete at the European level for policies that conform to their own interests and approaches.[10]

---

5   Delanty and Rumford, p. 2.

6   Ibid., p. 7.

7   Ibid., pp. 18–20.

8   Kevin Featherstone and George Kazamias, *Europeanization and the Southern Periphery* (London: Frank Cass, 2001), p. 5.

9   Tanja A. Börzel, "Pace-Setting, Foot-Dragging, and Fence-Sitting: Member State Responses to Europeanization," *Journal of Common Market Studies* 40, no. 2 (2002), p. 193.

10  Adrienne Héritier, Christoph Knill and Susanne Mingers, *Ringing the changes in Europe: regulatory competition and the transformation of the state. Britain, France, Germany* (Berlin: De Gruyter, 1996), p. 17.

Three different strategies of member states that are pursued as a response to Europeanization are defined by Börzel under three headings: "pace-setting, i.e., actively pushing policies at the European level, which reflect a member state's policy preference and minimize implementation costs; foot dragging, i.e., blocking or delaying costly policies in order to prevent them altogether or achieve at least some compensation for implementation costs; and fence sitting; i.e. neither systematically pushing policies nor trying to block them at the European level but building tactical coalitions with both pace setters and foot draggers."[11] Their response to Europeanization is shaped first by their policy preferences and second by their action capacity. This capacity very much depends on the economic power of the country.

Scholars of international relations first used the term "Europeanization" as a reflection of the evolution of EU foreign policy coordination itself. This kind of usage and analysis of the transformation of the member countries' foreign policies, however, were rare since the development of EC competences in this area were late and modest. The term "Europeanization" initially developed to define the changes in the member countries for the policy areas in the first supranational pillar of the Treaty of European Union.[12] Europeanization as a process of domestic adaptation in the area of foreign policy became a more frequently used term with the growing importance of the European Political Cooperation process in the late 1980s and the development of the Common Foreign and Security Policy after the Maastricht Treaty.[13] Participation within the CFSP rarely requires adaptation in the constitutional or legal framework and there are several instruments and procedures in the hands of foreign policy decision makers.[14] So, in analyzing the concept of Europeanization in relation to foreign policy cooperation and coordination, we have to keep in mind the relative weakness of the EU in this area in comparison with other areas of EU integration. Foreign policy is less vulnerable to the effects of Europeanization in comparison with other issue areas. European cooperation in foreign and security policy initially was established outside of the European treaties with the aim of avoiding the creation of common institutions. The aim here was to create a framework of collaboration working through direct contacts between counterpart ministers in member countries.[15] Consequently, changes in this area are difficult to observe. Although there is a lack of legal regulations or *acquis communitaire* that the candidates should adopt in this sphere, the candidate countries should have settled all their border problems which require legal regulations.

In analyzing the relationship between European integration and the changes in the member countries, we should be careful in differentiating European sources and other sources of the change. The changes in the foreign policies of the member countries also may result form the effects of globalization or the domestic need for

---

11 Börzel, p. 194.

12 Claudia Major, "Europeanization and Foreign and Security Policy, Undermining or Rescuing the Nation State," *Politics* 25, no. 3 (2005), p. 182.

13 Featherstone, "In The Name of Europe," p. 10.

14 Michael E. Smith, *Europe's Foreign and Security Policy, The Institutionalization of Cooperation* (Cambridge: Cambridge University Press, 2004), p. 58.

15 Major, p. 183.

reform. The significance of the pressure of Europe for change is sometimes difficult to determine. Especially the social constructivist approach, which is analyzed by Delanty and Rumford pays great attention to the conditions created by globalization. They even argue that Europeanization is a particular and cosmopolitan response to globalization.[16] Here European integration might be seen as a sub-system within the international system.

In analyzing this issue, Manners and Whitman ask four basic questions: What is the current European condition; what are the impacts of the European political, economic, societal environment on the foreign policies of member states; to what degree foreign policy formulation is being Europeanized as part of more recent developments in the EU; and whether there are similar forces at work in the variety of member states under analysis which have a common impact upon their foreign policies.[17]

Some scholars prefer the concept of coordination instead of Europeanization. They argue that the term Europeanization is used in variety of ways and consequently it does not have a precise meaning. Beside this, this term represents a one way, top-down relationship between the Union and the member states.[18] The concept of coordination offers a broader focus enabling the exploration of both the administrative and institutional impact of European integration on member states. This concept also provides an opportunity to understand the contribution of the member states to the functioning and capacities of the Union. This coordination process produces pressures towards convergence and also countervailing pressures towards divergence among the member states. Kassim argues that analysis of the coordination process provides four main findings: The first is that European integration exerts powerful pressure on the governments and EU policy making has become an important locus for domestic coordination for governments. Second, national responses to the demands of the EU require the redefinition of the traditional functions of some actors and also the recalibration of inter-institutional relationships. Third, there are important similarities between the ways in which the member states coordinate their European policies. The fourth finding is there is also important diversity among the member countries in this respect.[19]

There is no single way of institutional behaviour among the member states in adaptation to the European standards. National traditions and the peculiarities of the states also function in the adaptation process as intervening variables and this process is called "domestic adaptation with national colours."[20]

---

16 Delanty and Rumford, pp. 8–9.

17 Ian Manners and Richard Whitman, "Introduction," in *The Foreign Policies of European Union Member States,* edited by Ian Manners and Richard Whitman (Manchester: Manchester University Press, 2000), pp. 1–2.

18 Hussein Kassim, "Conclusion," in *The National Coordination of EU Policy, The Domestic Level,* edited by Hussein Kassim, Guy Peters and Vincent Wright (Oxford: Oxford University Pres, 2000), p. 236.

19 Ibid., pp. 236–7.

20 Maria Green Cowles, James Caporaso, and Thomas Risse, "Europeanization and domestic change: Introduction," in *Transforming Europe: Europeanization and Domestic Change* (edited by Maria Green Cowles, James Caporaso, and Thomas Risse (London: Cornell University Press, 2001), p. 20.

In the coming pages, I analyze the theoretical approaches towards Europeanization and examples from several countries. The theoretical framework and the examples of this chapter will be applied to the Turkish case in later chapters. In considering the definitions and uses of the term Europeanization, I will refer to this term as the changes in the foreign policies of the member and candidate countries in general and the changes in Turkish foreign policy in particular. In this respect, the second part of Featherstone and Kazamias's definition of Europeanization suits my analysis. In terms of Borzel's top-down and bottom-up dimensions of the definition, the top-down dimension will be more dominant in my analysis since I will focus on the impact of the membership and candidature of the EU on countries. In this respect, the changes in the perceptions of the decision makers in foreign policy, the changes is the process of policy making and the changes in the policy actions will be analyzed.

## A New Analytical Framework of Foreign Policy

Although the European Union attempts to have a common policy, the foreign policies of the member states were not abolished by the Maastricht Treaty and the CFSP does not replace the national foreign policies. In considering the existence of national foreign policies along with the European one, it is not very easy to locate the European Union foreign policy within the classical foreign policy analysis schemes. For this reason, it can be said that analysis of European foreign policy does not easily fit into the existing foreign policy analysis theories and requires new analytical frameworks.

In order to analyze the EU member states' foreign policies, Manners and Whitman constructed a new framework consisting of a series of six questions divided into three sections. These sections attempt to delineate three different forces shaping the foreign policies of member states. These are foreign policy change, foreign policy process and foreign policy actions.[21] There are two questions in each of these sections. In the section of foreign policy change, "adaptations through membership" and "socialization of foreign policy makers" are two issues that are discussed. "Adaptation through membership" tries to understand the way in which the EU member states adapt their foreign policy through membership of the EU towards the EU itself and also towards the other member states of the Union. "Socialization of foreign policy makers" analyzes the role of social interaction in shaping the practices, perceptions and interests of policy makers and tries to answer whether the sharing of information and common practices among decision makers leads to socialization and the transformation of the common perceptions of policy makers.[22]

The second section is titled "foreign policy process" and analyzes the domestic factors and bureaucratic factors in the policy process. The first part deals with the interaction between the domestic and international arenas and the impacts of domestic political forces on the foreign policies of member states. The second part deals with the legal design of the bureaucratic structures in member state's foreign policy making structures and the relations between the civil servants and the ministries.[23]

---

21  Manners and Whitman, pp. 6–7.
22  Ibid., pp. 7–8.
23  Ibid., pp. 8–9.

The third section deals with "foreign policy action" by analyzing the policies of the member states with the EU and without the EU. The first part of the section looks at the way in which participation in the CFSP of the EU alters the foreign policy of member states. Does this participation create constrictions or opportunities? The second part looks at EU member states' polices that are considered as special relations.[24]

Another effort to understand the relationship between the CFSP and national foreign policies and the impact of the EU on member states comes from Christopher Hill. In his analysis, Hill focuses on several issues in constructing his research: the state's attitudes towards the CFSP, the impact of the socialization effect; shifts in the public and elites' opinion; the states' attitudes towards countries other than EU members and institutions other than EU that complicated their participation in the CFSP; effects on the state of convergence between economic relations and the CFSP; the administrative and domestic political factors that strained the cooperation with the EU members; the states' response to the increasing importance of security issues within the CFSP; and the states' views on the institutional changes regarding the CFSP; responsibility handling, especially that linked to the Presidency.[25]

Similar to the schemes provided by Manners and Whitman and Hill, Michael Smith also proposes a scheme to analyze how participation in the CFSP feeds back into EU member states and reorients their foreign policy cultures along similar lines. Smith constructs his analysis on four factors: "Elite socialization, bureaucratic reorganization, constitutional change, and the increase in public support for EPC."[26] Elite socialization refers to the level of trust among the decision makers in member countries that emerged after several years of informal environments of meetings, EPC working groups, and staff exchanges between several countries. So, the elites became more familiar with each other's positions regarding foreign policy. Bureaucratic adaptation refers to the establishment of new offices within the member states, the expansion of the diplomatic services and the re-orientation of national foreign policies towards Europe. Constitutional changes are also an important part of the effects of Europeanization. The changes in the international environment and the participation in the military and humanitarian interventions required some changes in some member states. Public support for the increasing cooperation of foreign policy is related to the increasing awareness of the general public about international events and the need for European response to these developments. Especially, the developments in the Balkans and Eastern Europe increased public awareness of European foreign policy.

Brian White also contributed to the attempts of theorizing the analysis of European foreign policy. He tried to test the compatibility of Foreign Policy Analysis (FPA) scheme, which differs from traditional schemes by highlighting the difference between states, to the case of European foreign policy. Departing from the

---

24  Ibid., pp. 10–11.

25  Hill, "Introduction," pp xi–xii.

26  Michael Smith, "Conforming to Europe: The Domestic Impact of EU Foreign Policy Co-operation," *Journal of European Public Policy* 7, no. 4 (October 2000), p. 614.

assumption that the EU is understood as a unique type of institution,[27] he analyzes the foreign policy of the Union from the perspectives of several approaches. He argues that the structuralist approach of conventional IR theories leave little room for the units within the system and for this reason, they have difficulties in explaining the behaviour of the unit, be it a state or some other actor, when the unit does not act in accordance with the dictates of the system.[28] There are some changes in the attitude of conventional IR theories towards the analysis of European foreign policy and paying attention to other actors than states along with the attempts on the side of the EU to have a more common foreign policy.

White argues that Foreign Policy Analysis (FPA), which offers an actor rather than state perspective and focuses on the international level, might be adapted to new conditions and may shed light upon European foreign policy with the following six questions about European foreign policy:[29] The actors of European foreign policy, the nature of the process, the issues of the agenda, the instruments deployed, context and the outputs of the policy. White mentions four problem areas in the application of the FPA approach to the European case: "the inadequacy of the traditional focus on the state, the need to focus on the politics of identity, the limitations of its treatment of the policy and the role of the domestic factors in foreign policy making, and the inadequacy of the links between FPA and other approaches in explaining policy making at the international level."[30] This adapted version of the FPA proposed by White is eclectic epistemologically and concerned with bringing the actors and the agency back to the scene in the analysis of foreign policy.

Featherstone and Kazamias analyze Europeanization in the southern periphery of the European Union. Although their analysis is focused not only on the issue of foreign policy, their analysis provides another approach to the topic of Europeanization. In their analysis, they give the six dimensions below as necessary for a good analysis of the issue: institutional adaptation within government, transformation in the structural power of domestic actors, the adjustment of the domestic macroeconomic regime, new dynamic with the domestic party system, pressure to redefine the national identity and a strategic tool in the pursuit of foreign policy interest.[31]

## Increasing Cooperation among the Member States

Similar to the arguments of Manners and Whitman, and Smith, Ben Tonra also stresses the increasing socialization of decision makers in foreign policy and the results of it.[32] This socialization has led to a coordination reflex among the European partners for new initiatives and the language used in the CFSP has increasingly

---

27 Brian White, "The European Challenge to Foreign Policy Analysis," *European Journal of International Relations* 5, no. 1 (1999), p. 39.

28 Ibid., p. 40.

29 Ibid., p. 46.

30 Ibid., p. 54.

31 Featherstone and Kazamias, pp. 15–16.

32 Ben Tonra, *The Europeanization of National Foreign Policy: Dutch, Danish and Irish Foreign Policy in the European Union* (Aldershot: Ashgate, 2001), p. 261.

become common. National foreign policy making increasingly has come to be seen as driven by the European agenda.[33] Tonra concludes that the relationship between national foreign policies and the CFSP has been a reciprocal one which expresses itself in two ways. First, the formulation and output of national foreign policies have changed as a direct result of participation in the process. Second, policy makers in the member countries see the process as constraining all participants and at the same time providing significant added value.[34] So, participation in the CFSP has created some opportunities like the empowerment of their positions and also has created some constraints by forcing them to act together, like having a consensus. The foreign policies of member states are constrained by participation in the process of a creating a collective foreign and security policy. Decision makers do not act without reference to the views of their colleagues. So, the output of the policies has been compromised in pursuit of a consensus. On the other side, the foreign policies of member states are empowered if the member states are successful in pursuing the same foreign policy objectives in a common framework. This has an international impact that is far greater than the state could hope.[35]

Several meetings among the ministers of the member states and bureaucratic structures within the CFSP add up to the framing of political cooperation. The effects of these institutions are described as vital since they provided stable arenas and temporal rhythms to social interaction between diplomats from different national diplomacies.[36] Similar to the functions of these institutions, the previous political stances, common positions and common actions also have their effect on political cooperation. These are referred to as *acquis politique* and provide restrictions and opportunities for the diplomats.[37]

Several years of cooperation among members since the establishment of the EPC have created its own procedure and type of cooperation. Smith argues that, instead of a bargaining process as in the CFSP domain of the EU, a problem solving process that involves an appeal to common interests and the use of ostracism or peer pressure to sanction potential defectors has emerged.[38] Smith lists four norms that support the corresponding changes in the EU and have improved the environment of cooperation. First, regular communication and consultation on foreign policy issues have increased the cooperation among member states. Second, the CFSP discussions are confidential, states cannot use information shared during them to embarrass or blame other states. Third, CFSP discussions usually are conducted by consensus and any state can block a discussion of a sensitive matter with little justification. And fourth, there are some subjects considered off-limits owing to the objections of one or more EU states.[39] These norms help to build trust among member states that help the formation of common positions.

---

33  Ibid., p. 263.
34  Ibid., p. 280.
35  Ibid., pp. 285–6.
36  Glarbo, p. 646.
37  Ibid.
38  Michael Smith, "Conforming to Europe," p. 615.
39  Ibid., pp. 615–16.

Similar to the arguments of Smith, Christopher Hill also defines four reasons for increasing cooperation among the member states and the convergence of foreign policies.[40] These four ways are described as follows: Rational calculations might lead the member states in due course to conclude that the advantages of the politics of the scale outweigh the temptations of selfishness. External demands and perceptions could gradually force Europeans to speak with a single and comprehensive voice, the evolution of international society could push and pull the EU into greater actorness in politics and a convergence of values leads to a redefinition of national interests according to a genuine sense of collective identity. We can say that, the developments in the second part of the 1990s and in the early years of twenty-first century validate most of these arguments for the CFSP, despite the likelihood of defection possible.

Some scholars make general statements about the attitudes of the member states towards the common foreign policy and group these countries according to the convergence of foreign policy. Hill divides the EU members' attitude towards common foreign policy prior to the largest enlargement of the 2004 into three groups.[41] The first group of countries welcomes the discipline and protection of the CFSP and Benelux countries are in this group. The countries of the second group are generally supportive of the CFSP, not to anxious to break ranks for the sake of it, but still with distinctive concerns that limit convergence. The majority of the members are within this group, like Spain, Portugal, Italy, Germany, Finland, Ireland, Sweden, and Austria. In Hill's classification, Britain, France, Denmark and Greece are at the uncooperative end of the spectrum. Also the changes in the foreign policies of the member states differ from each other since their points of departure are different. The changes in the foreign policies of member states are analyzed by several scholars like Manners and Whitman, Hill, by grouping the states into big states like Germany, UK and France; small states like the Benelux countries, or neutral states like Ireland, Austria, Finland, etc.

## Europeanization in Candidate Countries

The limitation of the Europeanization process only to the period after the integration process is labelled "too static" by some authors.[42] This kind of a definition does not sufficiently take into account the dynamics of Europeanization and integration. Signs of Europeanization appear during the integration process and these can be progressive.[43] Europeanization not only affects the member states, but also the candidates of the European Union. Could we use the framework applied to member countries also for candidates, is it the same process, what are the differences? Or is this framework suitable for Turkey since Turkey's case is generally labelled as a special case? These are important questions for the case of Turkey. The candidates

---

40 Christopher Hill, *Convergence, Divergence and Dialectics, National Foreign Policies and CFSP*, EUI Working Papers, RSC No. 97/66 (December 1997), pp. 4–5.

41 Ibid., pp. 2–3.

42 Bastien Irondelle, "Europeanization without the European Union? French military reforms 1991–1996," *Journal of European Public Policy* 10, no. 2 (April 2003), p. 210.

43 Ibid., p. 211.

are more open to the pressures from the Union since they want to become the members, and consequently have limited effective pressure on the current members and other institutions of the Union. The impact of Europeanization on Eastern European countries and the countries in the Mediterranean are analyzed from different perspectives. I believe that these cases will provide some clues for the Turkish case.

The different type of Europeanization in candidate countries is defined by Grabbe with two factors; power asymmetry and conditionality.[44] First, since they are not members, but candidates, this asymmetric relationship gives the EU more coercive routes of influence and provides the candidate countries more incentive to adopt. Second, the uncertainty in the accession process requires the candidate countries to comply with the conditions.[45] The economic and diplomatic powers of the candidate countries are limited in comparison with the economic and diplomatic power of the EU. The organized structure of the EU and the institutionalization give the Union more leverage against the candidates. Since the membership promises several rewards, an important number of countries in Europe have become candidates to and members of the Union. This asymmetry and the conditionality of the accession process are two crucial factors that make members different from candidates.

During the accession process, there is little possibility that the candidate countries influence EU decision making. Beside this, the uncertainty about the nature of the accession negotiations makes the candidate countries vulnerable. The EU has benefits to offer like the accession to membership, aid, technical assistance and trade. In contrast to this, the offers of the candidate countries are limited. The asymmetrical relationship enables the EU to set the rules of the game.

It is argued by some scholars that the Europeanization effect is strong externally, until the accession of the states to the EU.[46] In considering the opposition of some member countries to Turkey's membership, the policies of the Greek and Cyprus governments refusing the Annan Plan for the solution of the Cyprus problem after securing EU membership, and threatening Turkey to have some concessions from Turkey prior to membership, the importance of this power asymmetry and conditionality becomes clear. The pressure on the current applicants for the adaptation and policy convergence is greater than those on previous applicants, since the Union advanced in different policy areas within several years.

The creation of formal accession conditions has given the EU more leverage to get these applicants to comply with its demands than it had with previous ones. This fact also has reduced the ability of applicants to negotiate concessions like transitory periods and derogations.[47] The conditions are set in advance and the national governments have to meet them before their membership is approved. So,

---

44 Grabbe, p. 303.

45 Ibid.

46 Simon J. Bulmer and Claudio M. Radaelli, "The Europeanization of National Policy?" *Queen's Papers on Europeanization*, no. 1 (2004), p. 2, available [online]: http://www.qub.ac.uk/schools/SchoolofPoliticsInternationalStudiesandPhilosophy/FileStore/EuropeanisationFiles/Filetoupload,5182,en.pdf [28 December 2005].

47 Grabbe, p. 305.

the bottom-up process of Europeanization does not work in the case of candidate countries. The bottom-up process might be suitable for the member countries and the application of this process to the candidates requires some adjustments.

The EU accession involves several processes that affect institutions and requires policy transformation in the candidate countries. These are instrumentally used by the EU. Grabbe defines these processes as "mechanisms" and gives five mechanisms of Europeanization.[48]

Models: provision of legislative and institutional templates; money: aid and technical assistance; benchmarking and monitoring; advice and twinning; gate-keeping: access to negotiations and further stages in the accession process.

These mechanisms are used by the EU in the negotiations to adjust the candidate countries to the Union. The last two mechanisms, twinning and gate keeping, have greater effect on the Europeanization of candidate countries.

The nature of the CFSP makes the adaptation of candidate countries different from other aspects of integration. The CFSP matters required no specific legal changes in the national law, as the CFSP constitutes pillar II of Treaty on European Union and does not operate as the legal instruments in the pillar I, such as directive and regulations. The CFSP is equipped with instruments like common positions, common policies and joint actions. Candidate countries are required to adapt to *acquis politique*, which means they will ensure that their national foreign policies comply with the positions of the member states within the framework of the CFSP. Contrary to the adaptation to the European standards by *acquis communitaire* during the accession process, there are limited things that the candidates should do, like promising not to do unexpected things like attacking their neighbour. Although the settlement of border problems and having good neighbourly relations is a condition for the candidates, there are limited things that a candidate country should do in terms of legal changes. Instead, it promises to refrain from irrational foreign policy actions.

In this area of accession, some institutional changes like the appointment of required personnel and the creation of some posts required facilitating political cooperation, such as establishing the European Correspondent, political director to facilitate political dialogue, or delegating officials to the meetings of working groups in Brussels are carried out.

The negotiations over the CFSP chapter in most cases went smoothly and were quickly brought to an end. These negotiations did not resemble the classic negotiations that took place in other policy areas. The intergovernmental nature of the CFSP made it easy to negotiate. In this area of coordination and Europeanization, national governments are the key actors. As mentioned before, the CFSP is different from other areas of cooperation and has an intergovernmental structure. This situation refers to one in which the policy process is not subject to European law, where the decisions are subject to unanimity amongst the governments. In these cases the Europeanization for the member states is much more voluntary and non-hierarchical.[49]

In cases where member states are unable to agree on a common policy, such as occurred in 2003 on the Iraqi war, then the Europeanization of policy is in danger. The

---

48 Ibid., p. 312.
49 Bulmer and Radaelli, p. 7.

lack of supranational powers results in a "horizontal" pattern of Europeanization in some issue areas like that of the CFSP.[50] Despite the lack of Europeanized policy on some issues, coordinated actions like over the Palestinian issue represent the horizontal process. This coordinated action does not come from the hierarchical governance of the EU, but from horizontal exchanges between member governments.

In issue areas where the EU does not work as a law making system but as a platform for the convergence of ideas, then the learning process prevails. In these cases, the member countries learn from each other with the help of an open method of coordination (OMC).[51] OMC means spreading best practice and achieving convergence towards the EU goals. In this process, the EU works as a transfer platform rather than a law enforcing agent. And if Europeanization occurs in this area of cooperation, this is a result of a process of learning among the national elites. This kind of cooperation is suitable for the Justice and Home Affairs, Schengen Process and the CFSP. However, the CFSP shows that the member governments are very reluctant to compromise their powers to agree on a common policy, as revealed during the early 1990s on the former Yugoslavia and during 2003 on the war in Iraq.[52]

## The Results of Europeanization

In the pages above, several theoretical frameworks for the analysis of Europeanization of the foreign policies of EU member and candidate countries were discussed. Among them, the most extensive one was Manners and Whitman's framework. The conclusions of these writers are important for my analysis. In this part, I will give some examples of results of the Europeanization from different sources on different countries but mostly benefiting from the theoretical framework constructed by Manners and Whitman. According to them, EU adaptation plays an important role in the modernization of foreign policies of member states to come to terms with the challenges of the twenty-first century.

*Foreign Policy Change*

The member states adapt themselves to the realities of the post-Cold War era. From the point of "adaptation through membership," scholars found that some member countries resist adaptation more than some others. The resistance is related mostly to the notion of maintaining the national symbols of the past. They argue that resistance to the change was found in particular in the cases of Britain, France, Greece and Denmark.[53] Greece is mentioned among the countries that are less Europeanized. Some academics summarize the reasons for this reality as follows: being a peripheral country (geographically, with no borders with other members), situated in a turbulent

---

50  Ibid.
51  Ibid., p. 11.
52  Ibid., p. 12.
53  Ian Manners and Richard Whitman, "Conclusion," in *The Foreign Policies of European Union Member States,* edited by Ian Manners and Richard Whitman (Manchester: Manchester University Press, 2000) p. 246.

region, under an external threat (Turkey) and spending large amounts of money on defence, a different historical and political development pattern, a Christian Orthodox religion and culture, economically weak and long-standing controversies about accession to the EU.[54]

In contrast to the case of resistance to the change and Europeanization, some countries embraced adaptation and Europeanization by using the EU to overcome their fascist or authoritarian past, or colonial past, non-aligned past or a past marked with economic problems. Overcoming a fascist and authoritarian past is true for the cases of Germany, Italy, Portugal and Spain. The help of the EU in forgetting a colonial past is valid for the cases of Britain, France, Portugal and Belgium. For example, in the case of Britain, the loss of former colonial power and decline of the country in terms of political and economic power were the main reasons for the application for the EU membership.[55] Beside this, the issue of security played an important role in the decision of the elites of the country and the USA supported this application.[56] Membership in the European Community is seen as a way to protect the role of the Britain in world politics.

Europeanization also enabled the elimination of foreign policy problems related to economic problems. This is true for the cases of Italy, Ireland, Greece, Spain and Portugal. Europeanization also affected the foreign policy behaviours of post-neutral EU members like Finland, Austria, Sweden and Ireland. In this process of Europeanization, the attitude of the members was more determining than the time that passed after membership.[57] This means, the EU's youngest members' foreign policies might be more Europeanized than the oldest members because of the differences in their attitudes. Since the Ministries of Foreign Affairs in the post-Communist countries are in the process of re-structuring, it might be easier for these structures to adapt themselves to the new conditions and also the European agenda may work as an incentive for reform.

Beside the economic problems, historical experience also has played a role in Greece's Europeanization, despite being late in comparison with the other EU members. Greeks believe that their country was at the epicentre of the political earthquakes in the First and Second World Wars and during the Cold War period. This historical background and the developments in the Balkans in the first part of the 1990s also played a role in the conforming of Greece's foreign policy towards the other members of the Union.[58]

In the case of Italy, the impact of Europeanization in overcoming the negative memories of the past is obvious. Italy's contribution to the founding of the Union is related to the fact that it lost during the WWII and there is a search for legitimacy.

54 Panos Kazakos and Panayotis Ioakimidis, "Introduction," in *Greece and EC Membership Evaluated,* edited by Panos Kazakos and Panayotis Ioakimidis (London: Pinter, 1994), p. x.

55 Timothy Garton Ash, "Why Britain is in Europe," Speech given at St. Antony's College, University of Oxford, 1 June 2006.

56 Ibid.

57 Manners and Whitman, "Conclusion," p. 248.

58 Panos Tsakaloyannis, "The limits to convergence," in *The Actors in Europe's Foreign Policy,* edited by Christopher Hill (London: Routledge, 1996), p. 196.

There was an accumulation of frustration and the need for eventual peace.[59] From the beginning, Italy's participation in the EPC was considered as the optimum way to underline the traditional political support for multilateralism on the basis of post-Second World War choices, and to participate in NATO and the EC.[60] This "European" umbrella provided a stable incentive for the problematic domestic divisions on the foreign policy issues. This multilateralism helped to minimize the radical political confrontation over international events, like those in the Middle East, which could have disturbed the domestic political climate.[61]

Spanish participation in the EPC and the CFSP also resulted in a dramatic change, especially in perceptions. It is argued that the membership means for Spain the end of a "national trauma" which began in 1898.[62] The colonial disaster in 1898 turned Spain into a small state and the fascist system until the death of Franco in 1975 isolated the country from Europe. Despite the earlier presumptions that Spain would be a new Greece in common foreign policy for historical and geographical reasons (Spain's good relations with the Arab world and Latin America), most of the time Spain acted along with the general approach in the community.[63] Spain did not recognize Israel until becoming member in 1986 and this was a part of accepting the *acquis politique*.

Another reason for the Spain's welcoming of the Europeanization process in overcoming the negative aspects of the past was related to Spain's relations with the USA. During the era of Franco, the impact of the USA on the country was great and European membership was seen as a solution, as an alternative, to the dependent relationship with the USA especially on the issue of military bases.[64] The point might be interesting in the analysis of Turkey's relations with the USA, especially in terms of the use of airbases for the operations in the Middle East. The socialists in Spain played the crucial role in anchoring the country to Europe and forgetting the fascist past. The differences between socialists and the rightist surfaced during the invasion of Iraq in 2003. The Aznar government supported the coalition and even proposed a second UN Security Council resolution along with the USA and the UK. Although they withdrew their proposal later on, Spain was one of the members of the coalition. However, after the Madrid bombings on 11 March 2004 (which had an effect on the elections) and the government change after the elections, the policy of Spain changed. The new socialist government withdrew Spanish soldiers from Iraq.

The socialization of foreign policy makers is another aspect of the analysis of the Europeanization of the foreign policies of member states. At this point, the important issue is the effect of membership on the shaping of ways of thinking among the policy making elites. The EU membership affects the reflexes, norms and identities

---

59 Guliano Damato, "Britons and Italians in Europe," Speech given at St Antony's College, Oxford, 23 February 2006.

60 Gianni Bonvicini, "Regional assertation, the dilemmas of Italy," in *The Actors in Europe's Foreign Policy*, edited by Christopher Hill (London: Routledge, 1996), p. 94.

61 Ibid., p. 95.

62 Esther Barbe, "Spain, the uses of foreign policy cooperation," in *The Actors in Europe's Foreign Policy,* edited by Christopher Hill (London: Routledge, 1996), p. 108.

63 Ibid., p. 110.

64 Ibid., p. 119.

in the foreign policy formation. It is argued by Manners and Whitman that the socialization process in the foreign policy formation is less pronounced in the larger states like Germany, Britain and France. By contrast, the impact of socialization is more noticeable in smaller states like Portugal, Netherlands, Belgium, Finland, Sweden, Denmark and Ireland.[65]

*Foreign Policy Process*

Another aspect of the analysis of the Europeanization of the foreign policies of the member states looks at the foreign policy process. Here domestic factors in the foreign policy process and the bureaucratic factors in the policy process are two important issues. Manners and Whitman locate the constitutional design, the role of the sub-national governments, the relationships between government and parties, the role of special interest groups and the breakdown of the domestic-foreign distinction under the heading of domestic factors in the foreign policy process.[66]

The constitutional design is important since it determines the nature of the government, who is responsible for the foreign policy, the role of political parties and the role of the parliament. The nature of the political system, whether it is parliamentary, as in most of the European countries, or semi-presidential, as in the cases of France and Finland, is important for the nature of the roles of the several actors in the foreign policy.[67] In parliamentary systems the decision making regarding foreign policy has clearer lines. The coalitions in the parliamentary systems may result in a condition in which the Prime Minister and the Minister of Foreign Affairs, who are responsible for the foreign policy, may come from different parties.

Another element determining the role of domestic factors in the foreign policy is related to the state structure, whether it is centralized or decentralized. Here EU member countries represent very different positions on a wide spectrum of degrees of centralization.[68] Although sub-national units do not have determining effects on the foreign policy, federal units have their say in countries like Belgium, Germany, Austria, and Spain and also in Britain, which has devolution.[69] The change in Spain in terms of providing new rights for the local authorities is an example of this case.

The impact of the political parties on foreign policy formation is another domestic factor. It is argued that party political orientation has decreasing relevance for the shaping of foreign policy and that parties throughout Europe generally have similar views on foreign policy issues.[70] Beside the political parties, another domestic element that has an impact on the formation of foreign policy is interest groups. Although it is difficult to judge the level of impact of these groups on foreign policy, these economic or non-economic groups try to influence the foreign policies of member countries.

---

65  Manners and Whitman, "Conclusion," p. 251.
66  Ibid., p. 252.
67  Ibid., p. 253.
68  Ibid., p. 254.
69  Ibid., pp. 254–5.
70  Ibid., p. 255.

Another impact of the Europeanization is the breakdown of the distinction between domestic and foreign issues.[71] It is no longer possible to make a clear distinction between European foreign and domestic policy. However, here the role of globalization also should be taken into consideration. The role of globalization and the increasing importance of NGOs are somehow interrelated. With the transformation of the concept of sovereignty, the state's control over society is decreasing and the number of actors in domestic and foreign policy is increasing. Although the transfer of several rights of sovereign states to Brussels is a part of the Europeanization process, globalization also makes some borders more permeable.

There are three major questions under the heading of the role of the bureaucratic politics in the foreign policy process. These are questions of autonomy and command, the relationship between the foreign ministry and other ministries, and the question of who is responsible for coordinating foreign policy.

Under the title of the autonomy and command, the important point is the relationship between the high level decision making bureaucracy and the staff below. The nature of these relations is crucial in determining the efficiency and the flexibility of the foreign policy. Here there is no single pattern and departments of Foreign Policy have greatest autonomy in the Netherlands, Denmark, Ireland, Spain, Portugal, Greece and Germany.[72] In the case of Greece, as a result of the Europeanization process, the foreign policy making structures of the Ministry of Foreign Affairs (MFA) were reorganized in order to better reflect the pillar structure of the EU.[73] There has been some kind of revolution especially in the foreign ministries of smaller EU states in terms of re-organization and expansion to cope with the political cooperation workload.[74]

On the issue of coordinating the foreign policy, two dynamics are at work in the member countries. On the one hand, the member countries have been consolidating their EU policy coordinating mechanisms in the office of Prime Minister after the success of French and British systems. On the other hand, in most of the member states the external relations of the domestic ministries are expanding as they increasingly conduct their own foreign policies with other member states' domestic ministries.[75] As the activity and autonomy of other ministries increases, the influence of the Ministry of Foreign Affairs decreases.

In the coordination of the foreign policy, the traditional structures of the foreign ministry generally have been maintained. With the increase of external relations of other ministries, the role of coordinating these relations generally belongs to a European minister, who always is subordinated to the foreign minister.[76] Here the

---

71  Ibid., p. 257.

72  Ibid., p. 259.

73  Stelios Stavridis, "The Europeanization of Greek foreign policy: A literature review," available [online]: http://www.lse.ac.uk/collections/hellenicObservatory/pdf/Stavridis-10.pdf, p. 18. [10 July 2006].

74  Michael Smith, "Conforming to Europe," p. 622.

75  Manners and Whitman, "Conclusion," p. 260.

76  Ibid., p. 261.

autonomy and power of the ministries of finance and economy also are increased in relation to the importance of the EU's economic power.

*Foreign Policy Actions*

The analysis of Europeanization from the perspective of foreign policy actions are covered with two headings, actions within the EU and without the EU. Acting within the EU in terms of foreign policy generally generates two opposing conclusions: whether it constricts the actions of the states or creates opportunities for them. Acting with the EU as a member of the Union is used by some countries to modernize their foreign policy outlook. This is especially the case for countries like Ireland, Italy, Greece, Spain and Portugal.[77] For example, in the case of Italy, participation in the EPC mechanism has helped to enlarge the country's range of action.[78] Despite the fact that Italy traditionally has acted in accordance with the European attitude, it some times has taken a more independent position as it did during the post-Cold War period when the EU was not very active. In the case of Italian participation in the UN mission in Somalia, old fashioned concepts of "spheres of influence" emerged in the writings of the Italian press in relation to Somalia.[79]

The general attitude of Britain towards the EPC was not very warm. The decision makers in this country believed that the foreign policy of their country was not wholly dependant on the EPC. This situation was especially true for the Thatcher government.[80] However, Britain's initially desperate situation during the Falkland War enabled the Thatcher government to discover that the EPC could be turned into an advantage and the UK welcomed the support of other EC members.[81] During the Thatcher period, the UK followed a selective approach towards the EPC by supporting many joint initiatives and ignoring others. Despite this trend, there was a gradual evolution of Britain's foreign policy towards working with its European partners.[82]

Although EU membership may affect the foreign policy of some countries that have extensive agendas like Britain and France negatively by constricting some policies, for other countries, EU membership has provided an opportunity to hide difficult decisions. In selected areas, this issue also has helped big states like Germany. It is difficult for Germany to criticize the policies of Israel in Palestine openly because of the historical baggage. However, it is easier to make criticism of Israel and Palestine through the EU framework. In contrast to the cases of Britain and France, smaller states that do not have the capacity to pursue extensive foreign policy agendas and states with historical reasons have been happy with a common approach. Ireland, Portugal, Italy, Belgium, Spain, Greece, and Denmark can be analyzed within this second group of countries. For example, for the case of Greece,

---

77  Ibid., p. 262.

78  Bonvicini, p. 96.

79  Ibid., p. 100.

80  Christopher Hill, "United Kingdom, Sharpening Contradictions," in *The Actors in Europe's Foreign Policy,* edited by Christopher Hill (London: Routledge, 1996), p. 72.

81  Ibid., p. 75.

82  Ibid., p. 76.

it is argued that membership in the EC served both as a diplomatic lever and as a restraining mechanism.[83] After becoming a member of the EC, Greece invoked its veto in EPC matters several times during the 1980s. Here the anti-European attitude of the PASOK Party was influential. At the end of the 1980s, PASOK started to change its position towards a more common approach with other members. It is argued that the reason behind the change was the belief that the EC could provide the answers to Greece's threat perception mainly caused by Turkey.[84] The change in Athens' rhetoric also was related to the aim of the Greece to join the West European Union (WEU). To accomplish this goal, Greece demonstrated its readiness to abide by the strictures of the nine members of the WEU.[85] It is argued that Greece staked so much on the EC (EU) to solve intractable security questions, but had fewer realistic chances to accomplish the goals.[86]

The real Europeanization in the foreign policy of Greece came when Costas Simitis became Prime Minister in 1996.[87] Beside the personal choices of the decision makers like Simitis or George Papandreou, policy failures also played a role here. For example, the support of Greece of the PKK and the sheltering of Öcalan, head of PKK, in a Greek embassy were big mistakes in foreign policy which resulted in the resignation of Pangalos, the then foreign minister of Greece. The negative attitude of Greece during the disintegration of the former Yugoslavia and criticisms from its allies were other reasons for this change. In the last years, Greece preferred to Europeanize its links with its Balkan neighbours, as in the case of the Stability Pact. Greek foreign ministry officials now emphasize the strength and advantages of a Greece that belongs to the EU club.[88]

Some other member countries traditionally have pursued their foreign policy agenda within the general framework of international organizations along with the European context. These are generally post-neutral states like Austria, Finland and Sweden.[89] Sweden has a tradition of international citizenship as a middle power. The developments during and after WWII led to the neutral and defensive policy of Austria. Finland had a defensive position against the USSR until its demise.

Other country responses to the EU membership are removing many of their activities to Brussels, rescuing their foreign policies by making their positions stronger with the help of the EU and the re-nationalization of foreign policies in response to the failure of the EU in some crises.[90] In "rescuing" foreign policy, the EU was perceived as an intergovernmental mechanism in strengthening the position of the country. The reassertion of traditional national foreign policies by some

---

83  Theodor Couloumbis, "The Impact of EC (EU) Membership on Greece's Foreign Policy Profile," in *Greece and EC Membership Evaluated,* edited by Panos Kazakos and Panayotis Ioakimidis (London: Pinter, 1994), p. 191.

84  Tsakaloyannis, p. 191.

85  Ibid., p. 193.

86  Ibid., p. 299.

87  Stavridis, p. 12.

88  Ibid., p. 18.

89  Manners and Whitman, "Conclusion," pp. 263–4.

90  Ibid., pp. 264–5.

member states in dealing with the failures during the crisis times can be seen as the re-nationalization of the policies.

The last factor analyzed by Whitman and Manners in relation to the foreign policy was about the policies that the member states pursued separate from the European context. In the absence of any higher authority to implement a common policy, the member states continued some special relations. These special relations are encompassing the issues of national security (e.g., nuclear states of the UN Security Council like Britain and France, Greece's security issues in the Balkans and the security issue of formerly non-aligned countries like Austria, Finland, Ireland and Denmark), bilateral relations (e.g., Britain's relations with the USA, relations among Nordic countries), European multilateralism (e.g., the EU's policy towards the Middle East).[91]

In the case of Greece, national issues related to security in the near environment are immune to the process of Europeanization.[92] Some scholars argue that this is true for most issues of Greece's foreign policy. They believe that Greece uses the EPC/CFSP frameworks mainly for satisfying its national interests, when that is not possible, for stopping unpleasant developments imposed by its partners instead of using these frameworks as stages and platforms for adapting its foreign policy to the European logic.[93] Stavridis argues that among the "national issues" in the case of Macedonia, Greece's foreign policy was Europeanized and Greece moved towards the position of the EU; and in the case of Cyprus (including Turkey), the EU moved closer to the initial position of Greece.[94] Here the role of the European Parliament is stressed by the same author.

In case of Britain, the protection of national interests and objectives in international relations required sometimes to opt out of a common European approach. When special relations are at stake, Britain generally judges the issues case by case and their style is defined as "Britain first and Europe a more distant second."[95]

Spain's special relations with some countries or regions before membership were affected partly by the Europeanization process. In some cases, like the Western Sahara, Spain diverted from its former position of supporting the Polisario Front to improve relations with Morocco.[96] Although this "European commitment" can be labelled as an alibi before the public opinion, Spanish foreign policy sought to have a place in the EPC by defining the its own priorities like the Mediterranean and Latin America within it, against the general tendency for Eastern Europe.[97] The Mediterranean and Maghreb were included on the list of joint actions area for the EU.

---

91 Ibid., pp. 266–8.

92 Dimitris Kavakas, "Greece," in *The Foreign Policies of European Union Member States*, edited by Ian Manners and Richard Whitman (Manchester: Manchester University Press, 2000), p. 159.

93 K. Kouveliotis, *The Impact of European Integration on the Europeanization of Greek Foreign Policy* (Athens: Institute of International Economic Relations Occasional Paper no. 20, 200), p. 1, quoted in Stavridis, p. 21.

94 Stavridis, p. 21.

95 Hill, "United Kingdom, Sharpening Contradictions," p. 86.

96 Barbe, p. 122.

97 Ibid., p. 123.

The Spanish governments, however, defined their relationship with Latin America in terms of "brotherhood" and "family" and tried to maintain room for manoeuvre for this special relationship.[98] Britain's relations with the Commonwealth states and France's relations with the North Africa also can be included in these examples of other geo-cultural relations. Even the names of institutions exemplify the importance of these relations, since the name of the British ministry of foreign affairs is "Foreign and Commonwealth Office."

In terms of general conclusions from their analysis, Manners and Whitman argue that the analysis of the foreign policies of EU members is separable but not separate from the EU context. The social context in which the foreign policy situated involves relatively a small number of and high level personnel. The role of the ministries of foreign affairs is evolving towards the coordination of the foreign policies of other ministries. The study also argues that the member states conduct all but the most limited foreign policies objectives inside an EU context.[99]

Given all of these different theoretical approaches to the Europeanization of foreign policies of the members and the candidates of the EU, I benefit mostly from the theoretical framework designed by Manners and Whitman. Their focus on countries and the comprehensive structure they constructed are helpful for my analysis. They begin their analysis by defining the current condition of Europe, they continue by analyzing the impact of the European environment on member states, the results of this process and they also look at several cases in order to make comparisons. Beside this framework, I also benefit from the theoretical approaches of Hill, Tonra, Smith and White.

Although the first attempt to analyze the impact of EU membership came from Hill during the time of the EPC before the introduction of the CFSP, the framework provided by Manners and Whitman combines examples from different member states with a comprehensive framework. Both Hill and Manners and Whitman make some generalizations about the changes in the foreign policies of the member states and their position within the CFSP. Whereas Hill groups the member countries according to their responses to the CFSP from cooperative to uncooperative, Manners and Whitman base their grouping of the member states on the size or the countries as big or small or according to their pre-membership foreign policy in the global context.

All of the authors dealing with the Europeanization of foreign policies refer to the increasing cooperation among the member states as a result of increasing communication and contacts. Smith and Hill mention several practical and pragmatic reasons for the member countries to divert from their earlier national policies and cooperate with other member states in foreign policy. The constructivist approach contributes to the analysis by highlighting the importance of the identity issue in the foreign policy analysis. The constructivist's stress on globalization and the historical process of modernity in which Europeanization takes place also is useful in considering the general atmosphere of world politics.

Börzel's conceptualization of the top-down and bottom-up aspects of Europeanization provides a new avenue in the attempts of explanation of the process.

---

98  Ibid., p. 125.
99  Manners and Whitman, "Conclusion," pp. 269–71.

However, it should be noted that the likelihood of bottom-up Europeanization is limited for the candidate countries. In analyzing the responses of countries towards Europeanization, Börzel's grouping of countries as pace-setting, foot-dragging and fence-sitting is also a very useful conceptualization.

I believe that the framework developed for the candidates will be helpful in analyzing the changes in Turkish foreign policy. Also the framework for the members can be adapted to candidate countries with some exceptions. The changes in the foreign policies of the member states will provide some clues for us to predict the possible changes in the Turkish case.

# Chapter 3

# European Integration and the CFSP

In this part, I will briefly cover the transformation of the European Union and the emergence of the need to construct a common foreign and security policy. In this respect, my greatest attention will be on the post-Cold War era. When talking about European foreign policy, I mainly refer to the foreign policies of the member states and policies of some bodies of the European Union. Since some examples about the policies of the member states are given in another chapter, here my focus will be on the Common Foreign and Security Policy of the EU.

The collapse of the Soviet Union and the transition to democratic and market-economy systems in Eastern and Central Europe required the EU's contribution. Without the European Union's economic and political support this transformation could not have materialized. In addition, the ethnic conflicts in the Balkans and the failure of the European Union in managing these crises made the need for a common policy and means to solve crises close to its borders obvious for the EU member states. And last, the developments in the Middle East, especially in Palestine and Iraq, made this issue a priority for the EU. The desire of the EU to have a say on these issues played a role in these attempts. In comparison with the other areas of increased European integration of the 1990s, the developments in the area of the CFSP seem primarily to have been problem driven rather than a spill-over from the institutional setting.[1] In this respect, the CFSP is a bit different from other areas of integration.

The transformation of the EU and attempts at the construction of a common foreign and security policy were not limited to the post-Cold War period and were driven not only by domestic but also by external forces. When discussing the search for a common foreign and security policy in Europe, we should keep in mind the general atmosphere of the international relations. The first attempts in this respect came during the Cold War period and trans-Atlantic relations and NATO are important factors that we have to keep in mind in analyzing the development of common foreign and security policy during and after the Cold War. Beside these external factors, the differences between the member states about the security issues played an important role on the path to be taken. The differences between member states resulted from several points of views. Some member states were the driving force behind the formation of the common foreign policy, like France. Some other states were less enthusiastic because of their perception of different interests and

---

1 Helene Sjursen, "The Common Foreign and Security Policy: Limits of Intergovernmentalism and The Search for a Global Role," in *Making Policy in Europe,* edited by Svein S. Andersen and Kjell A. Eliassen (London: Sage, 2001), p. 187.

strategic relations with other countries, like Germany and the UK. The factors that affected the development of a common foreign and security policy are summarized by some scholars under three headings: "the search for legitimacy, the interests of the member states and the demand for environmental stabilization."[2]

The Common Foreign and Security Policy of the EU has its bases in the Treaty on European Union (Maastricht). With this treaty, the European Communities became a Union and the legal basis of the CFSP was laid down. The inclusion of the CFSP in the treaty owes very much to the demands of France and Germany. With this treaty, the wider objective of a political union was materialized. The German unification at the end of Cold War played an important role in the transformation of the EU. France was determined to secure the economic and monetary union and gave its consent to the unification of Germany with the condition of the deepening of the European integration with political integration.[3] Consequently, for France and Germany, the CFSP was more important as symbol than as substance. And the proposals for the substance of the CFSP were slow. It was difficult to relate the different interests of the members within the overall scheme.[4]

**The Development of the CFSP**

Initiatives to forge a common foreign policy go back to the 1950s. Attempts to establish a European Defence Community in the early 1950s failed and this development led to the strengthening of the NATO framework for European security. Consequently, the security aspect of a common European policy developed along the lines of NATO and the central element in the framing of foreign policy at the European level was that of "civilian power."[5] The civilian diplomacy used the methods of soft power like that of economics and the hard security measures were left to NATO. Although the end of the Cold War created a suitable atmosphere to deviate form this stance, the idea of a global civil power was supported in some self-reflective discussions.[6] The most important aspects of this role are related to aid, trade relations and formalized economic relations. The argument is supported with the fact that the EU members collectively provide 57 percent of the world's development assistance and the European Community alone was the fourth largest aid donor in 2001.[7]

---

2    Michael Smith, "The Framing of European Foreign and Security Policy: Towards a post-Modern Policy Framework?" *Journal of European Public Policy* 10, no. 4 (August 2003), p. 566.

3    Daniel Cohn-Bendit, "Europe's Crisis: What Is To Be Done?", Speech at St. Antony's College, Oxford, 2 November 2005.

4    Simon J. Nuttal, *European Foreign Policy* (New York: Oxford University Press, 2000), p. 271.

5    Michael Smith, "The Framing of European Foreign and Security Policy: Towards a post-Modern Policy Framework?" p. 559.

6    Ian Manners and Richard G. Whitman, "The 'Difference Engine': Constructing and Representing the International Identity of the European Union," p. 388.

7    Ibid.

The 1961 Fouchet Plan proposed a European Political Union. This proposal aimed to coordinate foreign policy on intergovernmental principles, with a European Political Commission to be based in Paris. This plan was perceived as a Gaullist plot to undermine the European Community and in June 1962 it was rejected by a Dutch veto.[8] The European Political Cooperation was created at the Hague Summit of 1969 and inaugurated with the Luxembourg Report of 1970 that proposed the establishment of a European Political Cooperation as an intergovernmental process with no institutional base.[9] The aim here was to provide a mechanism for foreign policy cooperation and coordination to give political direction to the EC's external relations. The desire on the side of the Europeans to have a common foreign policy in the early 1970s were driven especially by three factors: "the enlargement of the communities to include Britain, the increasing perception of risk attached to US foreign policies, and the increasing politicization of apparently economic issues such as those of oil supplies and high technology trade."[10] The EPC prepared the ground for the incoming CFSP.

Despite these factors, the efforts to have a common policy did not bring the desired results. The member countries occasionally agreed on a common stance on some issues, such as the 1980 Venice Declaration, in which member states recognized the Palestinians' right to self-determination and declared that the Palestinian Liberation Organization should be associated with peace negotiations.[11] Although the EPC was not very influential in the formation of a common policy among the members, it is argued that its gradual expansion in institutional framework and policy content played a role in coordinating the western European states and setting the overall agenda during the Helsinki process in the early 1970s.[12] In the early days of the EPC, national interests constituted the major parts of the policy. However, alongside these national policies, formal routines and substantial domains of cooperation contributed to the emergence of a constructed dimension of EPC. Towards the mid-1970s, a firm agenda and relatively consolidated coordination reflex was constructed.[13]

The Single European Act of 1987 provided a treaty basis for the EPC as an intergovernmental process. The emergence and development of the EPC and the CFSP were difficult in comparison with the other issue areas within the community. The basic reasons of this situation arose from the difficult nature of foreign policy cooperation and lack of well-defined bureaucracy dealing with this issue.[14]

---

8 Kenneth Glarbo, "Wide-awake diplomacy: Reconstructing the Common Foreign and Security Policy of the European Union," *Journal of European Public Policy* 6, no. 4 (1999), p. 640.

9 Ibid., p. 650.

10 Michael Smith, "The Framing of European Foreign and Security Policy: Towards a post-Modern Policy Framework?" p. 560.

11 Karen E. Smith, "EU External Relations," in *European Union Politics,* edited by Michelle Cini (Oxford: Oxford University Press, 2003), p. 234.

12 Sjursen, p. 189.

13 Glarbo, p. 645.

14 Michael E. Smith, "Rules, Transgovernmentalism, and the Expansion of European Political Cooperation," in *European Integration and Supranational Governance,* edited by Wayne Sandholtz and Alec Stone Sweet (Oxford: Oxford University Press, 1998), p. 305.

*Post-Cold War Era*

With the end of Cold War, security challenges for Europe drastically changed and threat perceptions focused on diffuse issues like international crime, ethnic conflicts, illegal migration, terrorism, the spread of nuclear weapons and environmental threats. These kinds of soft threats dominated the agenda of Europe. With these changes in threat perceptions, the modest EPC was left behind and replaced by the Common Foreign and Security Policy.[15] The transformation of the European Community into the European Union brought significant changes in the direction of the establishment of the CFSP. With the Treaty on European Union in 1991 (Maastricht), the CFSP was established as an intergovernmental pillar of the Union (Pillar II). The CFSP pillar replaced the EPC in the Maastricht Treaty.

One of the objectives of the Union as asserted in the Maastricht Treaty is "to assert its identity on the international scene, in particular through the implementation of a common foreign and security policy including the eventual framing of a common defence policy, which might in time lead to a common defence."[16] The responsibility for the practical application of the policy is delegated to the West European Union. The new role of the West European Union is made clear by the Petersberg Declaration of 1992. According to this declaration, the military units of the WEU can be employed for humanitarian and rescue tasks, peacekeeping tasks, and tasks of combat forces in crisis management, including peacemaking.[17] Petersberg Tasks were fundamentally humanitarian in nature. Some members of the Union, like Ireland, were militarily neutral and want to keep this characteristic of the country. Treaty on European Union promised that the prospective advancement of the CFSP shall not prejudice the specific character of certain member states.[18] The Maastricht Treaty also makes it clear that the obligations of some member states under NATO will be respected. So, despite the changes in the security environment, trans-Atlantic cooperation is still important for Europe and it is maintained.

Besides the civilian and military part of the European foreign policy, it is argued by some scholars that the EU also should be considered as a normative power.[19] The idea of the pooling of sovereignty, the importance of a transnational European Parliament, the requirements of democratic conditionality, the focus on the protection of human rights are described as the constitutive norms of the EU, which is different from existing states and international relations.[20] The examples of this normative power might be seen in the policy of the EU towards the Middle East. Here the EU has always stressed the importance of international law in the solution of problems.

---

15  Sjursen, p. 190.

16  Nuttal, p. 177.

17  West European Union's Petersbeg Declaration, http://www.weu.int/documents/920619peten.pdf. [24 December 2005].

18  Laura C. Ferreira-Pereira, "The Military Non-Allied States in the CFSP of the 1990s," *European Integration Online Papers* 7, no. 3 (2004), p. 1, available [online]: http://eiop.or.at/eiop/texte/2004-003.htm [24 November 2005].

19  Ian Manners and Richard G. Whitman, "The 'Difference Engine': Constructing and Representing the International Identity of the European Union," p. 389.

20  Ibid.

A growing dissatisfaction with the effectiveness of the diplomatic statements on the side of the EU members led to the adoption of common positions and joint actions.[21] The Treaty on Europe brought two new instruments for the CFSP, common positions and joint actions.[22] However, the member states failed to agree on a list of common interests. In this agreement, in order to increase the possibility of pursuing a common policy, there are provisions for joint actions with Qualified Majority Voting to be applied at the implementation stage. As for all questions related to the CFSP, except for procedural questions and some aspects of joint actions, decisions are taken unanimously. The treaty also states that, "with regard the Council decisions requiring unanimity, Member states will, to the extent possible, avoid preventing a unanimous decision where a qualified majority exists in favour of that decision."[23] After the Treaty on Europe, there were several attempts during 1992 to figure out the common interests and the geographical areas in which joint action could be undertaken. In the short term Central and Eastern Europe, the Commonwealth of Independent States (CIS), the Balkans, the Mediterranean, and in particular the Maghreb and the Middle East were identified as these areas. This means that the CFSP would deploy its instrument of joint action to its geographical neighbours.[24] The CFSP secretariat was incorporated into the Council Secretariat. The Treaty on European Union made references to common defence as an aspiration for the future. With this agreement, the Union made a formal commitment to ensure the overall consistency of external activities.

Within the framework of the CFSP, the Council made decisions on the basis of unanimity and also played a more important role in preparing the decisions. In CFSP matters, the right of initiative currently is shared by the Commission and the member states in accordance with Article 22 of the TEU. However, the Commission's supranational right of initiative is partly deprived of its practical impact due to the organization of European foreign policy bureaucracy which is currently split between the Commission's Directorate General and the Council Secretariat's Directorate General.[25] The weak institutional basis created some problems when the EU faced serious foreign and security issues. The general inability of coordinated action of the EU became particularly clear in relation to the developments in the former

---

21 White, "The European Challenge to Foreign Policy Analysis," p. 50.

22 Some examples of joint actions; support of humanitarian help to Bosnia (November 1993), sending a committee of monitors to the Parliamentary Elections in Russia (November 1993), support for the Middle East Peace Process (19 April 1994), monitoring the election of Palestinian Council and coordinating international activities during the elections (25 September 1995). To reach some of the common positions by the EU, see http://www.consilium.europa.eu/cms3_Applications/applications/search/metaDoSearch.asp [24 July 2006]. In order to reach the list of ongoing joint actions of the EU, see http://ec.europa.eu/comm/external_relations/cfsp/fin/pja_cpcm.htm [6 November 2006].

23 Nuttal, p. 184.

24 Ibid., p. 237.

25 Ingolf Pernice and Daniel Thym, "A New Institutional Balance for European Foreign Policy?" *European Foreign Affairs Review* 7 (2002), pp. 377–8.

Yugoslavia.[26] The early 1990s witnessed increasing expectations on the side of the European countries to become influential in international politics, but the capabilities gradually adjusted to have such an important role. So, there was a capabilities-expectations gap at the heart of the CFSP. This gap reflected the contradiction between the ambitions of the EU member states to play a larger international role and their reluctance to move beyond an intergovernmental framework in doing so.[27] The problems in the implementation of the CFSP occurred especially in three areas: "the nature and content of common positions and joint actions and the extent to which CFSP activities could properly incorporate those of the Community, the financing of CFSP, and the degree of commitment of the member states."[28]

The relevance of NATO to European security became obvious once again at the NATO summit in Berlin in June 1996. At this summit, it was agreed that the European Security and Defence Identity (ESDI) should be developed within the framework of NATO. The creation of the Combined Joint Forces (CJF) by this summit, which would be available to the WEU for European operations, in situations where the United States itself would not wish to participate, was interpreted as a victory for the Atlanticists in Europe.[29]

The Treaty of Amsterdam in 1997 clarified and strengthened the CFSP provisions. According to this agreement, common strategies were to be determined by the European Council and the Policy Planning and Early Warning Unit were to be established in the Council Secretariat.[30] Although the fundamentals of decision making remained unchanged, it was written into the treaty that, after unanimous agreement on common strategies, the Council could proceed with majority voting for joint actions and common positions. This provision was restricted by a provision allowing member states "for important and stated reasons of national policy" to oppose the adoption of a decision by qualified majority voting.[31] Consequently, the practice of voting in the Council very much depends on the balance of these principles and therefore on the willingness of the member states to refrain from blocking consensus. In considering these facts, it is argued that the provisions on the qualified majority voting by and large remained a dead letter.[32]

The Amsterdam Treaty also created the post of the High Representative for the CFSP to help formulate and implement policy decisions and head the Policy Unit. This reform was accepted by the Commission, and also by France and Britain, as the most important change in the CFSP with the Amsterdam Treaty. However, the

---

26  Svein S. Andersen and Kjell A. Eliassen, "Introduction: The EU as a New Political System," in *Making Policy in Europe,* edited by Svein S. Andersen and Kjell A. Eliassen (London: Sage, 2001), p. 7.

27  Hill, "Actors and Actions," p. 5.

28  Nuttal, p. 257.

29  Sjursen, p. 191.

30  Charlotte Bretherton and John Vogler, *The European Union as a Global Actor* (London and New York: Routledge, 2002), p. 173.

31  Sjursen, p. 192.

32  Wolfgang Wagner, "Why the EU's Common Foreign and Security Policy Will Remain Intergovernmental: A Rationalist Institutional Choice Analysis of European Crisis Management Policy," *Journal of European Public Policy* 10, no. 4 (August 2003), p. 589.

authority and influence of the High Representative still very much depends on the personality nominated.[33] Former NATO Secretary General Javier Solana seemed the most suitable person for the position. Besides the position of High Representative, the member states also agreed to appoint some special representatives for various regions like the Middle East and Macedonia. In addition to increasing the visibility of the Union's foreign policy, the delegation of representative powers has contributed to the continuity of EU policies.[34]

*Institutionalization of the CFSP after 1999*

The efforts at the institutionalization of the CFSP gained momentum after the autumn of 1998. Until this date, the discussions on this issue had declared NATO as the centrepiece of European security. But, with 1998 onwards there were developments that represented a new turn for a greater role for the EU. British Prime Minister Tony Blair changed the position of his country and declared its support for a more independent role for the EU. The British and French governments came together at St. Malo to sponsor new proposals for an ESDI building on Amsterdam Treaty arrangements.[35] The St Malo declaration revealed the first signs that the EU would try to develop its own military capabilities outside of NATO in search of a greater international role.[36] After the change in the British attitude, the important blockades to the strengthening of the CFSP were overcome. Until St. Malo, the militarily non-allied states had counted on Britain to sustain the historical defence taboo within the integration process. The change in the policy of Britain created difficulties for these states.[37]

After the St. Malo declaration, at the European Council meeting in Cologne in June 1999 a new course for the CFSP was identified. The Cologne Summit conclusions stressed that the EU must develop the necessary capabilities to fulfil the objective of a common security and defence policy, and that the EU must have the capacity to act autonomously and be supported by a credible military force.[38] Since the Cologne Summit, the implementation of the common foreign and security policy has followed two main patterns. First, the Union sets the goals for military and police forces, later the member states struggle to meet these goals through voluntary contributions of personnel and assets, and candidate countries also complement the process.[39]

The appointment of Javier Solana as High Representative for the Common Foreign and Security Policy in 1999 and the decision to establish a 60.000 troop Rapid Reaction Force (RRF) was another step in the direction of the CFSP. Although

---

33  Sjursen, p. 194.

34  Wagner, p. 587.

35  Michael Smith, "The Framing of European Foreign and Security Policy: Towards a post-Modern Policy Framework?" p. 562.

36  Esra Çayhan, "Towards a European Security and Defense Policy: With or Without Turkey?" *Turkish Studies* 4, no. 1 (Spring 2003), p. 37.

37  Ferreira-Pereira, p. 8.

38  Cologne Summit Conclusions, available [online]: http://europa.eu.int/council/off/conclu/june99/annexe_en.htm [9 December 2005].

39  Antonio Missiroli, "The European Union: Just a Regional Peacekeeper?" *European Foreign Affairs Review*, no. 8 (2003), p. 494.

this force was not a European Army, it gives the Union a political and military tool for carrying out specific types of tasks, humanitarian and rescue missions, peace keeping operations and other crisis management tasks including peacemaking outside Europe. The crisis in Kosovo in that year and the dissatisfaction with the EU's role during the crisis was an important contributor for the decisions above. The Kosovo trauma influenced the attitudes of member countries and helped in the implementation of the Amsterdam Treaty. So, the Cologne and Helsinki Summits represented turning points in the history of the development of the CFSP. In March 2000, temporary structures that would prepare the future Political and Security Committee of ambassadors, the European Military Committee of senior officers and European Military Major Staff, started to operate in Brussels. The same year, in November, member countries came together to specify their commitments to the military capability goals set by the Helsinki European Council.[40]

By the end of 2001, the Laeken European Council declared that the capabilities of common policy are operational, although it was clear that many of the commitments remained to be fleshed out.[41] In spite of these attempts, the Union was still lacking some very important military capabilities and needed NATO's contribution. Another point that should be kept in mind is that the Petersberg tasks of the EU have nothing to do with collective defence. NATO remains the cornerstone of European security and whenever the strategic interests of both EU and North America make it necessary to handle a security crisis, NATO will take the lead.[42]

The problem of the link with NATO was very important for Turkey and the discussions with Turkey on the access and use and release of NATO assets for EU-led operations became problematic for EU. This negotiation was finalized at the end of 2002 and with this so called "Berlin-plus" agreement the EU has gained access to the NATO capabilities and it can work on the assumption that it has access to the NATO capabilities it requires, even when the formal decision will be taken on a case by case basis.[43] The "security strategy paper" titled "A Secure Europe in a Better World" delivered by the High Representative for the CFSP in December 2003, set the new general parameters for future common external action.[44] This paper gives much more attention to potential threats to European security, like the proliferation of weapons of mass destruction and international terrorism, and describes three strategic objectives for EU: cooperation against international terrorism, the prevention of proliferation of Weapons of Mass Destruction (WMD)s and intervention in regional problems. Consequently, it is argued that the Union should develop a strategic culture to respond rapidly to these needs.

The European Union launched its first peacekeeping operations within these parameters. These operations test the Union's ability to apply the stated goals in the

---

40  Çayhan, p. 38.

41  Michael Smith, "The Framing of European Foreign and Security Policy: Towards a post-Modern Policy Framework?" p. 562.

42  Çayhan, p. 44.

43  Missiroli, p. 495.

44  European Security Strategy, A Secure Europe in a Better World, http://www.iss-eu.org/solana/solanae.pdf [12 December 2005].

field. The European Union is engaged in police and military operations in Bosnia and Macedonia, respectively. The police operation in Bosnia started on 1 January 2003 as the European Union Police Mission (EUPM). This was the first civilian crisis management operation under the ESDP. The Union took over the responsibility from the UN, and a total of 531 police officers, eighty percent from member states and twenty percent from other states, perform monitoring, mentoring and inspection activities. The mandate of the mission is for three years. This mission is based on a Council decision and endorsed by the UN and entered into force also with the agreement of the Bosnian authorities.[45] Another ESDP mission of the Union is the "Concordia" mission in Macedonia. The EU took over this mission from NATO and ensuring the implementation of the Ohrid Agreement of August 2001. Here the EU force is patrolling the Macedonian borders with Albania, Kosovo and Serbia. Thirteen EU members and fourteen non-members participate in this operation with 350 military personnel. While Concordia constitutes an EU led mission, the Union draws on NATO assets and capabilities under the Berlin-plus agreement.[46] This case also represents a test for the strategic EU-NATO partnership for crisis management. In the case of Macedonia, no member state unilaterally defected from the common positions agreed in the Council and the EU showed that it learned some lessons form results of the German defection in the early recognition of Croatia and Slovenia in the late 1991.[47] The EU also led another military operation in 2003 in the Democratic Republic of Congo for the improvement of the humanitarian situation in the country.

## Success-Failure of the CFSP

Despite the lack of financial resources and personnel, the record of the High Representative and the Policy Unit has been perceived by some scholars as a success, especially contributing to the Middle East Peace Process and peaceful solution of the problems in the Former Yugoslav Republic of Macedonia.[48] This success is evaluated according to the soft power capabilities of the EU like that of peacekeeping and peacemaking as specified in Petersberg declaration. The EU-led missions in Bosnia, in Macedonia and in the Democratic Republic of Congo showed that the EU is capable of reacting to ongoing humanitarian crisis and to contribute to peace enforcement and stabilization.

These military activities came during a big crisis within the Union over Iraq. The member countries could not agree on a common policy towards the US policies and the invasion of Iraq. However, these three military operations showed that the member countries also share some common interests. Consequently, it seems that it is easier to achieve a common position whenever and wherever there is no major disagreement with the US and NATO.[49] The institutional status quo of the

45  Missiroli, p. 498.
46  Ibid., p. 498.
47  Wagner, p. 583.
48  Karen E. Smith, p. 238.
49  Missiroli, p. 501.

European foreign policy does not guarantee successful European crisis management. Whenever member states can not agree about appropriate policy in a conflict, no effective common policy is likely to emerge.[50]

But some other scholars argue that the CFSP is not successful and explained this failure by three factors:[51] The first is the decline of socialization of the foreign policy decision makers of the member states. Some meetings of the EPC have been transferred from the capital of the Presidency to Brussels and the importance of hospitality factor in the socialization of decision makers evaporated. The second factor is the increasing reliance on EC instruments. The third factor is incorporation of the EPC Secretariat in the Council. This means the Council Secretariat ethos has prevailed; leading to a bureaucratization and legalization of CFSP proceedings. The EU does not have military capabilities at its own disposal and very much depends on the contributions of the members. Besides this, significant command and control capability shortfalls among member states mean that any complex, high end operation would have to depend on NATO capabilities.[52]

Another issue that makes the CFSP seem unsuccessful is related to the decision making procedures. The competencies in European Foreign Policy decision making are still dispersed among several actors like Commission, the six month Presidency, and most recently, the High Representative.[53] There also is no higher authority to impose sanctions in case of non-compliance with the common positions. For example, the rotating six-month presidency plays an important role in the foreign policy of the Union. The presidency not only chairs Council meetings and prepares the agenda, but also represents the Union externally, by expressing the position of the Union in international organizations, conferences and treaty negotiations. This rotating presidency has become a source of imbalance hindering strategic long-term orientations and sometimes even undermining the efficacy of the CFSP.[54] However, smaller states generally are opposing proposals for longer-term presidencies with the fear of losing their impact in the foreign policy. Each presidency tries to add its own political priorities to the CFSP program.

In the elimination of the negative sides of the rotating presidency and the creation some kind of continuity, a troika system has played an important role. The need for a troika system emerged after the first Greek presidency in 1993. This system ensures that ongoing business is not overlooked and that representational and negotiating roles are not neglected or abused. It is argued that the troika system ensured the consultations during Greek presidency on the sensitive issues related with Turkey and Macedonia.[55]

The issues of financing of the operations of the EU missions and the participation of third parties, non member states, candidates may also create some problems for

---

50  Wagner, p. 589.

51  Nuttal, pp. 273–5.

52  Missiroli, p. 501.

53  Wagner, p. 577.

54  Pernice and Thym, p. 392.

55  David Allen, "The European Rescue of National Foreign Policy", in *Actors in Europe's Foreign Policy,* edited by Christopher Hill (London: Routledge, 1996), pp. 293–4.

the future activity of the Union. A proper analysis can be made after several other EU-led military peacekeeping or stabilization operations.

*Identity in Europe's Common Foreign Policy*

One of the problems of the CFSP also is related to the issue of identity. Personal identity, which is subject to change over time, is composed of social factors such as religion, nation, family, social strata, occupation, and education. There is interaction between personal identity and social factors.[56] The last century was the century of nation states and national identity was the most important identity among other identities. The definition of identity according to a nation state contributes to the division between "inner identity" that refers to the common characteristics of the citizens of a nation state and "outer identity" that refers to the differences between the given nation state and other nation states.[57] The central role of the national identity creates some problems for the European identity and consequently for European foreign policy.

A foreign policy rests on a shared sense of national identity, common definitions of enemies, friends and aspirations. These common assumptions are embedded in national history and change very slowly. It is easy to define these requirements for a nation state. The debates on foreign policy take place within constrains of these symbols. However, the shared history and identity of the EU is still weak and the forging of common identities takes time and requires common experiences. This identity issue, on which the foreign policy rests, is also an obstacle to the development of the CFSP.[58] Despite the non-existence of a fully-fledged European identity at the level of foreign policy, it is argued that an institutionalized concert is evident within the political cooperation.[59]

The debate about the European identity has led to confusion. Some scholars argue that it is not clear whether the European identity refers to a collective identity, interlinking collective identities, an aggregation of personal identities, a cultural category, and an EU political identity.[60] They believe that framing the European society in a way described by Hill is a result of thinking that the existence of European society is or will be a product of EU integration in a neo-functionalist sense.[61] They also argue that society is an area which lies beyond the scope of the EU project and there is no direct link between European integration and European society.[62] These scholars believe that European societies are becoming more and more interlinked, however a European society is not emerging and this interpenetration is not confined to Europe but is a result of the globalization process.[63]

56 Zeynep Dağı, "Ulusal Kimliğin İnşası ve Dış Politika," *Demokrasi Platformu* 2, no. 5 (Winter 2005), p. 58.

57 Ibid., pp. 59–60.

58 Hill, "Actors and Actions," p. 8.

59 Glarbo, p. 650.

60 Delanty and Rumford, p. 50.

61 Ibid., p. 4.

62 Ibid., pp. 4–5.

63 Ibid., p. 12.

In order to feel like European citizens, people should first feel some basic geographic attachment to Europe. A survey carried out in 1999 found that the level of very and fair attachment to Europe is around 60 percent and the people in the UK are least likely attached with 37 percent, followed by the people in Greece by 41 percent and by the people in Netherlands by 49 percent.[64] According to the same survey, the level of attachment to Europe is highest among the citizens in Luxembourg. When asked about the definition of their identity by national and European elements, despite the existence of a European identity, we see the persistence of national identities. Although people generally refer to both their national and European identities at the same time, defining the identity only as European at very much lower rates in comparison with the definition only with the national identities. People in Luxembourg feel European only by 20 percent (the highest ratio) and people in the UK (67 percent), Sweden, Finland (both 61 percent) and Greece (60 percent) define themselves only with their national identities.[65] The same survey found that 38 percent of EU citizens agree that there is a shared European cultural identity, 49 percent disagree with this statement.[66]

There is a general trend among the citizens of the member states to identify themselves with Europe and the proliferation of Europeanized personal identities.[67] The impact of Europe on collective identities is lower in comparison with the impact on personal identities. However, this Europeanization of identities does not mean superseding or eliminating national ones. Generally, people refer to their both national and European identities when they are asked on this issue.[68] The persistence of national identities and the weak position of the European identity in comparison with the national identities create some setbacks for the European Foreign Policy. At the end, the definition of the European identity by Delanty and Rumford refers "to specific modes of self-understanding that have arisen from the increased interpenetration of European societies and from a certain liquidification of national identities."[69]

After reviewing several approaches related to the foreign policy of the European Union, some scholars proposed the term "international identity of the European Union" (IIEU) to conceptualize the global role of the European Union.[70] They draw six constitutive features of this international identity of the EU and these are described as follows:[71] First, the IIEU is constructed and described as pacific, despite the development of some military structures. Second, the IIEU has a principled international identity, meaning it is constructed around particular interpretations of

---

64 "How Europeans See Themselves", *Report of the European Commission*, p. 10, available [online]: http://ec.europa.eu./publications/booklets/eu_documentation/05/txt_en.pdf [18 September 2006].

65 Ibid., p. 11.

66 Ibid., p. 12.

67 Timothy Garton Ash, "Why Britain is in Europe," Speech at St. Antony's College, Oxford, 1 June 2006.

68 Ibid.

69 Delanty and Rumford, p. 55.

70 Ian Manners and Richard G. Whitman, "The 'Difference Engine': Constructing and Representing the International Identity of the European Union," pp. 381–2.

71 Ibid., pp. 398–400.

liberal-democratic principles. Third, the IIEU is based on consensus and acts in a slow and structural way instead of rapid reactions. Fourth, the IIEU is one of several networks, rather than a single entity, meaning it connects a variety of governance modes. Fifth, the IIEU is seen as open, meaning its decision making process and system of consultation and legislation is more open to outsiders than most political entities. Sixth, the IIEU is clearly contra-Westphalian, meaning the EU represents the antithesis of the state in the post-Cold War World.

The results of Eurobarometers point out that the citizens of the Union support the common foreign policy. According to a survey carried out in the spring of 2003, the support for common foreign policy is 67 percent in the current member states whereas the opposition to this policy is 19 percent.[72] As it could be expected, the weakest support for the principle of the CFSP is in the UK and the UK was the only member state in which less than half of the population appeared to support the CFSP.[73] Although public opinion supports a common foreign policy among the member states, the governments failed to have a common stance before the invasion of Iraq. The figures of support for the common foreign policy are just a few points below in the candidate countries. Support for a common defence policy is slightly higher in member states and in candidate countries in comparison with the support for common foreign policy.[74]

## The Effects of Global Conditions on the CFSP

The transformation of the EU and attempts at the construction of a common foreign and security policy were driven not only by domestic and but also by external forces. Domestically, the integration attempts were successful in several areas, like the economy and social policy. After completing this integration, there were differing views about the future of the European Union. There was a disagreement on the precedence of enlargement or deepening. After long debates, the road for both deepening and enlargement opened.

We also should consider that decision making in foreign policy includes several aspects like domestic constituency, external constituency, policies of other states and globalization. No actor could control all of these variables in making decisions and consequently, there should be a balance among these aspects. In addition there might be some changes in this balance according to the changes in the circumstances.

On the side of the external developments, events like 9/11 and the invasion of Iraq also had important repercussions for the CFSP. The 9/11 events resulted in changes in threat perceptions and the asymmetric threats of the post-Cold War era began to dominate the EU's foreign and security policy agenda. Beside this development, the foreign policy of the USA after 9/11 exposed the problems of the foreign and security policy of Europe. The crisis situations made the vulnerability of the CFSP of the EU obvious. In a crisis in international relations, there is a high threat against countries

---

72  Standart Eurobarometer, http://ec.europe.eu/public_opinion/archives/notes/csf_pesc_papr03_en-pdf. [22 September 2006].

73  Ibid.

74  Ibid.

and countries have short time to decide and act. But the framework of the CFSP of the EU prevented the Union from responding to the events promptly. The crisis situations underlined the diverging opinions among the member states and especially the distinctive positions of the new member states. The member countries wanted to become influential in the international scene, but they failed to cooperate.

The nature of crisis situations also explains why there are few incentives for delegating sovereignty to supranational agencies and thus why the EU's CFSP has not been communitarized and why it is unlikely to become so in the future.[75] On the one hand, member states pursue common political and economic policies and on the other hand, they maintain individual national stances on several issues. Consequently, they present a confusing and often incoherent face to outside world.[76]

In addition to the existing division among the former members about the importance of Atlantic relations for the Union, the invasion of Iraq in 2003 added new dimensions to this debate. In the unipolar world of today, the Iraqi crisis showed the difficulties of having a consensus within the EU on a specific foreign policy issue where national interests were conflicting. This crisis proved the weakness of the CFSP, but also contributed to developments like the publication of strategy paper, and the decision to give more substance to a common defence policy.[77] Most of the new members of the EU supported the US-led coalition along with some important members of the Union. The intergovernmental structure of the CFSP became obvious once again when member states could not agree on a common policy towards the invasion of Iraq. Although the capabilities of the EU limited the ability of the Union to act in crisis situations, the EU is still an important actor in cases of soft security operations and long term political stabilization activities like in the cases of the Balkans and Afghanistan.[78]

Despite these attempts to have a common policy, it should be kept in mind that the CFSP is not a single policy. The foreign policies of the member states were not abolished by the Maastricht Treaty and the CFSP does not replace the national foreign policies. Each member state wants to put its own priorities at the top of the European agenda. The member states' commitment was to "actively support the Union's external and security policy actively and unreservedly in a spirit of loyalty and mutual solidarity."[79] And European foreign policy is a system of external relations, a collective enterprise through which national actors conduct partly common, and partly separate, international actions.[80]

The interaction between European foreign policy and the complementary national actions remain of great political importance for the overall coherence and consistency of the European foreign policy. Since European civil servants can

---

75  Wagner, p. 584.

76  Allen, p. 289.

77  Sinan Ulgen, "Of Chaos and Power: Will Europe Become a Strategic Community?" *Turkish Policy Quarterly* 2, no. 4 (Winter 2004), p. 40.

78  Michael Smith, "The Framing of European Foreign and Security Policy: Towards a post-Modern Policy Framework?" p. 563.

79  Nuttal, p. 267.

80  Hill, "Actors and Actions," p. 5.

not perform every task related with the foreign policy, national civil servants will continue to have an important part to play in this area.[81] Member states continue their policies within the framework designed in the TEU. This treaty-based framework of the EU nominally restricts foreign policy to the realm of intergovernmental cooperation and coordination with limited roles for supranational organizations like the Commission and the Court of Justice.[82] Therefore, in considering the existence of national foreign policies along with the European one, it is not very easy to locate the European Union foreign policy in the classical foreign policy analysis schemes. As placed under the Pillar II of the TEU, the CFSP is intergovernmental in nature and consequently a realist approach of the IR is the dominant approach in analyzing the CFSP. The intergovernmental setting resulted in the fact that the interstate negotiation remains the norm within the present day CFSP. It is argued that the common positions and common actions of the EU are rarely forged because of the displays of national interests and there also are unilateral defections even after some common positions.[83] These realities have caused disappointments about the expectations of a supranational foreign policy.

---

81  Pernice and Thym, p. 390.

82  Frank Schimmelfennig and Wolfgang Wagner, "Preface: External Governance in the European Union," *Journal of European Public Policy* 11, no. 4 (August 2004), p. 658.

83  Glarbo, p. 635.

# Chapter 4

# The Middle East Policy of the European Union

The years following World War II witnessed the transformation of the European continent from historically divided nation states and ideologically divided blocs into an emergent unified economic and political power centre in the global competition. The transformation of the continent occurred in a multi-staged and dialectical process that was the result of an action-reaction relation between the intra-Europe forces and the international context.

Today's European Union began with a defensive strategic mentality as a response to the weak position of Europe in the international arena after the end of World War II. When the war was over, the power centre of the world was no longer Western Europe. The power rested at the two flanks of the continent: one on the other side of the Atlantic, in the USA; the other on the eastern flank of the continent, in the USSR. This was a new phenomenon for the politics of the continent at that time. In order to overcome this weakness and to make the continent powerful again, the wars had to be prevented and to secure this, the international coordination of economics and politics was necessary. The basic aim was to control the German-French rivalry and prevent a new war. The cooperation in the control of coal and steel, which were crucial raw materials for the war machines, spilled over to other areas and the road to today's European Union opened. The above-mentioned transformation was affected at every stage by the internal dynamics of Europe and by the external dynamics of the international system. Within this transformation not only institutions changed, also the mentality of the cooperation. In this evolutionary process several paradigmatic changes occurred: From national economies to regional economic union, from political structures based on national sovereignty to supranational political institutionalization, and from cultural homogeneity to multicultural society.

The transformation of the European integration was necessary in order to make Europe a unified political and economic actor in the current global era. In order to be considered as an important global actor, the EU had to have a credible common foreign policy. As an important actor in the global scale, the EU tries to create a common foreign policy and the Middle Eastern region is one of the most important regions for the EU in its foreign policy. Turkey, as a European and also a Middle Eastern country, has a place in the policy of the EU towards the Middle East. In this part, I will analyze developments in the formation of a common EU foreign policy, the place of the Middle East in this policy, different aspects of this policy and the role of Turkey here. I will focus mainly on the post-Cold War era since at this time European Community has transformed itself into the European Union and had taken a more institutionalized political structure.

When the EU's or the EU's member countries policies regarding the Middle East are analyzed, it is seen that Palestinian-Israel problem and the developments in Iraq after the Gulf War are the two most important issues for the foreign policy considerations. For this reason, my analysis also will mainly focus on these issues.

## The EU's Interest in the Middle East

Establishing a Common Foreign and Security Policy was on the agenda of European Union during the 1990s and the developments in this respect gained momentum after 1999. It is not easy, however, to establish a common foreign policy if we consider the persistence of the primacy of national foreign policies. Since the signing of the Treaty on European Union, there is a commitment for the CFSP. But it is accepted by several scholars that foreign policy integration is different from internal integration. Although several and differing opinions for the success or failure of the EU in the formation of a common foreign policy in the 1990s mentioned in the previous section, it is generally accepted that the EU's ability to do this is limited.[1] European policy towards the Middle East and especially towards the Palestinian-Israeli conflict, however, constitutes an ideal case for the analysis of the EU's ability to form a common foreign policy.[2] It is argued that "the EU has nevertheless made itself clearly visible on the Middle East stage, presenting a distinguished international identity."[3] The decisions for the establishment of a common foreign policy and the means required to implement this policy are strengthening the possibility of the ability of the EU to act in the Middle East. The EU's policies towards the region are organized under three main headings: the Middle East Peace Process, the Barcelona Process and Mediterranean Partnership, and the relations with the Gulf countries.

Although several arguments can be raised for the interest of the European countries towards the Middle East, the basic reasons for this interest can be given as proximity to the region, dependence on the region's energy sources, trade relations, the investments of European firms in this region, illegal immigrants and workers coming from this region, the relations of some European countries with the region as former colonial rulers, and the threat of spillover of instability from the region. The official documents of the EU stressed the points of geography, shared history, immigrants and interdependence between Europe and the Middle East and Mediterranean as the reasons of the interest of the EU in the region.[4] More than half

---

1   Ian Davidson and Philip H. Gordon, "Assessing European Foreign Policy," *International Security* 23, no. 2 (Fall 1998), pp. 184–186.

2   Costanza Musu, "European Foreign Policy: A Collective Policy or a Policy of Converging Parallels?" *European Foreign Affairs Review* 8 (2003), p. 35.

3   Ben Soetendrop, *Foreign Policy in the European Union: Theory, History and Practice* (London: Longman, 1999), p. 113, quoted in Ian Manners and Richard G. Whitman, "The 'Difference Engine': Constructing and Representing the International Identity of the European Union," p. 382.

4   Draft Final Report on an EU Strategic Partnership with the Mediterranean and the Middle East, p. 3, available [online]: http://register.consilium.eu.int/pdf/en/04/st10/st10246.en04.pdf [4 December 2006].

of Europe's import of oil comes from the region and exports of the EU to the Middle East and North Africa totalled 77.5 billion dollars in 1995.[5] Consequently, the EU cannot be indifferent to the developments in the region. Beside the factors mentioned above, the issues of democratization and human rights are becoming sensitive issues in relations between the EU and Middle Eastern countries.[6] The end of the Cold War increased the sensitivity of European countries to these issues. Currently the calls for democratization and respect for human rights are generally on the top of the agendas of European countries towards the Middle East.

Problems in the Middle East and the economic problems related to the oil crisis after 1973 were important for the European countries. One of the first functions of the emerging EPC of the EC and the informal semi-annual Gymnich meetings within the EPC was to work to remedy short term disagreements over the Middle East and energy politics.[7] Although Europe's interest in the region increased as a result of the 1973 oil crisis, the EC's Venice Declaration of 1980 can be labelled as the official beginning of a common approach to the Middle East. But there are some indigenous and exogenous factors that were encouraging or impeding the EU's ability to have a binding foreign policy for the Middle East. The pressures from the international arena on the EU to play a more active role as a global actor congruent to its economic capabilities and the pressures from the Arab states to balance the USA's support for Israel in Palestinian-Israeli conflict can be given as examples of exogenous factors.[8] For example, the former Iraqi leader Saddam Hussein argued in an Arab Cooperation Council meeting in Amman on February 24, 1990, that the dissolution of the Soviet Union was a complete disaster for Arabs and in order to balance the support of the USA to Israel, Arab countries should develop relations with the EU and Japan.[9] But the EU's contribution to the solution of the problems in the Middle East was far from satisfying the expectations of the Arab states. The EU did not and could not replace the Soviet Union. It is also questionable to expect the EU to play such a role. The characteristics of world politics changed in the post-Cold War era and the characteristics of the Soviet Union and the European Union are very much different.

In response to the pressures for more involvement on the side of the Arabs in the conflict, Israel and the USA press the EU not to get too much involved in the conflict. We should keep in mind that although Europe is dependent on the region for oil supplies, it is dependent on the USA in terms of some security issues. Although the trans-Atlantic relations were always important for the Europe, the end of Cold War increased the possibility of a more independent approach for Europe. The differences between member countries regarding the Middle East, the existence of

---

5 Rosemary Hollis, "Europe and the Middle East: Power by Stealth?," *International Affairs* 73, no. 1 (1997) p. 16.

6 Soren Dosenrode and Anders Stubkjaer, *The European Union and the Middle East* (London: Sheffield Academic Press, 2002), p. 146.

7 Glarbo, p. 642.

8 Musu, p. 38.

9 Robert W. Rodman, "Middle East Diplomacy after the Gulf War," *Foreign Affairs* 70, no. 2 (Spring 1991), pp. 2–3.

common institutions and the development of a common vision are some aspects of the endogenous factors that affect the EU's common foreign policy regarding the Middle East.

The EU's involvement in the Middle East and the aims for the establishment of a common approach to the region increased after the end of Cold War. In relation to the transformation of the European Union from an economic gathering to a more concrete political union, the EU's desire and ability to play a more effective role in the Middle East increased. One of the meanings of the end of the Cold War for the Middle East was US supremacy in the region's politics. There was no more USSR to balance the US presence there. The Arabs demanded a more active role on the part of EU to balance the US power, but the policy makers in the EU and the leaders of the member countries believed that the role of the EU was not to compete with the US, but to complement it.[10]

The lack of military capabilities and sufficient political instruments on the side of the EU induced the union mostly to focus on economic issues during the 1990s. The EU helped in the construction of the peace process between the Palestinians and Israelis. In this respect, the EU was the most important donor to the Palestinian Authority. There are arguments that neither the officials in Brussels nor the leaders of the member countries want to limit their involvement to the economic aspects of the peace process. Contrary to this view, however, other scholars believe that the members of the EU are unwilling for it to become a military power and believe that the end of the Cold War has taken away the most compelling reason behind the need for a common foreign policy.[11] The European Union is known for its "soft power" characteristics and its involvement in the Middle East was mostly with soft measures involving economic and diplomatic powers. In relation to that, some scholars argue that the EU is not a Westphalian type polity with hierarchical governance or fixed territory and consequently it is unlikely that the EU will develop a Westphalian role of military power.[12]

## The Palestinian-Israeli Peace Process and the European Union

The first common action of the European Community (EC) came after the oil crisis of 1973 with the declaration accepted at the meeting of the European Political Cooperation in November 1973.[13] With this declaration, the EC accepted the Palestinian question as a political question and called for the recognition of the

---

10  Volker Perthes, "Points of Difference, Cases for Cooperation: European Critics of US Middle East Policy," *Middle East Report*, no. 208 (Autumn 1998), p. 31.

11  Davidson and Gordon, p. 185.

12  Ian Manners and Richard G. Whitman, "The 'Difference Engine': Constructing and Representing the International Identity of the European Union," p. 391.

13  Robert E. Hunter, "Western Europe and the Middle East Since the Lebanon War," in *The Middle East after the Israeli Invasion of Lebanon*, edited by Robert E. Freedman (New York: Syracuse University Press, 1986), p. 103, quoted in Muzaffer Şenel, "Avrupa Birliği'nin Ortadoğu Barış Sürecine Etkleri," in *Filistin Ç ıkmazdan Çözüme,* edited by İbrahim Turhan (İstanbul: Küre, 2003), p. 137.

legal rights of the Palestinians by Israel, the withdrawal of Israel from the territories occupied after the 1967 war, and the recognition of the existence of Israel in the region by the Arab states as the essential conditions for the solution of the problems.

The Venice Declaration of the EC Council on 12–13 June 1980 is a milestone in the EU's policy towards the Israeli-Palestinian problem. With this declaration, the EC accepted the PLO as the legitimate representative of the Palestinians and recognized the right of self-determination for the Palestinians.[14] The EC also stressed the need for recognition of Israel by the states in the region. With this declaration the EC accepted that peace in the Middle East is a condition for the security and stability of Europe because of the geographical proximity and common interests in the region. This argument is stressed again by the official documents of the EU in the post-Cold War era within the framework of peace process and also in relation to the security in the Mediterranean. In the common strategy of the EU Council accepted in June 2000, the EU declared that "the EU is convinced that the successful conclusions of the Middle East Peace Process on all its tracks, and the resolution of the other conflicts in the region, are important prerequisites for peace and stability in the Mediterranean."[15] The acceptance of the PLO as the legitimate representative of the Palestinians was against the official policy of Israel, which described the PLO as a terrorist organization. Although Israel and the USA continued to see it as a terrorist organization, the PLO already had been accepted by the Arab League and in 1974 by the UN General Assembly as the official representative of the Palestinians.[16] The EC condemned Israel's occupation of Lebanon and argued that this action ended the hopes of peace in the region. In those years, the EC supported all of the peace initiatives for the solution of the Israeli-Palestinian problem like the Fahd Plan of 1981 and the Reagan Plan of 1982.[17]

The eruption of the first Intifada in the occupied territories in the December 1987 and the harsh response of Israel attracted the attention of the EC countries towards the region. The presidency conclusions of the 1989 Madrid Summit described four basic principles for the peace in the Middle East as follows: An international conference under the auspices of the UN, the participation of the PLO in the peace process, negotiations that would be supported by the EC based on the principle of "land for peace" and free elections in the occupied territories.[18]

---

14 For the text of the 12–13 June Venice Declaration of European Council see http://domino.un.org/UNISPAL.nsf/2ee9468747556b2d85256cf60060d2a6/fef015e8b1a1e5a6852 56d810059d922!OpenDocument [4 December 2006].

15 "Common Strategy of the European Council of 19 June 2000 on the Mediterranean region", Official Journal of European Communities, 22 July 2000, available [online:] http://www.consilium.europa.eu/uedocs/cmsUpload/mediEN.pdf [2 December 2006].

16 For the text of the UN General Assembly Resolution on this issue see http://daccessdds.un.org/doc/RESOLUTION/GEN/NR0/738/38/IMG/NR073838.pdf?OpenElement [8 May 2006].

17 Şenel, p. 150.

18 Andrzej Kornikowsky, "EU-Israeli Elections," in *The European Union and the Developing Countries: The Challenges of Globalization*, edited by Carol Cosgrove Sacks (London: Macmillan, 1999), p. 230.

During the Cold War period, the involvement of the EC in the Israeli-Palestinian issue had been limited and mostly had consisted of declarations. The main reasons for this had been the dominance of the security considerations of the period and the supremacy of NATO in security and foreign policy issues, and the economic nature of European integration.

The fall of the Berlin Wall represented the end of the security threat to the Europe from the east and this change affected the perceptions of threat, defence and security. Instead of invasion or inter-bloc warfare, new security threats for Europe are small but more dynamic in nature. Conflicts and civil wars in the near abroad of Europe are the new threats to the security of Europe. Beside the instabilities in the East Europe and the Balkans, political and economic instabilities in the Middle East and the Southern Mediterranean have been a source of concern for Europe in the post-Cold War period. In response to these challenges, the involvement of the EC (later the EU in this period) in the Middle Eastern problems increased.

The first attempt of the EC in this respect came during the Madrid Peace Process. Arab countries were generally positive about the participation of the EC in the international peace conference in Madrid under the auspices of the UN. In order to participate to the Madrid Peace Conference, however, the EC had to obtain the consent of Israel. After several negotiations with the Israeli side, the EC could participate to the peace process. The contribution of the EC to the process during and after the Madrid Peace Conference in 1991 concentrated on economic and diplomatic issues. During the Madrid Peace Conference different from the USA, the EC stressed the importance of international law and urged Israel to accept "land for peace" principle.

With the Treaty on European Union, the EC was turned into the EU and the EU started to develop its common foreign and security policy. Support of the Middle East Peace Process was one of the first common actions of the EU. Europe aimed to increase its influence with the help of economic aid mechanisms.

After the Declaration of Principles (Oslo Agreement) in 1993 for a peaceful settlement of the Palestinian-Israeli dispute, the EU was the most important donor to the peace process. Just after the Oslo Agreement, the Union accepted the Copenhagen Action Plan and provided a budget of 9.2 million ECU, for the infrastructural works in the region.[19] The EU provided 45 percent of the financial aid to the Palestinians within the framework of the peace process.[20] In order to increase its political impact on this issue, the EU decided in May 1994 to help in the organization and monitoring of the Palestinian elections in January 1996. Another initiative of the EU to strengthen its position in the Peace Process was the appointment of Spanish diplomat Miguel Angel Moratinos as the special envoy of the EU for the Peace Process in 1996.[21] Although he faced great difficulties in his job because of the mandate of the Council of Ministers, this development was the first attempt to reduce the difficulties and

---

19 Şenel., p. 155.

20 Hollis, p. 22.

21 Esther Barbe, "Balancing Europe's Eastern and Southern Dimension," in *Paradoxes of European Foreign Policy*, edited by Jan Zielonka (London: Kluwer Law, 1998), pp. 117–18.

inconsistencies of the CFSP due to the rotating EU presidency system.[22] Moratinos was replaced in July 2003 by Belgian diplomat Marc Otte, who was formerly advisor to CFSP High Commissioner Solana.[23]

## Mediterranean Partnership

In the post-Cold War era, beside the Arab-Israeli Peace Process, the European Union's interest in the Middle East and Arab countries continued under the umbrella of the Euro-Mediterranean partnership program inaugurated at the Barcelona Conference of 27–28 November 1995. The connections between security in the Mediterranean and in the Middle East are officially accepted by the EU as it is shown in the pages above. This attempt represented one of the first examples of how the EU would establish relations with countries, with which it does not share boundaries. This process also can be seen as an initiative to respond to the arguments of the clash of civilizations. The reasons for the Mediterranean partnership are described by Nicolaidis as follows:[24] The impact of the Gulf War, the Madrid peace process, the internal war in Algeria, enlargement of the EU to the East and the threat of illegal migration from northern Africa and the Middle East. This initiative was also a test case for the EU's capacity as a normative power.

The aims of the Euro-Mediterranean Partnership are officially described as:

- to create a common area of peace and stability through political dialogue;
- construct a zone of shared prosperity through an economic and financial partnership and the gradual establishment of a free trade zone;
- promote the rapprochement between peoples by encouraging social, cultural and human exchanges between cultures and civil societies.[25]

The purpose of the Barcelona Process was to have common projects in areas of politics and security, economics and finance, social, cultural and humanitarian relations within the framework of bilateral and regional agreements between the EU and Mediterranean littorals. However, the lack of common strategic security perception among the participants prevented the emergence of an act similar to that of the 1975 Helsinki Act, which in time turned into the OSCE. Consequently, partnership focused on the economic development of the region.[26] The trade figures between the EU and the region verify this argument. Europe accounts for nearly 50

---

22 Musu, p. 46.

23 Dışişleri Güncesi, July 2003. p. 112, available [online]: http://www.mfa.gov.tr/NR/rdonlyres/2F815293-BCB4-4638-8AD4-8A8B250D38A9/0/temmuz2003.pdf [9 July 2006].

24 Kalypso Nicolaidis, "Europe as a Normative Power: Why is the Euro-Med Partnership in Crisis and What Should be Done About It?" Paper Presented at European Studies Centre, University of Oxford, 16 January 2006, Oxford.

25 European Union Factsheet, The Euro-Mediterranean Partnership, available [online]: http://www.consilium.europa.eu/uedocs/cmsUpload/MEDIT.pdf [2 December 2006].

26 Şenel, p. 155.

percent of the imports and exports of the region according to 2003 figures.[27] Another reason for the failure of an institution similar to the OSCE is the fact that Brussels made all of the important decisions. Europeans insisted on keeping a distinction between the partnership program and the peace process.

The EU signed the Euro-Med Partnership Agreement with Israel on 20 November 1995. Another agreement concerning trade relations between the EU and Israel came into effect on 1 January 1996. A commerce and cooperation agreement between the EU and the Palestinian Authority was signed on 24 February 1997.[28] With these agreements, the EU was trying to contribute to the political dialogue in the region and to help in the construction of security and stability. Although some members of the EU like Germany, France and the UK opposed to the opening of tunnels under the Temple Mount in 1996 and called Israel to close the tunnels that would endanger the Masjid el Aqsa, a coordinated effort on the side of the EU was difficult to achieve. When Arafat asked to meet with the troika in Luxemburg before going to New York to meet with Israeli Foreign Minister David Levy and asked for help on 6 October 1996, Irish Foreign Minister Dick Spring was visiting Israel and saying that they were against the involvement of the EU in the Peace Process as his country was holding the EU presidency for six months.[29]

The policies of Netanyahu government diminished the impact of the EU in the peace process. With the Israeli government's decision in 1997 to construct new settlements in the occupied territories, the members of the EU criticized the policies of Israel. EU special envoy Miguel Moratinos, with the cooperation of the US special envoy Dennis Ross, prepared a ten-point "code of conduct" for the elimination of the deadlock in the peace process and presented it to US President Clinton as a complimentary attempt of the EU to the US efforts.[30] The response of Netanyahu to this initiative was negative and he argued that the role of the EU in the Middle East peace process was confined to the economic sphere.[31] The negative attitude of the Netanyahu government to the role of the EU created a setback for the effective involvement of the Union since it lacked the capacity to pressure Israel to return to the negotiations.

The attempt to overcome the deadlock in the Peace Process came from the US. With the US pressure on Israel, Netanyahu and Arafat agreed to work for the end of diplomatic impasse with the Wye River Memorandum of 23 October 1998. Special envoy Moratinos followed the Wye River Memorandum on behalf of the EU. The change of government in Israel and the attitude of the new Israeli Prime Minister Ehud Barak created hopes for the solution of the problem. There were great expectations for a settlement when the parties came together at Camp David in July 2000. When

27 European Union Factsheet, The Euro-Mediterranean Partnership, available [online]: http://www.consilium.europa.eu/uedocs/cmsUpload/MEDIT.pdf [2 December 2006].

28 Esa Paasivirta, "EU Trading with Israel and Palestine: Parallel Legal Frameworks and Triangular Issues," *European Foreign Affairs Review* 4, no. 3 (Fall 1999), p. 306.

29 Hollis, p. 21.

30 Şenel, p. 157.

31 Ibid., p. 158.

the discussions between Barak and Arafat for a settlement of the problems failed, each side blamed the other and a new phase of the conflict began.

## The Second Intifada

After the breakdown of the negotiations at Camp David, the government in Israel was in danger and the elections in early 2001 resulted in a hard line government. Likud leader Sharon visited Masjid el Aqsa along with several policemen and this action sparked the fire of the second (el Aqsa) Intifada. For the revival of the peace attempts, representatives from Israel, Palestine, Egypt, Jordan, the USA and the EU came together in Sharm el Sheikh and decided to establish a committee, known as the Mitchell Committee, for the finding of the facts in the region. Members of the committee, which was established on 7 November 2000, included former Turkish president Süleyman Demirel and the EU High Commissioner for Foreign and Security policy Javier Solana. The inclusion of the EU High Commissioner for the CFSP in the committee is a sign that the EU was becoming a political actor in the peace process. The report prepared by the committee urged a re-start of the negotiations, an end to the violence and the co-working of Israel and Palestinian Administration for confidence building.[32]

The attempts of the EU special representative Moratinos enabled the start of new negotiations between the two sides but the elections in Israel on 6 February 2001 resulted in victory for the Likud Party. Ariel Sharon, head of Likud Party, declared that he would not recognize the results of the negotiations; the negotiations failed, despite the desire of the Arab states to continue the process.[33]

The visit of Israeli Prime Minister Sharon in the first half of 2001 to several European countries made the differences between European capitals and Tel Aviv in approaching the issue more obvious. In his visits to Paris and Berlin, Sharon blamed Arafat and the Palestinians for the failure of the peace negotiations. The European politicians urged him to deal with Arafat and warned about the negative consequences of the plans for sending Arafat to exile.[34] Sharon had to cancel his visit to Belgium because of a legal case against him in relation to his role in the massacres of Sabra and Shatilla.

The developments in this period showed that the Israeli government was not willing to negotiate with the Palestinians according to the framework of the peace process which had begun with the Oslo Declaration of Principles and was trying to impose its own terms for the re-start of negotiations. The Sharon government pursued a policy of de-legitimizing Arafat and refusing to negotiate with him. Earlier plans for sending Arafat into exile turned into limiting his movements. The EU members generally opposed this policy and advised Israel to deal with Arafat as the elected, legitimate representative of the Palestinians. Such kind of an atmosphere declined the influence of the EU in the Middle East peace process since Israel was pursuing a

---

32  For the text of the Mitchell Commission, see http://www.mideastweb.org/mitchell_ report.htm [4 December 2006].

33  Şenel, p. 162.

34  *Radikal*, 7 July 2001.

new framework for the solution of the problem. The capabilities of the EU were more appropriate for the conditions of peace and stability, and the deadlock in the problem limited the options of the EU. The negative attitude of Israel towards the diplomatic initiatives of the EU was the biggest obstacle for an active role of the EU.

## 9/11 and its Aftermath

The attacks of 9/11 and the US foreign policy after this event affected the developments in the Israeli-Palestinian conflict. Sharon's government portrayed Arafat and the Palestinians as the allies of Osama bin Laden and tried to end the international support for the Palestinians. The US supported this policy of the Sharon government, but the EU members argued that the peace process could not work without Arafat and that the weakening of Arafat might have negative consequences. When the EU governments criticized Israel's policy on this issue, the Israeli officials accused the EU as being anti-Semitic.[35] This historical baggage has always negatively affected the policy of the EU in this process. When Israel is criticized by the European countries for its policies, Israeli officials quickly respond by referring to the persecution of the Jews in Europe.

During these years, the role of the EU was limited because of the objection of the Sharon's government to re-start negotiations without preconditions. The general policy of the Israeli government was to start negotiations for a settlement from the beginning since the conditions were changed. But the EU opposed to this argument and was angry about the destruction of the Palestinian infrastructure, which mostly was constructed with European funding.

Another initiative in which the EU took part was the Road Map proposed by the Quartet (USA, Russia, the UN and the EU) on 30 April 2003 for the settlement of the Palestinian-Israeli problem.[36] The essence of the plan was to normalize the conditions in the region and start negotiations with the aim of a two state solution to be achieved until 2005. Similar to the support of the USA to the peace process after the Gulf War to eliminate the criticisms of double standards, the USA tried to create the image that it was not ignoring the Palestinian problem, which had continued for more than fifty years, and focusing on Iraq. Here, similar to the other initiatives, the role of the USA was decisive. Other members of the Quartet, and the EU among them, welcomed this initiative of the US and participated in it to increase the legitimacy of the initiative. This fact signifies the argument which was mentioned before, that the EU actions in the Middle East fall within the general framework determined by the USA. Another characteristic of the role of the EU in the Palestinian-Israeli problem became obvious during the initiative of the Quartet, which is the economic contribution of the EU to the process. The EU donated 100 million Euros as emergency aid for the implementation of the Road Map and the

---

35 *Radikal*, 23 April 2002.

36 Press Statement of the US Department of State, see http://www.state.gov/r/pa/prs/ps/2003/20062.htm [9 July 2006].

total aid provided by the EU for 2002–2003 equalled 570 million Euros.[37] Although the EU acts within the general framework designed by the USA, its participation in the Quartet represents its international role, especially in the Palestinian problem.

The negotiations between Israel and Palestine began after the acceptance of the Road Map by Israel on 25 May 2003. The first summit of this initiative took place in Sharm el Sheikh in Egypt on 3 June 2003 with the participation of parties and the representatives of the Quartet, including Bush.[38] However, after the emergence of several problems in the implementation of the plan, Israel started to pursue its own unilateral plan of withdrawal from some of the occupied territories.

The developments in the summer of the 2006 verified the argument that the EU is acting within the framework of US policies. Similar to the arguments of the US, the EU suspended its donations to the Palestinian Authority after the formation of the Hamas government in Palestine with the demand that Hamas should recognize Israel's right to exist. The consequences of this decision were critical for the Palestinians. However, later on with the initiative of France, the Quartet tried to create a mechanism to restart the donations bypassing the Hamas government and this decision is interpreted as a confession that the EU members realized their mistake.[39] When Israel harshly responded by destroying the electrical infrastructure of Gaza to the killing of two of its soldiers and capture of another one by the Palestinians, the EU capitals even failed to criticize Israel. The course of events during the crisis in Gaza and Lebanon were determined by the US not by the EU and Israel acted freely with the open support of the US. The European leaders, as in the case of Blair, asked the US to play a role for the end of conflict. The EU was able to play its role only after the end of conflict by sending troops to protect the peace. This fact verified the argument that the EU's foreign policy is not effective during crisis situations and the union plays a role in the protection of the peace and re-structuring in post-conflict situations. The limitations of the CFSP negatively affect the role of the EU in the Middle East and also in other places during crisis situations.

## Relations with the Gulf Countries

Since the focus of my research is on the policies of the EU towards the issues of the Palestinian-Israeli problem and Iraqi problems, I will briefly touch upon the relations of the EU with the Gulf countries. The oil crisis of 1973–1974 made the dependence of the European countries on the Gulf region obvious. Energy needs made the relations between the Gulf countries and the Europe an important part of the European interest in the Middle East. Similar to the Euro-Med partnership program, the European Union tried to increase its economic relations with the Gulf countries. In this respect, an agreement entered into force between the EU and the Gulf Cooperation Council (GCC) in 1990. The aim of the EU here was secure

---

37 Dışişleri Güncesi, July 2003, p. 112, available [online]: http://www.mfa.gov.tr/NR/rdonlyres/2F815293-BCB4-4638-8AD4-8A8B250D38A9/0/temmuz2003.pdf [9 July 2006].

38 Dışişleri Güncesi, June 2003, p. 20, available [online]: http://www.mfa.gov.tr/NR/rdonlyres/AB5F397B-1E53-4A45-AE52-89BC9CA80E49/0/Haziran2003.pdf [9 July 2006].

39 *The Guardian*, 6 July 2006.

future energy supplies and to increase its share in the Gulf market.[40] But the level of economic integration that was aimed at by the agreement could not be materialized. Although this cooperation agreement between the EU and the GCC countries contains commitments for the establishment of a free trade zone, the negotiations on this topic are still continuing. The trade relations between the EU and the GCC are increasing since the 1980s and the EU exports to the GCC countries were around 40 billion Euros whereas the EU imports from the GCC countries were around 25 billion Euros according to the figures of 2004.[41] Along with the developments in the post 9/11 world and the changes in the threat perceptions of the European countries, currently the political context of the joint meetings between officials of these two organizations are focused on other issue like counter terrorism and non-proliferation of Weapons of Mass Destruction.[42]

There are some criticisms of the EU's policies regarding both the Barcelona Process and the EU's relations with the GCC. The criticisms of the EU mainly concentrate on the following points: Security and political concerns dominate the EU's dealing with the countries of southern Mediterranean, the EU prefers to deal with these nations on an individual basis instead of a cooperation or partnership model, the EU aims to continue a unidirectional nature of relations, Europe focuses on preventing conflict rather than helping to solve existing problems like the Palestinian conflict.[43] These factors and other related issues affect Europe's ability to play an active role in the region in comparison with the USA. Some scholars argue that the Barcelona Process was initiated to prove that the EU is a different actor in world politics, using different tools.[44]

In explaining the failure of the Barcelona Process, Nicolaidis gives the internal problems of the EU below, besides other reasons:[45] One of them is the consistency question between the internal and external actions of the EU. The EU did little to promote democracy in the region. Second, the EU's relations with the NGOs in the region have been limited. Third, in opposition to the general principle of the EU for the free movement of people, there have been developments that limit the movement of the people. Fourth, there are disagreements among the member states on the Mediterranean policy, like the issue of Cyprus and the Palestine-Israel conflict.

Other reasons that have affected the success of the Barcelona Process negatively are issues of enlargement, constitutional debate and the discussions for the deepening of the integration.[46] Security issues are more important for Europeans

---

40 Nivien Saleh, "The European Union and the Gulf States: A Growing Partnership", *Middle East Policy* 7, no. 1 (October 1999), p. 9.

41 http://ec.europa.eu/comm/external_relations/gulf_cooperation/intro/index.htm [4 December 2006].

42 Ibid.

43 Emad Gad, "The EU and the Middle East: An Egyptian View," *Perceptions* 8, no. 2 (June-August 2003), pp. 22–3.

44 Kalypso Nicolaidis, "Europe as a Normative Power: Why Is the Euro-Med Partnership in Crisis and What Should Be Done About It?" Paper presented at European Studies Centre, University of Oxford, 16 January 2006, Oxford.

45 Ibid.

46 Ibid.

nowadays, especially after 9/11, 7/7 and the cartoons crisis, and a dominant exclusionary discourse is dominant in several European countries. On the other side of the coin, leaders in most of the countries in the region, especially the traditional monarchies in the Gulf, also are against any change in the direction of democracy. Their unwillingness to adopt democratization and change also contribute to the perpetuation of this negative atmosphere.

The European Union's position in the Palestinian-Israeli conflict stresses the importance of international law in the solution of the problem. But the problem here is to enforce the parties to comply with the international law. Although the EU participated in several peace initiatives, it has become clear that in order for the EU to play a political role, both of the parties should accept this role. Given the Israeli rejection of any country except the USA to play such a role, the EU's role is mostly dependent upon economic measures.

The EU's lack of military capabilities prevents it from playing a role similar to the American one in this problem. This reality has caused great disappointment on the side of Arab countries, which were expecting the EU to balance the overt support of the USA to Israel. And given the importance of the Palestinian issue for the Arab countries, this situation causes a belief among the Arabs that the EU is still a prisoner of the US policy in the region.[47] Here the position of the European Union is described as a "payer" since it has insufficient political power to broker political agreements.[48]

This payer position of the European Union however, has helped the Palestinian Authority not to go to bankruptcy. Under these conditions, the EU has had to play its role within a political framework that is designed by the USA. In the first years of the post-Cold War period, the policies of USA and the EU regarding the Middle East were coincided broadly with each other. Consequently the EU member states generally supported the USA's policies and initiatives in the region as long as the USA pursued a policy that guaranteed stability, the flow of oil at a reasonable price and supported the peace process.[49] In recent years, however, the effectiveness of the USA's policies in the region has been questioned by some of the European countries and a divergence has emerged between the USA and the EU countries especially in relation with the US' sanctions policies in the region. In order to gain the ability to manoeuvre independently in the region, the European countries have readjusted their security and strategic concerns in the region. The relations of the European countries in that period mostly concentrated on economic issues in order not to conflict with vital US interests in the Middle East.[50]

**The EU's Policy on Iraq and Changing Priorities of the Member States**

During the 1990s, the situation in Iraq was the other important problem in the Middle East. The developments prior and after the invasion of Iraq and the fall of Saddam

---

47  Gad, 24.

48  Dosenrode and Stubkjaer, p. 151.

49  B.A. Roberson, "Introduction," in *The Middle East and Europe,* edited by B.A. Roberson (London: Routledge, 1998), p. 12.

50  Ibid.

Hussein regime were other sources of concern for the European Union. After the end of Gulf War in 1991, UN sanctions were imposed on Iraq. At the time of the Clinton administration, US followed a policy of "dual containment." This policy imposed sanctions against Iraq and Iran and the US insisted on the continuation of these sanctions during the 1990s. But many European countries were against this idea and tried to develop economic relations with these countries despite US criticism. France and Germany took the lead in this policy and sought to develop relations with Iran, Iraq and Syria. Russia also took part at these initiatives. These countries attempted bypassing the UN sanctions against Iraq. The initiatives of countries that were against the US policies in the region helped to ease the sanctions and the introduction of the "oil for food" program. These points of difference showed the Europeans the need to develop a more independent foreign policy and the means to follow such a policy.

The relations between the EU and Iraq are less developed in comparison with the Mediterranean partnership and Gulf countries. There is not a contractual framework for the relations with Iran and the EU documents stress that "the economic and social characteristics of these countries call for instruments different to the programmes used within the Barcelona framework."[51] However, the relations with these countries still dominated by the bilateral relations of the member countries.

The differences among the member states in relation to Iraq became obvious before and after the invasion of Iraq in 2003. The divisions among the EU members were serious blows for the Union to act as a unified actor. As in several other crisis situations, the capability of the EU to play an active role was limited and the Union focused on the post-invasion reconstruction of the country. The EU hosted the first donors' conference in October 2003 and the EU collectively pledged 1.2 billion Euros to Iraq.[52] The Union also contributed to the building of democratic structures in the country by financially supporting the elections and educating the judges and police in Iraq for the establishment of the rule of law.[53]

The 1990s witnessed on the side of the European Union the activities to develop a more coherent foreign policy. With the Treaty on European Union, the road for this development opened. The events in these years brought a gradual harmonization of foreign policies of the member states. Governments shifted their preferences to make them compatible with those of other governments. Beside this development, bureaucratic formalization also helped the development of common foreign policy.

The 1990s also changed the priorities of the European Countries and the EU regarding the Middle East and Mediterranean regions. During the Cold War period security concerns and reliable access to energy sources had been the top priorities. In the post-Cold War era, the security problem perceived on the side of EU mostly has been

---

51 Draft Final Report on an EU Strategic Partnership with the Mediterranean and the Middle East, p. 8, available [online]: http://register.consilium.eu.int/pdf/en/04/st10/st10246. en04.pdf [4 December 2006].

52 European Union Factsheet, EU-US Cooperation in Iraq, available [online]: http://www.consilium.europa.eu/uedocs/cmsUpload/1Iraq_final_150605.pdf [2 December 2006].

53 Ibid.

related to soft security issues like mass migration.[54] Instability caused by socio-political problems has created the threat of the spillover of these problems into Europe.

In order to summarize the factors that have affected the EU's relations with the Middle East we should take into consideration several issues. The end of the Cold War and the rivalry between the USA and the USSR changed the strategic perceptions of the Europeans and the road into a more active role for Europe in the Middle East. This development was directly related to the changes in the nature of transatlantic relations and the transformation of European integration. In the post-Cold War era, the US expected a strong support from the European Union in security issues, but at the same time not be a rival against it. The US preferred the development of European defence and security architecture within the NATO framework.[55] The developments in the dissolution of the former Yugoslavia made this necessity obvious. The tragic events in Bosnia and later in Kosovo showed that European security still very much depends on the contributions of NATO and the USA.

Although polices of Europe and the USA generally coincide on many global issues, there was an increasing divergence for these policies in the second half of the 1990s. The Middle East was no exception to this. Being the only superpower in the world led the US to follow a unilateral approach on many global issues. In response to this, the United Nations provided an appropriate framework for Europe to approach the Middle East.[56] This United Nations umbrella enabled the EU to mark some distance from Washington and also helped to establish a common ground for diverging national foreign policies. The European Union faced several challenges in establishing a common foreign policy. France took the lead in these initiatives against the supremacy of the US. Although Germany helped the activities of France, it followed a more cautious policy. The third big power within the union, Britain, paid great attention to the stability of the transatlantic relations and is sometimes seen as a Trojan horse within the EU.

Despite their frustration with their inability to play a political or military role matching their economic relations in the region, the EU countries operated within the framework of the US polices in the region. The points of difference, however, should be kept in mind. The focus on the differences between the EU and the US is important since these two actors generally share the same priorities in world politics and act in accordance with this. Beside this factor, the EU's struggle to establish a policy of its own towards the Middle East emerged against the US preferences in the region. Consequently the EU's differences at the points below contributed to the development of a European approach towards the Middle East.

One of them is the issue of relations with the Iraq and Gulf. Contrary to the US policies against Iran and Iraq, European countries, especially the big powers within

---

54  Dosenrode and Stubkjaer, pp. 158–9.

55  Madeleine K. Albright, "The Right Balance Will Secure NATO's Future," *Financial Times*, 7 December 1998.

56  Ghassan Salame, 'Torn Between the Atlantic and the Mediterranean, Europe and the Middle East in the post-Cold War Era,' in *The Middle East and Europe,* edited by B.A. Roberson (London: Routledge, 1998), p. 23.

Europe, probably continue to trade with Iran.[57] European countries opposed to the US Congress ban trade with Iran. In case of Iraq, the policy of Europe is fractured. France, Germany and some other north European members of the EU were opposed to the invasion of Iraq. Britain, Italy, Spain and the most of the new members of the EU, however, participated in the invasion of Iraq. Although this division within the EU showed the weakness of the Union to establish a common foreign policy, it is generally accepted that most of the Eastern European countries acted in accordance with the US policies since their memories are fresh with Cold War security threats. These countries still need US protection against Russia and are paying the price of their membership in NATO. Some of the older members of the union, who acted with the US in the invasion of Iraq, like Spain and Italy, changed their policies with the government changes in these countries. The unilateral attitude of the US in its policies against Iran and Iraq, however, has made the European countries search for greater unity on foreign policy issues.

Another point of difference between the EU and the US is related to the Palestinian-Israeli Conflict and peace process. If a chance emerges for the peace process, then these two actors may cooperate for the solution of the problem. In cases of failure and conflict, however, the US and the EU's policies towards this issue are diverging from each other and the capability of Europe to play a role is decreasing. Currently the peace process is inactive and in response to overt support of the US administrations to Israel, European countries try to follow a more balanced approach. The EU argues that it will not be possible to realise a common zone of peace, prosperity and progress unless a just and lasting settlement of the Arab-Israeli conflict is in place.[58]

One of the differences between the EU and the US in the post 9/11 world is related with the style of the needed reform process in the region. Although it is commonly agreed that political, social and economic reforms are needed in the region, different from the interventionist style of the US for the reforms, the EU argued that "the reforms can succeed only of they are generated from within the affected societies, they cannot and should not be imposed from outside."[59]

Given the arguments above, we can say that although the EU cannot impose its will in the Middle East, it has a potential to affect the developments in the region. European countries relations with the region are still dominated by economic concerns. The European Union's attitude towards the region is gaining strategic aspects similar to the American interests in the region. Despite these strategic aspects, currently the EU's policies towards the region are mostly related to "soft" security measures like economic problems and illegal migration.

---

57 Phebe Marr, "The United States, Europe and the Middle East, Cooperation, Co-optation or Confrontation?" in *The Middle East and Europe*, edited by B.A. Roberson (London: Routledge, 1998), p. 97.

58 Draft Final Report on an EU Strategic Partnership with the Mediterranean and the Middle East, p. 2, available [online]: http://register.consilium.eu.int/pdf/en/04/st10/st10246.en04.pdf [4 December 2006].

59 Ibid.

## Harmony between the Policies of Turkey and the EU

Despite the declaration of Turkey as a candidate country to the EU, the discussions about the formulation of the Common Foreign and Security Policy within the EU and the place of Turkey in this framework have caused setbacks in Turkey's relations with the EU. The European Union was planning to establish the CFSP and needed military capacities to implement such a policy. But the EU was lacking these capacities and required the use of NATO's military capacities. The problem here appeared in getting the permission of NATO members which were not the EU members, like Turkey and Norway. Turkey demanded to take part in the decision making process of international operations that the EU would carry out independent of NATO. Until 2001 Turkey's position regarding the CFSP was supported by the US. But the US came to the conclusion that the EU was determined to construct its military structure with Turkey or without it and with NATO or without it. This conclusion and the attacks of September 11 led to a change in the US policy and the US followed a more balanced policy about the issue of the CFSP. In December 2001, a compromise was reached on Turkey's position within the CFSP and in exchange to lift of its veto in NATO; Turkey received the right to participate in the discussions of the EU constitution convention.[60] Turkey's military capacity and the operational capability to participate in humanitarian intervention in the crisis regions are important assets in its hands. Closer relations with the EU have helped Turkey and increased its foreign policy options. These relations also have increased the bargaining power of Turkey vis-a-vis the US and Israel in the Middle Eastern policies.

Until the late 1990s Turkey's policies regarding the Middle East had very much in common with those of the US and Israel. In recent years, however, the situation has started to change and Turkey's Middle East policy has become closer to that of the European one. Besides the factors mentioned above, the end of support from some European countries of the PKK, the unilateral attitude of the Bush government, the effects of 9/11 and the general opposition to terrorist activities, the government change in Israel and the policies of the Sharon government in Palestine, the differences between the US and Turkey on the future of Iraq also have brought the Turkish foreign policy towards the Middle East closer to that of the European one.

Both the US and Israel are in favour of a weak and de-centralized Iraq, which is contrary to the security interests of Turkey. This difference came to surface before the US-led coalition's invasion of Iraq. The decision of the US-led coalition to intervene in Iraq also showed the challenges to establish a common foreign and security policy within the EU. Some of the new members of the EU acted along with the US despite the opposition from Germany and France. On 30 January 2003 UK, Spain, Denmark, Portugal, Italy, Czech Republic, Hungary and Poland declared that Europe should act along with the US.[61] A similar declaration came from the ten NATO candidate

---

60 "Turkey Accepts EU Military Force," *Facts on File World's News Digest*, 3 December 2001, p. 983.

61 *Milliyet*, 30 January 2003.

countries. Here, however, the case of Turkey was particularly unique.[62] Turkey had been an ally of the US for years and there was a general belief that Turkey could not oppose the demands of the US in considering the military, economic and political conditions of Turkey. But the Turkish Parliament did not allow the transfer of US troops to northern Iraq via Turkish territory or sending Turkish troops there on March 1, 2003. This decision seriously effected Turkey's relations with the US and also was accepted as the manifestation of greater democracy and weakening of pro-US military's power in the country. This decision of parliament also nullified the arguments that in the case of membership, Turkey would be a Trojan horse of the US within the EU. Turkey's current policy on the Cyprus issue also helped to change the negative attitude of some of the EU member countries towards Turkey and prevented the labelling of Turkey as a troublemaker.

The divisions among the members and the candidates of the European Union induced the Greek presidency of the time to convene a special summit on Iraq and the Middle East on 17–18 February 2003. In this respect, the Prime Minister declared that Turkey see its benefit in contributing to the EU's Middle East and Iraq policy. The members of the EU tried to agree on common position in this crisis and as the only candidate country bordering Iraq, Turkey's efforts for a peaceful solution to the problem was appreciated by the Union with a declaration after the Summit.[63] Turkey's possible role and contribution to the EU's foreign and defence policy was stressed by Nicolaidis with the argument that "the triangular relationship between Turkey, NATO and the EU in the context of Iraq War and the EU's role in the post-war Iraq should have functioned once again as a reminder that a future European foreign and defence policy would be crippled without the south-eastern flank of Europe."[64]

Turkey's foreign policy towards the Middle East in the post-Cold War era witnessed important changes from the traditional trend. Security concerns dominated Turkey's policy towards the region and Turkey was involved actively in the Middle Eastern politics. The security threat to the integrity of the country and the negative atmosphere with the neighbours paved the way to the increasing cooperation between Turkey and Israel. The US supported this rapprochement and the conditions of peace process made this cooperation easy. In the same period the EU also was satisfied with the peace process and financially contributed to this atmosphere. But Turkey's struggle with the PKK and human rights violations during this struggle, the role of the army in Turkish politics, the close cooperation between Turkey and the US, and Turkey's problems with Greece helped the perpetuation of a negative atmosphere between Turkey and the EU. This situation got worse when the EU declined Turkey's candidature to the membership in 1997. This decision limited Turkey's options and increased Turkey's dependency on the US and Israel in the Middle East.

---

62  Kemal Kirişçi, "Between Europe and the Middle East: The Transformation of Turkish Policy," *Middle East Review of International Affairs* 8, no. 1 (March 2004), p. 8, available [online]: http://meria.idc.ac.il/journal/2004/issue1/kirisci.pdf [17 July 2006].

63  Dışişleri Güncesi, February 2003, p. 85, available [online]: http://www.mfa.gov.tr/NR/rdonlyres/4DC42D46-4F41-4959-990C-AC6CBF6BE9CB/0/SUBAT2003.pdf [8 July 2006].

64  Kalypso Nicolaidis, "Turkey is European ... for Europe's Sake", *Turkish Policy Quarterly* 2, no. 4 (Winter 2004), p. 61.

Turkey's candidature coincided with the increasing initiatives of the European Union to form a CFSP. Given the deficiency of military capabilities on the side of the EU, Turkey's possible role in this structure increased. The road to membership created an incentive to Turkey to follow a more harmonized policy with the EU on international issues. Turkish officials stressed that if the Union wanted to become a global actor, it would have "to resort to stronger and more diverse political, economic and military capabilities and Turkey is in a position to contribute not only to the formulation and implementation of European foreign policy but also to its credibility and effectiveness in this wide spectrum".[65] The vice-president of the European Parliament also pointed out that, "in view of the urgent need to strengthen the EU's ability to influence its global and regional environment, the accession of a democratic, stable, highly populated country where a great majority of its people belongs to the Islamic faith would be a tremendously powerful message, confirming the ethical and political significance of the European project".[66]

The decrease of threat to Turkey's security and the EU's acceptance of Turkey in 1999 as a candidate country opened a new phase in Turkey's relations with the EU. Turkey's candidacy and the EU's initiatives to become a more unified political actor in the global scale ushered in a new era. These developments made Turkey's position closer to the European one in the Middle East. The latest developments during the Iraqi invasion showed the EU what kind of an asset Turkey could be in its policy towards the region. Turkey followed a policy similar to the core countries of the EU contrary to some new members of the EU. During the sanctions against Iraq prior to the invasion, Turkey tried to by-pass these sanctions together with some European countries.

In addition to the similarities in Iraqi policy, Turkey's policy in the Palestinian-Israeli conflict has much common with that of the EU. Both Turkey and the EU stress the importance of international law in the solution of problem and pay attention to the sufferings of the Palestinian people. Given the open support of the US to Israel and the differences of capacity between the US and other big actors in world politics, the EU's role in the peace process should be within the framework designed by the Americans. The EU contributed to the construction of the infrastructure of a future Palestinian state within the peace process and accepted Israel to some European platforms to break its isolation. Both Turkey and the EU favour the revitalization of the peace process since the EU's and Turkey's capacities enable them to operate in times of peace and stability. The latest Sharon government, however, destroyed the infrastructure of Palestinian Authority. Since the EU had paid most of the costs for this infrastructure, the European countries strongly criticized these actions. Also, the atmosphere of conflict in Palestine limits the manoeuvring capability of the EU. Turkey having a long history of relationships both with Palestinians and Israel and also being a candidate or member of the EU would contribute to the peace process. In this respect, it is commonly argued that given the insensitivities and the detachment

---

65 Oğuz Demiralp, "The Added Value of Turkish Membership to European Foreign Policy," *Turkish Policy Quarterly* 2, no. 4 (Winter 2004), p. 17.

66 Alejo Vidal Quadras, "EU-Turkey: A Good Match?" *Turkish Policy Quarterly* 2, no. 4 (Winter 2004), p. 23.

of the EU, it is not possible for the Union to play a greater political role in the region and with the accession of Turkey, the EU would gain a greater deal of legitimacy in its involvement in the Middle East and this legitimacy would be instrumental in decreasing the Israeli resistance to the EU involvement in the region by building more constructive channels of communication via Turkey.[67] I, however, believe that although Turkey would contribute to this kind of condition, this contribution should not be exaggerated. Turkey's membership will represent a message and will make communication easy but this role will not completely change the expected role of Turkey by Israel and Palestine.

The possible convergence of Turkey's Middle Eastern policy with that of the European one is related, beside its candidature or membership in the union, to the future policies of the big powers, especially the US. The unilateral attitude of the US after the 9/11 and its disregard for criticisms, bypassing the United Nations and international law alienated some of its allies like Turkey. This unilateral approach also alarmed other big actors like the EU and caused them reconsider their relationship with the US. Consequently, the stability of transatlantic relations has come under question and Europeans have tried to limit their dependency on the US on security issues. Such a situation has increased the status of Turkey within the security framework of Europe. The unilateral approach of the US has brought Turkey and the EU closer to each other.

The criticisms against the EU in terms of lacking a strategic culture which guides the foreign policy actions are made very often. This issue surfaced again before the invasion of Iraq. The formulation of the strategy paper of Solana at the end of 2003 just after the Iraq War and the proposals for the establishment of a post of EU Foreign Minister during the discussions for the constitutional treaty can also be evaluated within this perspective. The Turkish authorities also complained about this issue when I asked them about the possible harmonization with the EU in foreign policy. Instead of talking about a shared vision in the Middle East and other regions, the discussions were related to the Cyprus issue and the steps that Turkey should take on this issue dominated the agenda between Turkey and the EU for a long period of time after the opening of accession negotiations with Turkey.[68] The intergovernmental nature of the CFSP and the attempts of the members to dominate the foreign policy agenda in terms of their own national interests negatively affect the formation of a strategic culture. Beside the factors that are affecting the harmonization of foreign policies between Turkey and the EU positively, this kind of differences also should be taken into consideration in order to make a proper analysis of this issue. It is argued that the development of a strategic dimension within the EU should be, in principle, welcomed by Turkey and the fight against terrorism might constitute a case that the EU members will cooperate with Turkey.[69] Such a common approach would

---

67  Senem Aydın, "The Self-Definition of Europe: Where Does Turkey Stand?", *Turkish Policy Quarterly* 2, no. 4 (Winter 2004), p. 71.

68  Ahmet Davutoğlu, Prof. Dr. and Ambassador, Chief Advisor to the Prime Minister, interview by author, Istanbul, 28 May 2006.

69  Sinan Ülgen, "Of Chaos and Power: Will Europe Become a Strategic Community?" *Turkish Policy Quarterly* 2, no. 4 (Winter 2004), p. 44.

contribute not only Turkey's foreign policy concerns but also increase the added value of Turkish potential contribution to the EU as an important global actor.

Turkey's possible membership and role within the CFSP is becoming more important in the current threat perceptions of the EU. Although the EU also has developed its relations with the Middle Eastern countries under the framework of Euro-Mediterranean partnership and the history this relation goes back to 1970s, there is no possibility of membership for these countries. The EU's attitude towards the Middle Eastern and Mediterranean countries very much differs from its policies towards East European countries. The EU has been criticized for its policies regarding these countries. Current threats to the EU like illegal immigration are originated mainly from these countries. Besides the struggle with illegal immigration, Turkey also may contribute to the efforts of the Union in the struggle against the challenges to security like terrorism, organized trans-border crimes, and proliferation of weapons of mass destruction, xenophobia and racism.[70] Turkey constitutes the border between Europe and some Middle Eastern countries. A healthy relationship between Turkey and the EU may constitute an example for future relationships. Through Turkey's accession, the EU will be in a position to contribute to the peace in neighbouring countries which is also a benefit to the Union.

Turkey's proximity to the region and the impact of this location to its membership and the contribution to the EU are also issues of contention. Whether inclusion of Turkey to the EU means the inclusion of the Middle Eastern problems into the Union or Turkey neighbouring the Middle East will help the EU to play a more active role there. Whereas the groups in the EU that oppose the membership of Turkey support the former argument, Turkish officials and academics and the supporters of Turkey within the EU favour the latter. Turkey's active and positive role during the general elections in 2006 in Iraq in convincing the Sunni groups to participate to the elections, Turkey's facilitator role during the negotiations with Iran on nuclear issue are given as examples of Turkey's possible contribution to the EU's foreign policy. Turkey's participation to the United Nations Implementation Force in Lebanon (UNIFIL) along with several other European countries also can be given as an example here. Turkey's leading role along with Spain in the initiative of the Alliance of Civilizations, which was supported by the UN Secretary General Kofi Annan in July 2005, is presented as another example of Turkey's possible role.[71]

The EU is becoming a more integrated political entity and establishing the required infrastructure for the CFSP. Although this structuring takes some time, this development will increase the chances of Europe to act together in international relations and becoming a more powerful actor in the global arena. The EU is an actor which pays attention to democracy and international law. Turkey's reforms for democratization and increasing civilian control of foreign policy as a result of this democratization and decline of security threats make Turkey a reliable partner for the EU.

70 Demiralp, p. 17.

71 Dışişleri Güncesi, July 2005, p. 35, available [online]: http://www.mfa.gov.tr/NR/rdonlyres/6397723E-ADBC-4355-8A56-195ABDA0953F/0/TEMMUZ2005.pdf [13 July 2006].

# Chapter 5

# The Making of Turkish Foreign Policy

## Basic Factors and Formation of the Foreign Policy

This chapter will discuss the basic factors that affect Turkish foreign policy (TFP), a general history of Turkish foreign policy, evolution of TFP from the establishment of the Republic until today and the basic actors in the decision making procedures of TFP.

Turkey is a typical country of transition between East and West and between North and South from the point of politics, economics and culture and consequently, it has a multidimensional character depending on the perspective of analysis.[1] Turkey is a Muslim/Eastern country from the perspective of cultural/demographic character while it is a Western/European country from the perspective of political establishment and membership in international organizations like NATO, and the Organization for Security and Cooperation in Europe (OSCE). It might be perceived as a southern country because of the low income levels and high rates of population increase, but at the same time Turkey might be seen as part of the North with its customs union with the EU and membership in the Organization for Economic Cooperation and Development (OECD). This multidimensional character necessitated a new multidimensional foreign policy especially in the post-Cold War era.[2]

In analyzing Turkish foreign policy, we should begin by discussing the basic characteristics that affect it as they are very influential in its formation, whether they are obvious or obscured. These characteristics are described by Oran as strategic, cultural, historical and domestic structural dimensions.[3] The cultural and political characteristics that derive from the historical legacy appear especially in foreign policy.[4]

Historically, the Ottoman legacy influences Turkish foreign policy in Turkey's relations with the neighbouring regions and Europe. Except for Iran, almost all of the neighbours of Turkey were under the control of the Ottoman Empire in different periods. Despite the migrations and population exchanges, there are ethnic

---

1   Ahmet Davutoğlu, "The Intercivilizational and Interreligious Interaction in the Global Era: The Case of Turkey-EU Relations," paper presented at the Halki Seminar *Mediterranean Crossroads: Culture, Religion and Security*, Halki, Greece (8–12 September 2002), p. 6.

2   Ibid.

3   Baskın Oran, "Türk Dış Politikasının Teori ve Pratiği," in *Türk Dış Politikası Kurtuluş Savaşından Bugüne Olgular, Belgeler, Yorumlar,* edited by Baskın Oran (İstanbul: İletişim Yayınları, 2002), p. 20.

4   Hakan Yavuz, "İkicilik (Duality): Türk-Arap İlişkileri ve Filistin Sorunu," in *Türk Dış Politikasının Analizi,* edited by Faruk Sönmezoğlu (İstanbul: Der, 1998), p. 567.

and religious minority groups in Turkey's neighbouring countries that have close connections with Turkey. Although Turkey abstained from making the problems of these people issues of foreign policy and interfering in the domestic affairs of its neighbours during the early Republican and the Cold War years (Cyprus might be an exception here and also the Turkish minority in Bulgaria at the end of Cold War), the conditions after the end of the Cold War induced Turkey to begin to take an interest in the problems of these people. Instabilities in the neighbouring states strongly affected Turkish foreign policy in the post-Cold War years.

Turkey is a westernized Muslim country. This westernization process began during the late Ottoman times and accelerated with the republic. It is the only example of transformation to a western style democracy among countries of its region. In this respect, Turkey combines both western and eastern characteristics. This characteristic of Turkey is an important point of discussion in relation to the identity of the country and its foreign policy.

Strategically, Turkey is at the crossroads of the continents of Asia and Europe and a neighbour to the Middle East, Mediterranean, Black Sea, the Balkans and Caucasia. During the Cold War period, Turkey acted as the southern flank of the NATO and as a barrier against the Soviet threat. The Cold War period represented stability in international politics and Turkey did not pay very much attention to the developments in Caucasia, the Balkans and the Middle East out of the alliance framework. The Balkans and Caucasus were under Soviet control and Turkey did not want to interfere in Middle Eastern affairs. With the end of the Cold War, the regions adjacent to Turkey became sources of turbulence in international politics. These developments also created domestic problems for Turkey, especially in the south-east of the country. The problematic conditions in these regions affected the Turkic and the Muslim groups in each region. Public opinion in Turkey was sensitive to the conditions of these people and these concerns were reflected in the Turkish foreign policy. These can be given as the basic factors that affected Turkish foreign policy. The end of the Cold War signalled important changes in the influence of these factors. Although these factors continued to affect Turkey, a transformation in the global politics caused a change in their effects.

It can be argued that there are some basic premises of Turkish foreign policy that have been perpetuated for several years. Although some changes and diversifications in these premises may occur, the general tendencies remain in effect. These basic premises may be summarized as western orientation, the preservation of the status quo, and the elite formation of politics. The end of the Cold War required some adjustments in these basic premises in order to adapt to the environment. The forces of continuity proved powerful and only minor adjustments were achieved.[5]

In considering the factors above, we can analyze Turkish foreign policy from a historical perspective from the establishment of the republic to the end of the Cold War. Although the main responsibility for the formation and implementation of the foreign policy belongs to the Ministry of Foreign Affairs, there are also actors and

---

5   Bilge Criss and Pınar Bilgin, "Turkish Foreign Policy toward the Middle East," *Middle East Review of International Affairs* 1, no. 1 (January 1997), p. 2, available [online]: http://meria.idc.ac.il/journal/1997/issue1/jv1n1a3.html [21 April 2006].

institutions that participate in this process in several ways. The primary players in Turkish Foreign Policy are enumerated as the government, the presidency, the foreign ministry and the security establishment. Parliament, media, interest groups, ethnic pressure groups and the general public opinion are described as secondary actors in this process.[6] The role of the universities, non-governmental organizations (NGO) and independent research institutions are limited in comparison to the western standards. There are economic, political and structural reasons for this reality and this reality limits the participation of the public to the foreign policy formation despite the increasing importance of the public opinion in the last couple of years and it remains mainly an intra-elite issue.

The formation of Turkish foreign policy can be described as a "dynamic interplay between there factors: overall political context, the powers and traditions of institutions and the personalities and priorities of the leading players."[7] Consequently, the formation of Turkish foreign policy has been affected by different factors in different periods from the establishment of the republic until today. Not only domestic developments, but also the changes in the international atmosphere have caused adjustments in Turkish foreign policy. These factors can be given as the changes in the international atmosphere like the rise of fascist regimes during the 1930s, World War Two, the bi-polar rivalry between the USA and the USSR and the Soviet threats against Turkey, the Cyprus issue, the political changes in the Middle East and the wars in the region. Domestically, leadership factors; the rise and fall of effects of the bureaucracy; the role of the army, press and public opinion; and the effect of business community can be given as the important factors.

Some other scholars described the formation of Turkish foreign policy as the interplay of two variables: structural variables like geographical position, historical experiences, cultural background, and conjunctural variables like changes in the international system, domestic political change, and the personalities of specific decision makers.[8] Within the definition of structural variables, the same writer gives three traditional inputs of Turkish foreign policy as follows: the Ottoman experience and its long lasting legacy, the geopolitical realities of Turkey and the ideological foundations defined under the leadership of Atatürk.[9] İsmail Cem, former Minister of Foreign Affairs, argued that the "traditional" input has both positive and negative characteristics. The positive sides of this tradition are described by Cem as three principles devised by Atatürk: Peace at home peace abroad, the protection of oppressed nations, and accepting the passion of independence as an identity.[10] The most important negative aspects of this traditional input are given by the same writer as the lack of historical and cultural consciousness.[11]

---

6   Philip Robins, *Suits and Uniforms: Turkish Foreign Policy since the Cold War* (London: Hurst, 2003), pp. 68–88.

7   Ibid., pp. 52–3.

8   Mustafa Aydın, *Turkish Foreign Policy Framework and Analysis* (Ankara: SAM, 2004), pp. 9–10.

9   Ibid., p. 13.

10   İsmail Cem, *Türkiye Avrupa Avrasya* (İstanbul: İstanbul Bilgi Üniversitesi Yayınları, 2004), p. 10.

11   Ibid., p. 11.

The structural factors that have been perpetuated for several years have played a stabilizing role in Turkish foreign policy. The rationality of Turkish foreign policy is attributed to the heritage of the Ottoman Empire, which was forced to pursue its foreign policy amid tensions between its own interests and the interests of the big powers of the time.[12] Historically, the advance of the Ottomans in Europe ended with the Treaty of Karlowitz in 1699. From that point on, the Empire pursued a defensive strategy and tried to benefit from the intra-European balances as a part of its defensive strategy in foreign policy.[13] The wars and the peace agreements with Russia in 1774 and 1856 were also important cornerstones in this legacy. After 1774, Russia had some rights for the protection of the Orthodox population of the Empire and this resulted in the use of this protection as leverage against the state. The Crimean War and the Paris Treaty of 1853–1856 represented the first examples of the Ottoman-Turkish diplomacy tradition in the use of intra-European problems for the elimination of a threat.[14] This war and the peace treaty afterwards generally are accepted as the official inclusion of the Ottoman Empire into the European states system. This development is often referred to in the discussions on the European identity of Turkey. The pan-Islamist policy of Abdulhamid II and pan-Turkist policy of the Committee of Union and Progress had their impact on the Turkey's foreign policy preferences.

The foreign policy of Turkey is built on the legacy of the late Ottoman state and the international atmosphere of the time. The new republic built its foreign policy on the declaration of National Pact, which was more acceptable in the new international system. The National Pact was based on two basic principles: First, instead of an assertive, interventionist policy the protection of the borders and nation-state defined in the National Pact. Second, the new Turkish state would not be an alternative or opposition to the Western axis, but would be a part of this axis.[15] The geopolitical situation of Turkey as a neighbour to Europe, the Middle East and the former Soviet Union also necessitated rationality during the past and a multi-sided foreign policy more recently.[16]

The roles of the identities are increasing in the formation of foreign policy along with the advance of globalization and Europeanization. In addition to the factors mentioned above, we also should pay attention to the different identities within the country that have different ideas about the foreign policy to be pursued.

**Identity in Turkish Foreign Policy**

As stated in Chapter 1, in opposition to the definitions of the conventional theories of identity as essentially fixed and categorical, constructivist approaches focus on the impact of norms and ideas on the construction of identity and behaviour. The

---

12  Haluk Ülman, "Türk Dış Politikasına Yön Veren Etkenler-I," *Siyasal Bilgiler Fakültesi Dergisi* 23, no. 3 (1968), pp. 241–3, quoted in Aydın, p. 44.

13  Davutoğlu, *Stratejik Derinlik*, p. 66.

14  Ibid., p. 67.

15  Ibid., p. 69.

16  Aydın, *Turkish Foreign Policy Framework and Analysis*, p. 44.

change in the conceptualization of the identity of human beings is also true for the conceptualization of institutions like states. The unitary state of realist theory is challenged by the constructivist states as the intersubjectively constructed agents of socially constructed realities. Contrary to the stress on the importance on the structure of the actors and the international system, constructivism stresses the role of agents in the system. In this system, the cultural characteristics and identities of human beings gain importance in the analysis of international relations. Identity plays a crucial role in the direction of foreign policy. Consequently, identity-related issues become an important part of foreign policy analyses. The issue is also true for the case of Turkish foreign policy. Although we mentioned the western orientation and elite formation of policy among the basic premises of Turkish foreign policy, the rise of public opinion and the increasing importance of identity issues in the post-Cold War period have somehow shaken these premises. Since identities are not static but subject to change over time, foreign policy, as a tool or process representing this identity, would not be static.

*The Kemalist Identity*

Along with the rise of different identities, each of the groups has wanted to have its say in foreign policy formation. Aras argues that the identities that have the broadest presence in Turkish foreign policy are the Kemalist and the Islamist, along with nationalist and conservative identities.[17] The foundational elements of the Kemalist identity is given by the same author as the abandonment of the Ottoman past, the termination of Islamic power in the public sphere and the prevention of Islamic influence from functioning as a source of political legitimacy.[18] The motto of this identity is the "Peace at Home, Peace in the World" principle of Atatürk.

Similar to the definition above, Oran defines two basic principles of Turkish foreign policy as the preservation of status quo and western orientation.[19] In his definition, west is used not to refer to a specific geographical area, but to refer to civilization, which is constructed on capitalism and the supremacy of human rationality.[20] Oran argues that the imitation of the West in Turkey is easier in comparison to other underdeveloped countries and that the intellectuals of Turkey who have Western educations are admirers of the West and do not oppose the West. This admiration and application of the Western model in Turkey has led Turkish intellectuals not to think about any alternative to the West in foreign policy.[21] This policy of the elites is criticized by one of the former ministers of foreign affairs, İsmail Cem, in his book *Türkiye Avrupa Avrasya*. Cem argues that break with the past after the establishment and maturation of the republic led to a dominant approach which lacks historical depth, and fails to understand the special cultural identity of Turkey.[22] Cem believes

---

17  Bülent Aras, *Turkey and the Greater Middle East* (İstanbul: Tasam, 2004), p. 18.
18  Ibid.
19  Oran, "Türk Dış Politikasının Teori ve Pratiği," p. 46.
20  Ibid., p. 49.
21  Ibid., pp. 52–3.
22  Cem, p. 11.

that this simplistic approach is unable to comprehend the European and Eurasian aspects of Turkish culture and consequently the officials in Turkey forget that they are governing a European country and "aped" being European.[23]

Issues and discussions in the domestic politics related to the issue of culture have their impacts on foreign policy. Cem argues that the elite's orientation towards the West has led to the alienation of the foreign policy of the country from the East, Middle East, the Central Asia and Africa and has created the belief that interest in these regions represents "backwardness" and only creates problems.[24]

Despite this orientation towards the West and admiration of Western culture, there are also some concerns regarding the attitudes of the Western elites towards Turkey. Here, Aras mentions mistrust and a latent enmity towards the West inherited from the Ottoman administrative elite.[25] This distrust generally is labelled "Sevres Syndrome" in the daily discussions.

In several definitions, the elite refer to the military and civilian bureaucracy and also to the western-oriented intellectuals and big businessmen. The general complaints of the Turkish elite towards the criticisms of the Europeans concentrate on the argument that the Europeans do not understand the special conditions of Turkey. For example, there were criticisms of the human rights record of Turkey after the coup in 1980 and also during the 1990s from several European institutions. The Council of Europe was among these institutions and the reactions of the elite towards the criticisms of this otherwise marginal institution also signified the attachment of the elite to Europe and the belief that the Europeans did not understand the conditions in Turkey.

Turkey became a member of the Council in 1949 and this membership is seen as a proof of Turkey's European identity by the Turkish westernizing elite.[26] For the Turkish elite, Turkey's relations with the West should not be reduced to a military alliance. Turkey should be a member of European Union as it was member of other European institutions.[27] In considering this attitude of the elites towards Europe, the criticisms of the Europeans towards Turkey may result from "Turkish inadequacy" to comply with the European norms, as most Europeans see it, or form "double standards of the Europeans", as most of the Turks understand it.[28]

It is argued that Turkish foreign policy is dominated largely by the Kemalist elite and conducted via cooperation between the military and foreign policy elite,

---

23  Ibid.

24  Ibid., p. 30.

25  Aras, *Turkey and the Greater Middle East*, p. 18.

26  Mustafa Aydın, "Twenty Years before, Twenty Years after: Turkish Foreign Policy at the Threshold of the 21st Century", In *Turkey's Foreign Policy in the 21st Century*, edited by Tareq Y. Ismael and Mustafa Aydın (Aldershot: Ashgate, 2003), p. 10.

27  Mesut Yılmaz, "The Political Aspects of the Ankara Agreement and Its Assessment from the Point of Our External Relations," *Journal of Foundation for Economic Development*, no. 59 (September 1988), p. 6; quoted in Nuri Yurdusev, "Perceptions and Images in Turkish (Ottoman)-European Relations," in *Turkey's Foreign Policy in the 21st Century*, edited by Tareq Y. Ismael and Mustafa Aydın (Aldershot: Ashgate, 2003), p. 80.

28  Ibid.

the military's subordinate allies.[29] Domestic societal groups outside the Kemalist identity have been excluded from foreign policy making since the beginning. The constitutional and legal framework legitimizes the role of these elite in the foreign policy formation, especially in considering the role of the military in the National Security Council (NSC). The level of popularity of the military is high among the public opinion and the security threats contributes to the legitimization of this role. Although the European agenda has curtailed some powers of the military elite, the popularity of the military and some very thorny foreign policy issues contribute to the legitimization of the role of the military in foreign policy.

*The Islamic Identity*

Aras argues that different from the official foreign policy of Turkey, the Islamic and nationalist identity favours a more assertive foreign policy.[30] The Islamic approach generally prefers increasing cooperation with the Muslim world and has initiated some projects like Developing 8 (D-8) in this respect as an alternative foreign policy direction. The end of ideological confrontation between Eastern and Western blocs and the rise of the cultural issues in the post-Cold War era enabled the rise of the Islamic consciousness along with other cultural characteristics. In Turkey the 1990s witnessed the rise of the Islamic identity in domestic politics and the ramifications of this for foreign policy. The clashes in the neighbouring territories (formerly Ottoman) in the 1990s after the end of the Cold War created some challenges for the official identity of Turkish foreign policy. There were several demands on the side of the public opinion for a more assertive and interventionist foreign policies, especially in times of crises in the vicinity of Turkey, since several societal groups in Turkey have connections with the people in the Balkans, Caucasia and the Middle East. However, it is argued by Aydın that the role of Islam in Turkish foreign policy from the late 1980s onwards was confined mostly to the justification of the policies for which the government opted for other reasons.[31] The economic factors were much more influential in the attempts of closer cooperation with the countries in the Middle East.

The general tendencies on the side of the Islamic identity towards Europe were cautious and suspicious. It is argued that for the supporters of this identity, the support and interventions of the Europeans for the rights of the Kurds but disregarding the rights of Islamists is not different from the nineteenth century European intervention into the domestic affairs of the Ottomans on behalf of the non-Muslim subjects of the Empire.[32]

---

29 Ümit Cizre Sakallıoğlu, "The Anatomy of the Turkish Military's Autonomy," *Comparative Politics* 29, no. 2, pp. 151–166., quoted in Aras, *Turkey and the Greater Middle East*, pp. 17–18.

30 Aras, *Turkey and the Greater Middle East*, p. 20.

31 Aydın, "Twenty Years before, Twenty Years after: Turkish Foreign Policy at the Threshold of the 21st Century,", p. 13.

32 Yurdusev, p. 90.

However, this stance started to change after the "soft coup" of the 28 February process in 1997. The split within the Welfare Party led to the emergence of a new movement which embraced EU membership and liberal economic values. The traditionalist wing continued the former rhetoric about the foreign policy whereas the modernist wing left the movement and pursued a conservative stance in politics. The victory of the Justice and Development Party (AKP) in the elections in 2002 also had consequences for the foreign policy of the country. Turkey's current policies in the Middle East and Cyprus represent a shift from the general pattern. I believe that the popular support for the government played an important role in the implementation of the reforms for the EU agenda and the changes in the foreign policy. Although one of the most important aspects of the official identity is Western orientation, there are some kinds of concerns of the elites from the point of democratization in relation to the reforms. And it would be very difficult to pursue a reform agenda on the road to the EU without the support of the traditionalist-conservative segments of society.

*The Nationalist Identity*

The Nationalist identity is referred to as pursuing a model of Turkish nationalism beyond the Kemalist territorial nationalism and favouring cooperation with Turkic peoples abroad.[33] However, the earlier expectations after the end of Cold War did not come true. The tragic events in the Balkans and Caucasus after the end of Cold War and the dissolution of the Soviet Union and Yugoslavia resulted in questioning the Western identity of Turkey, given the weak response of the Europe to these crises. Aydın argues that these events led to the promotion of pan-Turkist and neo-Ottomanist ideas by the right leaning intellectuals.[34]

I believe that the rise of the Turkish nationalism and the effect of this identity in foreign policy are related mostly to the domestic developments instead of the developments abroad. The real reason behind the rise of the Turkish nationalism is the activities of the PKK. The main representative of the nationalist identity is Nationalist Action Party (MHP) and the declarations of the officials of this party regarding foreign policy focus on the continuation of the former policy of Turkey in Cyprus. They are opposed to EU membership because of the demands for democratization which will result in granting some rights to the Kurds within the country. The interventionist side of this identity mostly emerges not in relation to the Turkic peoples, but in relation to the developments in the Kurdish issue and northern Iraq. The nationalists were asking the government to intervene into northern Iraq in relation to the latest developments there.[35] For the nationalists, along with the Kemalists, the support of Europe for the Kurdish people is reminiscent of Eastern Question and Sevres Treaty.[36] In this respect, some segments of the Kemalist elite

---

33  Aras, *Turkey and the Greater Middle East*, p. 21.

34  Aydın, "Twenty Years before, Twenty Years after: Turkish Foreign Policy at the Threshold of the 21st Century," p. 15.

35  See Press Releases of MHP, http://www.mhp.org.tr/basinaciklamalari/basin2006/index.php?page=bsaciklama04092006 [14 September 2006].

36  Yurdusev, p. 90.

can be defined as nationalist left, whereas the MHP can be defined as the nationalist right in Turkey.

The reforms on the road of EU membership faced strong resistance during the coalition government (1999–2002) of the Democratic Left Party (which is known as left nationalist), the Nationalist Action Party (right nationalist) and the Motherland Party (conservative right). Opposition to the EU-led reform program was one of the reasons for the fall of the coalition government. The MHP tried to develop Turkey's relations with the Turkic world and had a minister (Abdulhaluk Çay) in the coalition government responsible from the relations with the Turkic world. Beside this, the *Türk İşbirliği ve Kalkınma ve Ajansı* (Turkish Agency for Cooperation and Development, TİKA) was associated with the Prime Minister's Office (during the coalition government, with MHP leader Bahçeli) instead of with the Ministry of Foreign Affairs as in the past.

*The Conservative Identity*

Tracing the conservative identity in the foreign policy formation is difficult in comparison with other identities since it did not appear as compact and autonomous identity but has been displayed as an attitude in several contexts.[37] The routes of the conservative parties in Turkey can be traced back to the introduction of the multi-party system in the country and the parties based on the legacy of the Democrat Party are within this category. Lacking clear cut principles of doctrine, the conservative identity has characteristics from the Islamist, Nationalist and Kemalist identities. The conservative identity favours increasing contacts with the Turkic and Muslim groups in the neighbouring regions of Turkey, but they are also not against to EU membership as long as this membership is not against the culture and identity of the Turks.[38] For example, the Democrat Party pioneered the idea of Europeanness in Turkey and the foreign policy of this party was totally in line with the Western and European countries. It is argued that personalities and the conditions play an important role in the conservative attitude of the foreign policy.[39] In terms of self-definition of the identity and the implications of this for the foreign policy, surveys of public opinion provide some clues for us. According to a survey conducted in the spring of 2004, 58 percent of the Turkish public define themselves by only their nationality, whereas 42 percent of the population accepts some European element identity.[40] In the same survey the support for EU membership was 71 percent. This result shows us that, although Turkish public opinion is in favour of EU membership, the place of Europe in the definition of identity is limited in comparison with the other European countries.

---

37  Aras, *Turkey and the Greater Middle East*, p. 23.
38  Ibid., p. 24.
39  Ibid.
40  Eurobarometer, *Spring 2004*, p. 23, available [online:] http://ec.europa.eu./public_opinion/archives/cceb/2004/cceb_2004.1_highlights.pdf. [22 September 2006].

*The Impact of EU Candidature on the Identities in Turkish Foreign Policy*

The changes in the policies advocated by different groups and the changing alliances between these groups signify the fact the identities are nor fixed and are subject to change over time. Beside this, the multiple identities of the people are the facts of the post modern world. The changes in the identities are driven not only by domestic political and economic developments, but also by global political and economic conditions. Similar to the changes in the Islamic identity after the 28 February process, along with the effects of globalization, the EU candidature and the reforms to meet the Copenhagen Criteria for membership resulted in the definitions of identities regarding the foreign policy and also some changing alliances among the different identity groups within Turkey. Domestic political reforms, changes in the foreign policy on Cyprus and also on Iraq contributed to the emergence of a *"Kızılelma Coalition"* (Red Apple) comprising the leftist nationalists and rightist nationalists. The erosion of the sovereignty of the state as a result of the process of globalization and the EU reforms decreased the control of the state over the society and consequently the dominant identities in the state structure. The common point in this coalition was the fear of disintegration of the country as a result of the changes in domestic and foreign policies. Some retired civilian and military officials also raised similar concerns, as in the cases of former high level judges and generals. Here the concerns of the Kemalist establishment and the nationalists coincided. The fears regarding the rights of non-Muslim minorities were another common point which was shared also by other identity groups.

The support for the membership in the European Union was high when Turkey became a candidate to the Union. The economic problems after the economic crisis in 2001 led to an increase in this support and 71 percent of the Turkish public was in support of membership in the spring of 2004.[41] The same survey pointed out a 3.5 percent increase in the support of the public for membership. However, the picture started to change when Turkey faced several problems in the opening of accession negotiations with the EU and when the issue of Turkey was hotly debated in relation to the referenda of the constitutional treaty in the member countries. Beside these factors, the increasing terrorist activities of the PKK from 2004 onwards created the feeling among the conservative and nationalist segments of the society that the reforms on the road to meet the Copenhagen Criteria were irrelevant for the demands of the some Kurdish groups and dangerous for the territorial integrity of Turkey. These feelings represented an important political problem for the conservative government that pursued the EU reform agenda.

Beside these domestic problems, the signals from the European elite and the public during the Cartoons Crisis and the Pope's speech on Islam in 2006 led to the questioning of the compatibility of the Islamic and western identities in the minds of some parts of the Turkish society. For example, the president of the European Commission Barroso argued that the enlargement of the European Union should stop after accepting Bulgaria and Romania as members before deciding on the fate

---

41 Eurobarometer, Spring 2004, p. 4, available [online]: http://ec.europa.eu./public_ opinion/archives/cceb/2004/cceb_2004.1_highlights.pdf. [22 September 2006].

of the Constitutional Treaty.⁴² In support of the Pope's speech on Islam, Barroso also argued that European leaders should support the Pope since he had the right to declare his own views and he was disappointed that the European leaders did not supported him as he had expected.⁴³

These problems and the attitude of the European leaders during these crises contributed to the negative image of the EU in Turkey. The official institutions of the EU also recognized the decline in the image of the EU in the eyes of the Turkish public opinion in the spring of 2006 in comparison with the previous years from 60 percent to 43 percent.⁴⁴ Although there is a general decline in the image of the Union at this survey, the decline in the Turkish public opinion is dramatic in comparison with other countries. This figure also has its ramification on related issues since the support of the Turkish public opinion weakened to 45 percent (a seven percent decrease) and here Turkey forms an exception among the candidate countries with the support for the EU membership below 50 percent.⁴⁵

After discussing the basic factors and the roles of different identities in Turkish foreign policy, I will continue with the evaluation of Turkish foreign policy from the establishment of the republic according to the important factors in the decision making process. The periodization is given to provide some idea about the influential factors in each period. This does not mean that that other actors and factors did not have any say in the making of foreign policy. But in each period, some actors were more influential than others in the making of policy.

## Periodization of Turkish Foreign Policy According to Influential Factors

In considering the factors above, the history of Turkish foreign policy has been analyzed by some scholars according to the influential actors in the decision making process as follows:

- The period in which the leader was decisive (1919–1950);
- The rise of the influence of the Ministry of Foreign Affairs (1950–1960);
- The rise of the influences of public opinion, opposition parties and intellectuals (1960–1980);
- The period of the September 12 Coup (1980–1983);
- The rise of the business community in foreign affairs (1983–1991);
- The rise of the army in foreign affairs (1990s).⁴⁶

---

42  http://www.zaman.com.tr/?bl=dishaberler&alt=&trh=20060926&hn=352994 [26 September 2006].

43  http://www.zaman.com.tr/?bl=sondakika&alt=dis&trh=20060924&hn=352395 [26 September 2006].

44  Standard Eurobarometer 65, Public Opinion in the European Union, (Spring 2006), p. 15, available [online]: http://ec.europa.eu/public_opinion/archives/eb/eb65/eb65_first_en.pdf [22 September 2006].

45  Ibid., p. 27.

46  İlhan Uzgel, "TDP'nin Oluşturulması", In *Türk Dış Politikası Kurtuluş Savaşından Bugüne Olgular, Belgeler*, Yorumlar, edited by Baskın Oran (İstanbul: İletişim, 2002), p. 74.

*From the Establishment of the Republic until the end of the Cold War*

In the first period during and after the War for Independence, Mustafa Kemal had the decisive role in the formulation of the foreign policy. Other important actors in this period were İsmet Pasha (İnönü) and Tevfik Rüştü (Aras). In those years, the Ministry of Foreign Affairs was in the making and an important part of the staff of the Ministry was former Ottoman diplomats. Tevfik Rüştü Aras was Minister of Foreign Affairs from 1925 until 1938. During his time, Atatürk's influence was decisive and Aras's position was to implement Atatürk's policy. During this period, the Ministry inherited a lot from the Ottoman diplomacy and followed a successful policy during the inter-war period. The army's role under the command of Fevzi Çakmak in relation to the foreign policy was confined to technical issues and it was kept out of politics. These bureaucrats had the experience of the late years of the Ottoman Empire and the memories of the Balkan Wars, World War I and the Independence War had left imprints on their perceptions. They followed a cautious diplomacy.

The international environment was deteriorating during the 1930s and Turkey tried to establish a security belt along its borders. In this respect, Turkey played a leading role in the formation of the Balkan Entente of 1934 and the Sadabad Pact of 1937. Also the Montreux Convention of 1936 helped Turkey to reinstate its sovereignty over the Straits.

The post World War II period represented drastic changes in world politics and these changes had important consequences for Turkish foreign policy. Turkey became one of the founding members of the United Nations in 1945 and the Council of Europe in 1949. With the transition to the multi-party system in 1950 and change of government, a new era in Turkish foreign policy began. The Democrat Party (DP) period was similar to the single-party period in terms of the dominance of the leader in foreign policy, but the role of the foreign ministers increased.[47] Fuat Köprülü (1950–1957) and Fatin Rüştü Zorlu (1957–1960) served as the foreign ministers during the DP governments. Since both Menderes and Köprülü were not experienced in foreign policy matters, they relied on the bureaucracy of the ministry. Despite this reliance, Menderes tried to be active on foreign policy issues like the Korean War, the Baghdad Pact and membership in NATO. Diplomatic background of Fatin Rüştü Zorlu and active support of some high level diplomats enabled an increase in the role of the Ministry in the second half of the 1950s. With the support of Menderes and the Ministry, Zorlu played an important role in the formulation of the 1959–60 Cyprus Agreements.[48] During this period, the roles of the army, public opinion and the press were limited in the formation of the foreign policy.

During the DP period, Turkey did not pursue a policy of neutrality and became an active member of the western camp. The end of neutrality in foreign policy began with the threats of Stalin against the territorial integrity of Turkey. Turkey's policy was consciously pro-western in the DP era. The reasons behind this policy were the Soviet threat against the territorial integrity of Turkey, ideological issues, pro-Americanism and regarding the countries in the neighbouring region inferior to

---

47  Ibid., p. 76.
48  Ibid.

Turkey.[49] Security concerns determined the framework of Turkish foreign policy in this period and Turkey missed some important political changes in the world. The period after World War II was the period of de-colonization in world politics and many former colonies declared their independence. Most of these newly independent states were anti-western and opted for policies of non-alignment. And some of them established close relations with the Soviet Union. Since the greatest threat to Turkey stemmed from the Soviet Union, the foreign policy priorities of Turkey did not conform to most of these countries. Turkey could not develop its relations with these newly independent states during this period. Turkey was accused by some Arab states in the region of "being the spokesperson of the imperialism".[50]

The coup of 27 May 1960 represented the beginning of a new era in Turkish foreign policy making, the rise of public opinion. The coup leaders did not pursue important changes in the direction of foreign policy. They tried to curtail the influence of the cadre that had worked closely with the DP. Until the 1965 elections, the policy of appointments of diplomats as foreign ministers continued.

The atmosphere created by the 1961 Constitution enabled the impact of the rise of the press and public opinion in foreign policy formation. This development also caused the politicization of foreign policy and foreign policy issues were discussed openly in comparison with earlier times. The connection between domestic and foreign became a reality of political life in Turkey. Another important change in this period was the increase in the role of army in foreign policy making. With the help of National Security Council, the army gained a direct and effective role in the formation of foreign policy. Another important development that had important consequences for Turkey's current foreign policy objective was Turkey's becoming an associate member of the European Economic Community in 1963.

A new development in this period was a change in the direction of foreign policy. Turkey started to follow a multi-dimensional foreign policy after 1965. The Johnson Letter made it obvious how fragile the policy of alliance with the US and western world in the Cold War realities was. With the Cyprus question, the requirement for the definition and defence of the national priorities except the Soviet threat became acute.[51] Turkey began to reassess its relations with the countries of the Warsaw Pact especially in economic terms. Turkey also realized its mistakes after experiencing the isolation in international arenas like the UN in relation to the Cyprus issue. In this period until the coup in 1980, Turkey followed a multi-dimensional foreign policy and tried to increase the level of relations with Third World countries and the Arab world. Important reasons for this preference were the issue of Cyprus, Turkey's economic problems, the disappointment created by the Johnson Letter and the pressure of public opinion. Turkey benefited from the détente atmosphere in

---

49 Hüseyin Bağcı, "Demokrat Parti'nin Ortadoğu Politikası," in *Türk Dış Politikasının Analizi,* edited by Faruk Sönmezoğlu (İstanbul: Der, 1998), pp. 101–102.

50 Melek Fırat-Ömer Kürkçüoğlu, "1945–1960 Ortadoğu'yla İlişkiler," in *Türk Dış Politikası Kurtuluş Savaşından Bugüne Olgular, Belgeler, Yorumlar*, edited by Baskın Oran (İstanbul: İletişim, 2002), p. 615.

51 Davutoğlu, *Stratejik Derinlik*, p. 72.

developing its relations with the Eastern European Countries and the Soviet Union, its northern neighbour.[52]

There were three important consequences of these changes for Turkish foreign policy:[53] First, Turkey changed its stance towards the Soviet Union and increased the level of relations. Second, Turkey renewed its security policy which would enable it to intervene militarily in Cyprus. Third, Turkey recognized that it could not develop relations with the members of the Third World and the Non-Alignment Movement. Turkey's policy during the Arab-Israeli Wars of 1967 and 1973 represents examples of this change. Contrary to the pro-Western and American policy, Turkey followed a policy of neutrality during these wars and did not allow the use of airbases by the American forces to help Israel. Turkey even enabled the use of its airspace by Russian planes for humanitarian help to the Arabs.[54]

The coup of September 12, 1980 resulted in a change in the direction of Turkish foreign policy. The period of the rule of the coup leaders represented the return of US impact on foreign policy. Some agreements concerning military issues and use of airbases were signed between Turkey and the US in this period. Beside the domestic issues, some regional issues also played important role in the re-strengthening of relations with the USA. These were the Soviet invasion of Afghanistan and the Iranian Revolution in 1979. In world politics, the 1980s are defined as the second Cold War and the increasing security threats decreased Turkey's options in foreign policy. The impact of several groups in foreign policy curtailed with the policies of the coup leaders and composition and authority of the NSC were revised to enable an increase in the role of the army in foreign policy.[55] Despite the constitutional changes that increased the role of the army in this area, the period in which the army became most decisive was in the 1990s. The economic policies followed after the return to civilian government in 1983 and the Özal's policies somehow curtailed the role of the army in foreign policy decision making during the 1980s.

In 1980, Turkey began to implement an economic policy based on export oriented development instead of import substitution. Consequently, we see the increasing impact of the business community in foreign policy. With the return to civilian government, the pressure of public opinion, the press and the intellectuals regained its former importance. Another important characteristic of this period was the rise of leadership, the role of Turgut Özal. When Özal was the Prime Minister (1983–1989) and the President (1989–1993), his leadership style dominated the foreign policy of the country. During this period the economy was incorporated into the international capitalist economy and the business community of Turkey had an important political power domestically. In this period, the personal style of Özal

---

52 Synopsis of the Turkish Foreign Policy, available [online]: http://www.mfa.gov.tr/ MFA/ForeignPolicy/Synopsis/ [20.06.2005].

53 Bülent Aras, "The Place of the Palestinian-Israeli Peace Process in Turkish Foreign Policy", *Journal of South Asian and Middle Eastern Studies* 21, no. 2 (Jan 1997), p. 55.

54 Meliha Benli Altunışık, "Soğuk Savaş Sonrası Dönemde Türkiye-İsrail İlişkileri", in *Türkiye ve Ortadoğu: Tarih Kimlik Güvenlik*, edited by Meliha Benli Altunışık (İstanbul: Boyut, 1999), p. 185.

55 Uzgel, p. 81.

was influential in foreign policy decision making and the power of the traditional bureaucratic structures declined. Özal believed that the chronic problems of foreign policy could be solved through economic vehicles and that the bureaucracy did not share his vision. Consequently, he sought to limit the influence of the bureaucracy in foreign policy decision making.[56] Although Özal tried to limit the impact and the rights of the Ministry of Foreign Affairs, he also worked very closely with some younger and educated members of the Ministry. In his second term, Özal changed the ministers often and tried to be influential in the handling of foreign affairs.

*The Post-Cold War Period*

At the beginning of the 1990s, with the Gulf War and the dissolution of the USSR and Yugoslavia, Turkey was faced with several opportunities and challenges. The number of Turkey's neighbours increased. Newly independent states, newly established "brother" republics and consequently ethnic and regional conflicts were included on the agenda of Turkish foreign policy.[57] The ideological rivalry of opposing camps was replaced by the increasing importance of regional issues. Turkey tried to be active in its environment by initiating and participating in several regional organizations. Turkey initiated the formation of the Black Sea Economic Cooperation Organization (BSEC) and also contributed to the formation of the Naval Task Force for the Black Sea (BLACKSEAFOR) among the coastal states to respond to soft security challenges. The membership of another regional organization, the Economic Cooperation Organization (ECO), was expanded by the initiative of Turkey.

The formation of Turkish foreign policy in the post-Cold War period is analyzed by Robins in several phases. In the first phase Özal dominated foreign policy between the mid 1980s and 1991.[58] The second phase was dominated by a collegiate, bureaucratic approach. During this phase, foreign minister Hikmet Çetin closely worked with the staff of the Ministry. The third phase began with 1994 when a fragmented and competitive approach dominated the foreign policy. However, we should keep in mind that most of the actors that were influential in the formation of the Turkish foreign policy were "state actors" like the president, prime minister, military commanders and the professional diplomats of the foreign ministry.[59]

The style of Özal in handling the policy during the Gulf War represented the peak of his leadership in foreign policy. During the crisis, Özal determined Turkey's policy by communicating with US President Bush. Özal acted not only as the president, but also as the de facto prime minister of the country. His attitude was criticized by the opposition parties and his former party, the Motherland Party, lost the elections in 1991. His style in foreign policy was more visionary and ready to take risks. Özal's dynamism in foreign affairs, especially in foreign economic

---

56  Ibid., p. 82.

57  Şule Kut, "Türkiye'nin Soğuk Savaş Sonrası Dış Politikasının Ana Hatları," in *En Uzun Onyıl*, edited by Gencer Özcan and Şule Kut (İstanbul: Boyut, 1998), p. 45.

58  Robins, *Suits and Uniforms*, p. 53.

59  Hale, p. 205.

relations, contributed much to Turkey. This dynamism brought fruitful results in areas such as the former Soviet Union and the Middle East. However, there were side effects of this dynamism. The negative consequences of Özal's approach for Turkey are grouped into two: First, Özal's calculations were not perfect. His policy during the Gulf War created negative outcomes for Turkey. Second, his style caused erosion in the institutionalized decision making in the country's foreign policy. The weakening of the bureaucratic structures of Turkish foreign policy would have more critical consequences in the mid 1990s.[60]

With the end of the bipolar ideological rivalry, the post-Cold War era in world politics signified the rise of cultures and norms such as democracy, market economy, and human rights. However, these changes were not completely applicable for the Turkish case. The problems of adaptation in foreign policy to the changes may be attributed to several factors, like lack of vision, and the resistance of bureaucratic structures but the most important reason was the security threat to the integrity of the country. The 1990s witnessed the rise of the army in foreign affairs in Turkey. While the end of the Cold War signalled a decrease in security threats and the decline of the role of armies for most of the countries in the world, this was not the case for Turkey. Because of several factors, but especially as a result of the terrorist activities of the PKK, the role of the army in Turkey's domestic and foreign policy increased. The struggle against the PKK, the political and economic instabilities during most of the 1990s, and the rise of the Welfare Party were the domestic factors which enabled the rise of the role of the army in Turkey. The instabilities in the neighbouring region of Turkey, the PKK's international networks and Turkey's participation in the UN and NATO's international missions were the external factors that contributed to the increasing role of the army in Turkey's politics.

Developments in communication technologies and private TV and radio channels contributed to an increase in the role of public opinion in foreign affairs. Turkish public opinion was sensitive to the developments that affected Turkic and Muslim communities in the world. The Turkish public was informed about the events in Bosnia, Azerbaijan, Chechnya and Eastern Turkistan, which created a pressure on the Turkish foreign policy.

This period saw changes and turmoil in world politics and the traditional cautious bureaucracy had difficulties in adapting to the change. The stable environment of the Cold War was replaced by several conflicts in the neighbouring regions of Turkey and dealing with all of these problems was difficult to manage.

Within these difficult circumstances, the period between 1991 and 1994 represented an orderly period between two periods of chaos. The impact of the president on foreign policy declined during this period and the close cooperation between the minister Çetin and the top bureaucracy of the Ministry contributed to a stable period for decision making in foreign policy. Also Prime Minister Demirel's low profile in foreign policy strengthened the hands of the Minister and the bureaucracy.[61] In this period, with the decline of the effect of leaders or personalities in the formation of foreign policy, we see a bigger role for institutions.

---

60  Robins, *Suits and Uniforms*, pp.60–61.
61  Ibid.

*The impacts of political and economic problems*     From 1994 onwards, a fragmented approach dominated decision making in Turkish foreign policy. Instability in the political system and weak governments coincided with high turnover in the foreign ministers. The weakness on the side of the political direction of the foreign policy led to an increase in the role of the military in foreign policy decisions. The examples of the increasing role of the military can be found in the issues of increasing the level relations with Israel, the S-300 crisis with Greece and Southern Cyprus, the threatening of Syria for the expulsion of Öcalan.

Despite several weak coalition governments which comprised parties with different foreign policy agendas, there was stability in the post of Foreign Minister after 1997. İsmail Cem served as the minister for five years (between 30 June 1997 and 11 July 2002) and this period represented stability in comparison with the previous period of fragmentation. In spite of the elections, changes in the government and economic crisis, the continuity in the post of the minister and the mild approach of Cem were factors of stability. Cem argues that the period of 1997–2002 differed from the historical pattern because of his "realist" approach.[62] In addition to this realism, he says that his government tried to improve Turkey's relations with several countries, benefiting from cultural and historical affinities. In this respect, he mentions five factors identified to support the goals of this policy: 1) A re-defined identity: Turkey as meeting point between East and West. 2) Cultural identity: the privilege of being both an Asian and a European nation. 3) A rapidly developing economy: a big potential in the areas of industry, commerce and tourism. 4) Peace and stability: being a factor of peace and stability in a region of great challenges and opportunities. 5) The Turkish model: combining Islamic traditions with democratic institutions, human rights, secular law and equality between the sexes.[63]

During this period, similar to the previous coalition governments and economic crisis, there were some problems in international relations. Although Cem acted as the Foreign Minister for a long time, the governments was comprised of several parties. The process of consensus and negotiation building among the members of the coalition took time and caused delays and difficulties in reaching conclusions on several issues. When Turkey was offered candidature status in December 1999, there were disagreements on the conditions of the offer within the government and even between the ministers from the same party about accepting the offer. The coalition made up of DSP, MHP, and ANAP was nationalist, with the DSP nationalist left and MHP nationalist right. This attitude of the government caused some delays in the implementation of reforms for the meeting of the standards of the Copenhagen Criteria. For example, some important reforms packages were accepted in the parliament just a few months before the elections in November 2002.

Beside the differences among the members of the coalition, the economic crisis also negatively affected the foreign policy of Turkey. Turkey entered the year 2000 with a new IMF backed economic program. The crisis in November 2000 and February 2001 resulted with the end of this program and the devaluation of the Turkish Lira 50 percent overnight. The economic crisis was severe and the damage

---

62  Cem, p. 24.
63  Ibid., p. 64.

to the credibility and the power of the country was huge. Most of the energy of the government was spent on economics and the weak economic conditions negatively affected the options of foreign policy.

Along with the differences among the members of the coalition on several issues, especially on the reforms to meet the Copenhagen Criteria, Prime Minister Ecevit's ailing health played a decisive role in the decision to go to early elections in November 2002. The results of the election changed the political arena of the country dramatically. All parties of the governing coalition failed to win seats in the assembly and the AKP won the election with enough seats to form the government. This development signified a new turn in domestic politics and also in foreign policy. Since 1991, the country had been governed by different coalitions and the political and economic instabilities had affected the foreign policy negatively.

The AKP promised democratization and reforms on the path to the EU membership. Several reforms were carried out to meet the criteria for the opening of accession negotiations and some of these reforms also were related with foreign policy in general and decision making in foreign policy in particular. In this respect, beginning with period of the Ecevit's coalition government and continuing with the AKP government, Turkey introduced eight legal reform packages between 19 February 2002 and 14 July 2004 to meet the European political criteria.[64] On 6 October 2004, the EU Commission in its annual *Regular Report on Turkey* indicated that Turkey met the political criteria and recommended that the Council open negotiations with Turkey.[65] After long negotiations on 17 December 2004, the Council decided to start negotiations with Turkey on 3 October 2005.

*Impacts of the EU reforms*    The reforms that began during the coalition government of Ecevit changed the composition, power and functioning of the National Security Council (NSC). These changes affected not only domestic politics, but also foreign policy and decision making in foreign policy. The constitutional changes in October 2001 were the first important steps in this direction and other legal changes followed. With the modification of Article 118 of the Constitution adopted on 17 October 2001, the role and function of the NSC in policy making in general, and in foreign policy in particular, changed. The new text emphasizes the advisory role of the NSC and introduces a majority of civilian members in it. Previously, the government had given *priority* to the NSC's decisions. The new version of the text was "The Council of Ministers shall *evaluate* decisions of the National Security Council concerning the measures that it deems necessary for the preservation of the existence and independence of state, the integrity and indivisibility of the country and the peace and security of society."[66] With the changes in the Law of NSC and

---

64 http://www.mfa.gov.tr/MFA_tr/DisPolitika/AnaKonular/Turkiye_AB/trab.htm [26 July 2006].

65 http://www.deltur.cec.eu.int/!PublishDocs/tr/2004Recommendation.doc [24 April 2006].

66 *Resmi Gazete* (Mükerrer), 17 October 2001, no. 24556.

on the Secretariat General of the NSC, the provision that "the NSC will report to the Council of Ministers the views it has reached and its suggestions" repealed.[67]

With the modification of Article 5 of the Law of NSC and on the Secretariat General of the NSC, the NSC was to meet only once in every two months instead of monthly meetings, and the prerogative of the Chief of General Staff to convene NSC meeting was abolished. The changes in the composition, functioning and role of the NSC Secretariat General also limited the role of military in decision making. According to the new version of law, the Prime Minister was to propose the nomination of the Secretary General, who henceforth could be a civilian, and the President of the Republic would confirm the nomination. The Secretary General's executive and supervisory powers were curtailed, including the follow up of the implementation of the NSC's recommendations, the correlative transformation of the Secretariat General into a purely advisory body, and the suppression of its right of access to the document of any civilian public agency or legal person.[68] Another sign of the development of the democratic process came form the Council of Europe Parliamentary Assembly. On 22 June 2004, the Assembly accepted that Turkey had fulfilled its obligations arising from membership of the Council of Europe and ended its surveillance of Turkey, which had been in action since 1996. The meaning of this decision is that Turkey met the standards of the Council of Europe in terms of democracy, respect for human rights and supremacy of law.[69] Although the Council of Europe is not an EU body, this decision confirmed the democratic standards in Turkey and contributed to the image of the country before the decision for the start of accession negotiations.

These legal changes on the path to the EU along with the declining threat of security diminished the role of the military in decision making regarding foreign policy. The changes in Turkish foreign policy became more visible during the new government of the AKP. The AKP government had to deal with three difficult foreign policy issues, namely Iraq, Cyprus and the EU. All three issues had been on the agenda for several years, but the developments in the previous few years in these three cases were very dynamic and important. With its "pre-emptive strike" policy in the aftermath of 9/11, the USA pressed Turkey to help in the plans for toppling the regime in Iraq. Beside this dynamic issue, Turkey's candidature to the European Union and the prospects of the settlement of the Cyprus problem after several years were the two other crucial issues in Turkish foreign policy.

In this problematic environment, the strength of the government came mostly from institutional coherence. With a decisive majority in the parliament, decision making became less cumbersome. This factor was especially important in considering the issues at stake, like the invasion of Iraq, the settlement of the Cyprus problem after several decades with the Annan Plan, and the starting the negotiations with the EU. Although there were some problems between the government and the armed and

---

67 Ibid.

68 Frederic Misrahi, "The EU and the Civil Democratic Control of Armed Forces: an Analysis of Recent Developments in Turkey," *Perspectives* 22 (2004), p. 25.

69 *Dışişleri Güncesi*, June 2004, p. 68, available [online]: http://www.mfa.gov.tr/NR/rdonlyres/82D08FA5-E3E2-4566-A147-A2EDCB8CFB3C/0/Haziran2004.pdf [10 July 2006].

civilian bureaucracy in the beginning, the government pursued its preferences with the help of the EU agenda. The fragility of the economy at the beginning of the term of the AKP government was another setback for foreign policy, especially in relation to Iraq and the relations with the USA. However, the stabilization of the economy during this period strengthened the hands of the government domestically and abroad. The active involvement of the Prime Minister along with that of the Foreign Minister was another important characteristic of this period. Similar to the approach of Özal, Prime Minister Erdoğan also favoured economic interdependence and not only relied on bureaucratic structures. NGOs, advisors and other non-bureaucratic agents were influential in the formation of foreign policy.

In a speech at the Diplomatic Academy of the Ministry of Foreign Affairs of the Russian Federation in February 2004, Foreign Minister Abdullah Gül defined the three main axis of the Turkish Foreign Policy as follows: First, relations with the Western world, Europe and Euro-Atlantic Institutions. Second, relations with the Middle East in the widest terms. Third, relations with the Eurasian world.[70] This definition did not refer to the foreign policy of his government, but was used to describe the general policy of Turkey from a historical perspective.

The set of principles followed by the Minister and advisers provide us important clues with which to analyze the new theoretical framework of the policy. Foreign Minister Abdullah Gül argues that Turkey is pursuing a "value based" foreign policy and aims to develop its soft power.[71] Gül states that, in spite of the existence of active and dormant problems in the vicinity of Turkey, Turkey does not look at its environment and to the international system from a security perspective.[72] Ahmet Davutoğlu, chief foreign policy advisor to the Prime Minister, describes the five principles of current Turkish foreign policy making as follows:[73] Balance between freedom and security, zero problems with the neighbours, multi-dimensional and multi-track policies, a new diplomatic discourse and transition to rhythmic diplomacy.

Kirişçi described the three characteristics of foreign policy approach of the AKP government as follows: First, willingness to be proactive and take risks. Secondly, to address and attempt to resolve bilateral problems and actively develop closer relations with neighbouring countries. Third, shift away from seeing the world from the perspective of "win-lose" to "win-win" games.[74]

The impact of EU candidature sometimes has strengthened the government's foreign policy agenda and sometimes has made the decisions of foreign policy difficult. The relationship between some of the principles above, especially the first three, and Turkey's EU candidature is useful in understanding the impact of

---

70 *Dışişleri Güncesi*, February 2004, pp. 88–90, available [online]: http://www.mfa.gov.tr/NR/rdonlyres/A6A242D1-417F-4B4C-8EFA-890880A6DD1C/0/Şubat2004.pdf [10 July 2006].

71 Abdullah Gül, "New Horizons in Turkish Foreign Policy," Boğaziçi Yöneticiler Vakfı, Dedeman Hotel, İstanbul, 22 May 2004.

72 Ibid.

73 Ahmet Davutoğlu, "Türkiye Merkez Ülke Olmalı," *Radikal*, 26 February 2006.

74 Kemal Kirişçi, "Turkey's Foreign Policy in Turbulent Times," *Chaillot Paper*, no. 92, (September 2006), pp. 49–51.

EU candidature on foreign policy. These principles, especially the first three, are in conformity with the EU agenda for any country and also for Turkey.

In the post-9/11 world, many countries, several global actors and even some NGOs have pursued agendas dominated by security concerns. As several countries have boosted their security arrangements, naturally many freedoms have been curtailed automatically. According to Davutoğlu, contrary to the measures of many countries, Turkey constitutes an exceptional case in this respect. Turkey has increased the domain of individual freedoms with political reforms. It is argued that Turkey has tried to expand the area of freedoms without endangering the security of the country.[75] These reforms have been carried out to meet the Copenhagen criteria and the impact of the EU candidature in the democratization is obvious. Without the EU agenda, it would not be easy for the government to pursue this policy.

The impact of democratization on foreign policy can be seen from the new attitude of Turkey in the current developments in Cyprus, Iraq and Palestine. Public opinion and NGOs have played increasing roles in the decisions. For example, the impact of public opinion and the role of pro-EU NGOs have been obvious in the change of stance on the Cyprus question. With the support of public opinion in Turkey and Northern Cyprus, the government has managed to pursue a new course in such a sensitive issue. Opposition parties and anti-EU NGOs and some other groups have been very critical of the changes in these policies. Turkey's EU agenda and the changes in the policy regarding Cyprus has been described by one of the opposition parties as "un-national" and the government has been warned about the consequences for the EU agenda and the results of it on the Cyprus question.[76]

We also have seen increasing impact of public opinion on the foreign policy in the cases of Iraq and Palestine. The refusal of transfer of US soldiers to northern Iraq and of sending of Turkish troops there in the Grand National Assembly is very much related to the impact of public opinion. Allowing the transfer of US soldiers via Turkish territory to attack Iraq could have create a handicap for a country on the road to the European Union with a government which was claiming to introduce a new direction in foreign policy. The Turkish public was opposed to such an action and the government did not press hard for the acceptance of the motion, since this might result in the division of the governing party. On the issue of Iraq, the opposition party, the CHP (Republican People's Party) in the Parliament opposed the motion and the deputy head of the party, Onur Öymen, a retired diplomat, argued that Turkey could transfer some of its soldiers to northern Iraq if the security of the country required doing so.[77]

The EU requires the applicant countries to settle their differences with their neighbours in a peaceful way before becoming members and have good neighbourly relations. Contrary to the general post-Cold War trend in global politics, Turkey's relations with its neighbours were problematic during most of the 1990s. This reality was very much related to Turkey's own economic and political problems and also to

---

75  Ibid.

76  http://www.mhp.org.tr/raporlar/kibris/kibrisraporu.pdf [24 November 2006].

77  http://www.chp.org.tr/index.php?module=news&page=readmore&news_id=319 [24 November 2006].

the threats to its security. These conditions led to a psychology of fear of encirclement by its enemies and policy prescriptions for a "two-and-a-half war strategy."[78]

In the past few years, Turkey has had positive relations with its neighbours, except for Armenia and (Southern) Cyprus. This policy has provided Turkey with an area of manoeuvre in the formation of foreign policy. However, Foreign Minister Gül has argued that Turkey's active involvement in its region and multilateral relations with the countries in the Middle East is not an option to replace its connections with Europe and that the security and stability of Europe and the Middle East are complementary.[79] An example of this attitude of the government came after the historic decision of the EU to start negotiations with Turkey, when Prime Minister Erdoğan visited Syria. The timing of the visit just after this event and at a time when US pressure on Syria was on the rise was a point criticisms, but there was also support for this visit since it signalled that relations with the EU are important but Turkey also is trying to improve relations with its neighbours.

During the Cold War period, Turkey obeyed the rules of the polarized nature of world politics and acted a committed member of the western alliance. It is impossible for Turkey in the dynamic conditions of global politics to follow static and mono-dimensional policies. In these global conditions, Turkey tries to develop its relations not only with the US and the EU, but also with Russia, Central Asia, East Asia and other parts of the world. The policy makers argue that none of Turkey's relations with one party is an alternative to its relations with another actor. Namely, Turkey's relations with the EU are not an alternative to its relations with the US. All of them are parts of this multi-dimensional foreign policy.[80]

Similar to the developments during the export oriented economic program of 1980s, the role of the business elite in foreign policy started to increase again. The relative decline of security threats and positive atmosphere with the neighbouring countries has contributed to this development. The expanding economic relations with Turkey's neighbours and the investments of Turkish businessmen in these countries have become important factors in relations between Turkey and these countries. Beside the increasing activities of Turkish businessmen, the increasing amount of foreign direct investment (FDI) in Turkey also contributed to the position of the business community. With the stabilization of economy backed by the IMF program and Turkey's EU agenda, the amount of foreign direct investment in Turkey reached to unprecedented levels. According to official data, the amount of FDI for the year 2004 was 2.883 million US dollars, for the year 2005 was 9.793 million US dollars and for the year 2006 (until the end of October) 15.804 million US dollars.[81] The average FDI before the year of 2000 was always below the 1.000 million US

---

78 This "two-and-a-half war" strategy is developed by Şükrü Elekdağ in referring to a possible confrontation between Turkey and Greece and Syria, along with the struggle with the PKK. For details see Şükrü Elekdağ, "İki Buçuk Savaş Stratejisi," *Yeni Türkiye*, no. 3 (March–April 1995), pp. 516–522.

79 *Dışişleri Güncesi*, February 2004, p. 54, available [online]: http://www.mfa.gov.tr/NR/rdonlyres/A6A242D1-417F-4B4C-8EFA-890880A6DD1C/0/Şubat2004.pdf [10 July 2006].

80 Davutoğlu, "Türkiye Merkez Ülke Olmalı," *Radikal*, 26 February 2004.

81 http://www.hazine.gov.tr/stat/yabser/ybs_bulten_ckim2006.pdf [30 January 2007].

dollars. Another important figure in these increasing foreign direct investments is the source of the investment. More than 90 percent of these investments are coming from EU member countries.[82] The investors and their partners in Turkey support the EU agenda of Turkey since they have their economic interests in this integration process. Consequently, this part of business community also wants to have their views reflected in the foreign policy of Turkey.

The roles of NGOs have been very constructive in Turkey's relations with the EU. These groups not only have supported the government in its EU agenda, but lobbied in the European capitals for the beginning of accession negotiations. NGOs like TÜSİAD (the Association of Turkish Businessmen and Industrialists), TOBB (the Union of Chambers and Commodity Exchanges of Turkey), and İKV (the Foundation for Economic Development) have lobbied for Turkey and these groups continue their efforts in eliminating the negative stance of some members. The aim of the foundation of İKV is described as to inform the Turkish public about the relations between Turkey and the EU and also to support the activities on the road to EU membership.[83]

Turkey's role in the project of the "Alliance of Civilizations" has been one of the foreign policy initiatives of this period, the aim of which has been to show the contribution of Turkey to an understanding between East and West. The Turkish authorities have tried to use this initiative as a foreign policy tool and have aimed to benefit from this project in their bid for EU membership. The support of the UN for this joint initiative between Spain and Turkey has contributed to the efforts of Turkey. Besides these kinds of initiatives to show its capacity to combine eastern and western characteristics, Turkey also has called for reforms in the Muslim world. An example of this initiative is a the speech by Abdullah Gül at the Organization of Islamic Conference (OIC) Meeting of Foreign Ministers in Tehran on 28–30 May 2003. Gül referred to the backwardness and problems of the Islamic world and argued that instead of blaming others, several reforms should be carried out to overcome these problems and that the reforms should come within the Islamic world. Gül later said that the response of the politicians and the intellectuals to the proposal of Turkey were very positive.[84] In addition to the calls for reform in the Islamic world, Turkey also played a positive role in the crisis related to the cartoons portraying Prophet Mohammed in Denmark.

The foreign visits of the Prime Minister and Foreign Minister in the last couple of years have increased drastically in frequency. Turkey's officials have paid attention to visiting and maintaining contacts with the neighbouring countries in relation to the "zero problems with the neighbours" policy. But the visits have not been limited to neighbouring states or not focused on one region. In order to get support for the Turkey's candidature for the 2009–2010 UN Security Council membership, the Prime Minister and Foreign Minister visited several countries in East Asia and Africa. The official figures provided by the Ministry for these visits give an idea of

---

82  Ibid.
83  http://www.ikv.org.tr/ikv.php [24 November 2006].
84  Gül, "New Horizons in Turkish Foreign Policy," 22 May 2004.

the scope of these travels. For example, Erdoğan visited Ethiopia and South Africa between March 1 and March 5, 2005.[85]

In the last couple of years, the interest of the public opinion in foreign policy has increased a great deal and foreign policy issues like Cyprus, Iraq and the EU are hotly debated domestically. The reason for this development may be a result of the importance of these foreign policy issues for the Turkish public opinion, but also it is related to the disappearance of foreign-domestic distinction as seen in the case of several EU members and candidates. As a result of this development, foreign policy issues became much more politicized and the interest of the public in these issues made the governments take ideas of the public into consideration.

The activities of Turkish foreign policy in the post-Cold War era before the EU candidature are grouped in general terms by Kirişçi under two main headings:[86] The first type of actions focused on the protection of Turkey from the surrounding instabilities and the control and prevention of instabilities. In this manner, Turkey tried to make the actions of the international community incongruent to the priorities of Turkish foreign policy. The second types of activities consisted of long-term efforts for the establishment of an international order that would replace the existing regional instabilities.

Under the first type of actions, Turkey was actively involved in efforts for the solution of the regional problems in the Balkans and the Caucasus. Regarding the dispute between Azerbaijan and Armenia in the Caucasus and the problems in the former Yugoslavia, despite the demands for unilateral actions, Turkey acted along with the international community. During these crises, Turkey demanded that the international community play a more active role in the solution of these problems. Under the second type of actions, Turkey's activities can be grouped as making contributions to the establishment of a system composed of several organizations in Europe, contributions to stability by promoting economic solidarity, enhancing the relations with the former Soviet republics and participation in the humanitarian aid initiatives.[87]

Turkey's contribution to these operations continued after the EU candidature. In this period Turkey participated in peace-making and peace-enforcing operations in Somalia, Bosnia-Herzegovina, Albania, Kosovo and Georgia. Turkey assumed the command of the International Security Assistance Force in Afghanistan (ISAF II) and contributed 1,400 troops between June 2002 and February 2003. Turkey assumed the command of ISAF IV between February and August 2005.[88] Turkey's contribution to these kinds of missions has not been limited to the confines of the framework of the UN. Turkey participates in the Balkans UN's KFOR (Kosovo Force) and UNMIK (UN Police Mission in Kosovo) and the European Union's (EU)

---

85 *Dışişleri Güncesi*, March 2005, p. 62, available [online]: (http://www.mfa.gov.tr/NR/rdonlyres/F63ECDA4-266F-4BE7-8EFA-F9CF06BAD054/0/MART2005.pdf) (15 April 2006).

86 Kemal Kirişçi, "Uluslararası Sistemdeki Değişmeler ve Türk Dış Politikasının Yeni Yönelimleri," in *Türk Dış Politikasının Analizi,* edited by Faruk Sönmezoğlu (İstanbul: Der, 1998), p. 618.

87 Ibid., pp. 618–28.

88 "Synopsis of the Turkish Foreign Policy," available [online]: http://www.mfa.gov.tr/MFA/ForeignPolicy/Synopsis/ [20.06.2005].

Police Mission in Bosnia-Herzegovina (EUPM) and the EU-led Police Mission "Proxima" in Macedonia.

The role of Turkey in the world politics since the 1990s has been a functional one with participation in peace making operations and as the smiling face of the eastern world.[89] Although such a role compliments the needs of the western alliance, Turkey should also develop its own long term strategy. Otherwise it may continue only to play the functional role in future transatlantic relations.[90] Turkey's active involvement in the neighbouring regions in the last couple of years may constitute the early signs of its own strategy.

Beside the EU candidature and the developments in this respect, Turkey's involvement in the Middle East and increasing relations with the regional countries is sometimes interpreted by some segments of society as a part of the secret agenda of the government in foreign policy affairs. Increasing contacts with the Muslim countries in the Middle East, with Syria, Iran and also with the countries in the Gulf and elsewhere, are seen as parts of this agenda. The government legitimized these relations with the arguments of economic interdependence and good neighbourly relations.

There are officially two major objectives of Turkish foreign policy for the future.[91] The first goal is to make Turkey an integral part of the European Union. Second Turkey aims proactively to pursue the goal of helping to create an environment of security, stability, prosperity, friendship and cooperation all around itself. Turkey's contribution in this respect will affect Europe, Balkans, the Middle East, the Caucasus, the Mediterranean and Central Asia positively. Turkey also aims to increase relations with Latin America and Africa.

---

89 Gülnur Aybet, "The Future of Trans-Atlantic Relations and the Place of Turkey," Paper presented at the European Studies Centre, University of Oxford, 15 June 2006.

90 Ibid.

91 "Synopsis of the Turkish Foreign Policy," available [online]: http://www.mfa.gov.tr/MFA/ForeignPolicy/Synopsis/ [20.06.2005].

# Chapter 6

# Turkish Foreign Policy towards the Middle East until the end of the Cold War

This chapter covers Turkish foreign policy towards the Middle East from the establishment of the republic until the end of Cold War. In order to analyze the changes in Turkish policy in the post-Cold War period and the impact of the EU candidature there, the historical background of the Turkish policy towards the Middle East should be provided. This chapter provides a transition from the general characteristics of the TFP to the developments in the post-Cold War and the post-Gulf War period in the region.

There have been many ups and downs in Turkey's policy towards the Middle East since the establishment of the republic. Turkey's predecessor the Ottoman Empire, ruled most of the Middle East until the first quarter of the twentieth century. In the second and third quarters of the twentieth century, Turkey's relations with the region were minimal, except for some initiatives like the Baghdad Pact. After understanding the negative impacts of this situation, Turkey's interest in the region started to increase in the beginning of the last quarter of the twentieth century. During this period, several issues and actors were influential in the formation of the Turkey's policy and this reality should be kept in mind in analyzing Turkish foreign policy towards the Middle East. Beside the regional developments like the Arab-Israeli Wars, oil crisis and the negative impacts of these on Turkey; the issues that had great importance for Turkey like the Cyprus problem, relations with the US and the European Union also caused changes in Turkey's policies towards the region.

Beginning with the establishment of the republic, Turkey did not want to be involved in Middle Eastern developments. Although the new republic focused on the institutionalization of the state and pursued a policy of westernization, as a country in the region, the developments affected Turkey. For example, Turkey's border with Iraq was not settled until 1926. However, Turkey's relations with its Middle Eastern neighbours in this period were generally cooperative and unproblematic. During this interwar period, several Middle Eastern countries were under the mandate of European powers. The most important foreign policy developments in this period were the Sadabad Pact and the unification of Hatay with Turkey.

**The Cold War and Security-Based Foreign Policy: 1945–1964**

During the Cold War and the post-Cold War period, Middle Eastern politics was characterized by four major issues: "Ideology based geopolitical polarization; oil based geo-economical structures, geopolitical division representing the global strategic rivalry and lastly regional conflicts arising from the establishment of Israel."[1]

Turkey gave up its neutral foreign policy in the aftermath of WWII and became a part of the western alliance. The main reason for this change was the perception of the Russian threat to Turkey's security. Security concerns dominated Turkish foreign policy in this period and Turkey's policy towards the Middle East also was influenced by this reality. Turkey paid great attention to the developments in the region in comparison to the early years of the republic. Turkey perceived the changes in the world system in the Cold War, tried to benefit from the conditions and wanted to play a leadership role for the countries of the region as the representative of the western world. But Turkey failed to realize another important development in this period, the impact of de-colonization, and could not develop relations with the newly independent states. It was criticized by the Arab states as being "the spokesmen of the imperialism."[2]

Turkey voted along with the Arab states in the General Assembly of the United Nations on 30 October, 1947 against the division of Palestine. It is argued that this behaviour was not a result of an Islamic solidarity with the Arabs, but the result of Turkish fears regarding the region.[3] Israel's neutrality was perceived as a deception and increased a secret threat of communism. Although Turkey opposed the division of the Palestine Mandate and acted neutral during 1948 War, it became a member of the Palestine Conciliation Commission after the war. Turkey followed a neutral policy and argued that the problem should be solved peacefully.

The reason behind the cautious policy of Turkey against Israel in the beginning was the USSR's support for the establishment of Israel and the migration of an important number of people from the USSR to Israel.[4] Turkish member of the UN Commission, Hüseyin Cahit Yalçın, presented a report to President İnönü in March 1949 after his visit to Israel and claimed the Israel's possibility of becoming a communist state was very low and that Turkey should recognize Israel immediately.[5] Turkey recognized Israel on 28 March 1949 as the first Muslim country to do so. US support of Israel played an important role in the decision of Turkey. We also should consider the effect of the Truman Doctrine and the assistance received by Turkey within the framework of this doctrine along with Turkey's wish to become a member of NATO. In this respect, Turkey's relations with Israel were influenced positively by the support of

---

1   Davutoğlu, *Stratejik Derinlik*, p. 135.

2   Melek Fırat-Ömer Kürkçüoğlu, "1945–1960 Ortadoğu'yla İlişkiler," in *Türk Dış Politikası Kurtuluş Savaşından Bugüne Olgular, Belgeler, Yorumlar*, edited by Baskın Oran, vol. 1 (İstanbul: İletişim, 2002), p. 615.

3   Gencer Özcan, "Türkiye-İsrail İlişkileri 50. Yılına Girerken," in *Türk Dış Politikasının Analizi*, edited by Faruk Sönmezoğlu (İstanbul: Der, 1998), p. 159.

4   Hasan Köni, "Mısır-Türkiye-İsrail Üçgeni", *Avrasya Dosyası* 1, no. 3 (Autumn 1994), p. 46.

5   Özcan, p. 160.

Israel for the decisions of the UN about the Korean War in opposition to the neutral policy of the Arab countries. US support for Israel and Turkey's membership to the western organization after the threat perceptions from the USSR made Turkey and Israel regional partners as a result of global alliance formations.[6]

In this period, decisions in Turkish foreign policy were consciously western oriented. The governing party viewed Turkey as the most important factor in the preservation of peace in the Middle East and a bridge between East and West. In relation to that, Turkey had to make every effort to pull the Muslim countries of the Middle East to Baghdad Pact against the Soviet threat.[7] The differences about the Soviets, however, between Turkey and its Arab neighbours became sources of conflict. Turkey's relations with the Middle East in this era were characterized by the factors of ideological differences, Soviet threat, pro-Americanism, accepting the Arab countries as inferior to Turkey.[8] Cem argued that Turkey's distancing itself from the Middle East was ideologically motivated and was the result of two factors: First, the advice and sometimes the pressures of the western powers; second, the choice of western oriented dominant ideology.[9] For the Turkish elite, the Middle East represented backwardness in cultural terms and it was an area of political risks that Turkey should refrain to intervene. The negative memories of World War I, especially related to the Arab revolt, dominated the general feelings towards the region.

The 1950s were one of the important times of contention between the two blocs. The instability began with the end of World War II and continued with the establishment of Israel. During this period, the end of the imperial policies of the European countries like the UK and France and the emergence of new independent states determined the features of the region. Regime changes in some of the new states like Egypt and Iraq, and internal struggles in the countries like Syria after independence were causes of concern for the policies to be pursued. The rivalry between the two superpowers for the region was also one of the determining factors that dominated the politics in the region.

Turkey's recognition of Israel and opposition to the USSR's Middle East policy made its relations with the Arab countries problematic. The Menderes government was unable to follow a balanced diplomacy towards the region. It is argued by some scholars that the real reason behind this failure was the non-existence of a clearly defined Middle East policy for the Turkish government.[10] Turkey's attitude towards the Middle East during the 1950s was dominated by the communist threat. Turkey's active involvement in the region was a result of the attempts to balance the rise of pro-Soviet regimes. Turkey's attempts at the formation of the Baghdad Pact, the tensions with Syria in 1957 and afterwards, the formation of the United Arab Republic between Egypt and Syria in February 1958 were some examples of

---

6   Davutoğlu, *Stratejik Derinlik,* p. 418.

7   Mahmut Bali Aykan, "The Palestinian Question in Turkish Foreign Policy from the 1950s to the 1990s," *International Journal of Middle East Studies* 25, no. 1 (February 1993), p. 92.

8   Bağcı, pp. 101–102.

9   Cem, p. 16.

10   Bağcı, p. 103.

reciprocal negative perceptions. Turkey's relations with the Arab countries in those years grew worse because of the different threat perceptions and the changes in world politics. Turkey faced a Soviet threat and become a member of the Baghdad Pact for the elimination of this threat, and supported the Eisenhower Doctrine of 1957, but the Arab states did not perceive a Soviet threat and accepted Israel as the biggest threat to their security. Beside the factors above, Turkey's support for the Eisenhower Doctrine of 1957, problems with Iraq during the 1958 coup and the permission for the use of İncirlik base during the crisis in Lebanon in 1958 negatively affected its relations with the Arab countries.

Another important development during the 1950s was the Suez Crisis. Israel's constant criticisms of the Baghdad Pact, which was very important for Turkey, created some problems between Turkey and Israel. Upset about these criticisms, Turkey decreased the level of its relations with Israel beginning with the summer of 1955 and after the Suez Crisis.[11] In order to save the Baghdad Pact, Turkey condemned Israel during the Suez Crisis and labelled this country as a threat to the Middle Eastern peace at a Baghdad Pact summit.[12] Despite these declarations, Turkey continued its relations with Israel. During the 1950s, the criticisms and demands of the Arab states and the intra-bloc influences of the Cold War period made Turkey's position difficult.[13] The intra-bloc solidarity was important for Turkey because of the Soviet threat.

The coup in Iraq in 1958 represented the end of the Baghdad Pact and Turkey signed a pact with Israel covering military, diplomatic and security issues during a secret visit of Israeli Prime Minister to Turkey in 1958.[14] During the meetings for the Pact, the Menderes government tried to get 150 million dollars, recognition in the international monetary markets and the support of the Jewish lobby on the issue of Cyprus.[15] The timing of this pact also coincided with the increasing Soviet influence in the region and pro-Nasserite movement in the Middle East.

Beside the issues above, some of the foreign policy decisions of Turkey in the 1950s were criticized and these criticisms prevented Turkey from becoming a leading player in the region. The most obvious problem for Turkey was failing to observe the emergence of post-colonialist states and failing to develop relations with these newly independent states as the first republic established after an anti-colonialist independence war. In this respect, Turkey voted against the independence of Algeria in the United Nations General Assembly in 1955. Turkey also remained neutral during the discussion of a proposal made by the African and Asian states for the self-determination of Algeria in 1957.[16] Turkey's active relationship with Britain, former colonial power in the region, within the framework of the Baghdad Pact was another

---

11  Çağrı Erhan-Ömer Kürkçüoğlu, "1945–1960: Ortadoğu'yla İlişkiler," in *Türk Dış Politikası Kurtuluş Savaşından Bugüne Olgular, Belgeler, Yorumlar*, edited by Baskın Oran, vol. 1 (İstanbul: İletişim, 2002), p. 645.

12  Altunışık, "Soğuk Savaş Sonrası Dönemde Türkiye-İsrail İlişkileri," p. 183.

13  Davutoğlu, *Stratejik Derinlik*, p. 418.

14  Nezih Tavlaş, "Türk-İsrail Güvenlik ve İstihbarat İlişkileri," *Avrasya Dosyası* 1, no. 3 (Autumn 1994), p. 9.

15  Köni, p. 47.

16  Criss and Bilgin, p. 6.

source of criticism and hindered Turkey's potential afterwards. Remembering the negative effects of the policies during the 1950s, Turkey worked hard in the second half of the 1990s in order to prevent a similar isolation from the region. With the decrease of security concerns after the capture of Öcalan, Turkey increased its dialog with several countries in the region.

## Diversification of Foreign Policy: 1964–1980

With the beginning of the 1960s, the one-dimensional pro-Western orientation of Turkish foreign policy is criticized. Several factors were influential in the questioning of its general orientation. These can be summarized as the participatory nature of the new constitution, the increasing effect of the public opinion on foreign policy formation, the 1962 Cuba Missile Crisis, the Johnson Letter of 1964, having problems in getting support for the Cyprus issue in the UN except from the Muslim countries and the increasing economic problems. During this period in reaction to the policy preferences of the 1950s, Turkey avoided involvement in the intraregional problems and tried to correct bilateral relations with all states regardless of ideology.[17]

In his famous letter, US President Lyndon B. Johnson informed Turkey that in the case of an intervention to Cyprus, the US would not help Turkey against the Soviet threat and warned Turkey not to use US-made weapons outside of NATO purposes. In addition, Turkey's limited police operation on Cyprus ended with a vote in the UN on 18 December, 1965. Turkey's western allies did not support it during the voting and only Iran, Albania, Pakistan and US supported Turkey. Syria, Egypt and Lebanon supported Turkey by remaining neutral during the voting. Since the direct and indirect support for Turkey came from the Muslim countries, some decision makers in Ankara questioned the orientation of their country's foreign policy and the Grand National Assembly of Turkey brought the matter under review.[18]

In this period, Turkey developed its relations with the Soviet Union, East European countries and members of the Organization of the Islamic Conference. The aim of the policy makers in this period was to have an independent, elastic and diversified approach regarding the Middle East.[19] Turkey's policy during the 1967 Arab-Israeli War signalled the change. Turkey did not allow the US use of İncirlik Air Base to help Israel and also actively participated in humanitarian assistance to the Arab countries. During the 1973 Arab-Israeli War, Turkey did not allow the US to use Turkish military facilities to aid Israel, but did allow the Soviet Union to re-supply aircraft heading for Egypt and Syria to use its airspace. This policy "marked a change in Turkish foreign policy in the direction of active support for the Arab cause

17  Philip J. Robins, "Avoiding the Question," in *Reluctant Neighbor*, edited by Henry J. Barkey (Washington DC: US Institute of Peace Press, 1996), p. 179.

18  Hakan Yavuz, "İkicilik: Türk-Arap İlişkileri ve Filistin Sorunu," in *Türk Dış Politikasının Analizi*, edited by Faruk Sönmezoğlu (İstanbul: Der, 1998), p. 572.

19  Aras, "The Place of the Palestinian-Israeli Peace Process in Turkish Foreign Policy," p. 55.

in the Arab-Israeli conflict."[20] Turkey acted along with the Arab states and also with the international community in the UN and demanded the end of Israeli occupation. In January 1975 Turkey recognized the PLO as the sole legitimate representatives of the Palestinians and in November 1975 it voted in favour of the UN General Assembly resolution equating Zionism with racism.

The main factors that drove the formation of Turkish foreign policy during this period were the increase in the price of oil after the oil crisis, a decline in Turkey's economic conditions, worsening relations with the European Economic Community, problems with the US because of the Cyprus intervention and coalition governments like the CHP-MSP Coalition. Under these conditions Turkey continued its policy of close relations with the Arab countries. Turkey followed a balanced policy in the region after the mid-1960s. On the one hand, Turkey established close relations with the Arab states and supported the Palestinians. On the other hand, despite great pressure from the Arab states, Turkey continued relations with Israel. After the Camp David Accords, Egypt also established diplomatic relations with Israel. Egypt is an important country in the Arab world and the criticisms for having relations with Israel focused on Egypt instead of Turkey after this development. Foreign and domestic issues like the isolation in the foreign policy, coups and polarization in the political spectrum and the economic problems were reflected in Turkish foreign policy regarding the Middle East.

**Economic Factors and the Search for a Balanced Policy: 1980–1990**

The early years of the 1980s were dominated by the tense relations between two camps of the Cold War after the invasion of the Afghanistan by the Soviet Union. Beside this invasion, the Islamic Revolution in Iran also contributed to the fears of the western camp. For Turkey these developments resulted in the strengthening intra-camp relations with the US. During this era, Turkey's Middle East policy changed with the impact of several factors. Issues like Israeli Knesset's declaration of united Jerusalem as its eternal capital and Turkey's economic problems induced Turkey to follow a policy close to the Arab countries. Turkey tried to develop relations with Israel after 1985, but *Intifada* negatively affected this development.

Turkey opposed the declaration of Jerusalem as the eternal capital of Israel by the Knesset and decreased its level of relations with Israel to the Second Secretary level. The reason behind this policy is explained by some scholars as a sign of solidarity with the members of Islamic conference to show its support of the Arabs on this sensitive issue.[21] It is argued by some other scholars that Turkey's decision was not a result of solidarity with the Arab countries, but a result of economic concerns. Turkey's decision to decrease relations with Israel came after a donation of 250 million dollars by Saudi Arabia.[22] As the Turkish economy integrated with the capitalist world economy after the implementation of a new economic policy

---

20 Aykan, "The Palestinian Question in Turkish Foreign Policy from the 1950s to the 1990s," p. 97.
21 Ibid., p. 101.
22 Özcan, p. 165.

based on increasing exports with the decisions of 24 January 1980, economic factors started to have increasing importance in foreign policy. Arab countries constituted an important market for Turkey's new export oriented economic policy; this resulted in continuation of a low-level relations policy with Israel. With the 1980s, Arab countries represented an emerging market characteristic for Turkey.

Turkey's policy towards the Middle East in this period is described as "the aim of Turkey was buying oil, paying the money for this oil as late as possible, attracting foreign investment and increasing Turkey's exports to those (Arab) countries."[23] In this era, Turkey's foreign policy was influenced greatly by economic factors. Some scholars argue that Turkey's foreign policy preferences during the late 1970s and 1980s very much look like the Japanese approach, meaning the overriding aim was material benefit.[24] This was true especially during the oil crisis and Iran-Iraq war. Turkey tried to pursue its relations as bilateral relations, instead of the general policies within the western alliance.

After Israel's invasion of Lebanon and the massacres of Sabra and Shatilla, there was a negative feeling in the Turkish public opinion against Israel. Israel's invitation to Turkey in participate to the elimination of the ASALA Camps in Lebanon was a positive sign of the warming of the relations.[25] Ankara government positively responded to Israel's invitation and Turkey also acted neutral in the UN on a resolution about Israeli occupied Golan Heights.

Turkey's relations with Israel started to develop in the second half of the 1980s and one of the aims of Turkey here was to limit the negative impact of lobbies in US politics against Turkey. In January 1986, Prime Minister Turgut Özal declared that Turkey's relations with Israel was the result of a practical need and that in order to play a role in the solution of the Middle Eastern problems, Turkey's contacts with Israel were needed.[26] The Intifada affected Turkey's relations with Israel and the Palestinians and increased sympathy of the Turkish people for the Palestinians and damaged Israel's image. Turkey supported the establishment of a Palestinian state and recognized the Palestinian state declared by the PLO in Algeria. Although Turkey recognized Palestine immediately, it opposed to a resolution in 1989 for the prohibition of Israeli representation in the UN. In response to this, Jewish lobbies opposed an Armenian resolution in the US Congress.[27] Jewish lobbies have always been an important factor in Turkey's relations with Israel and have contributed to the development of relations between Israel and Turkey. Jewish lobbies supported Turkey in the US against the Armenian and Greek Lobbies upon the request of Turkey. However, it is argued that the Turkish governments perceive these lobbies

---

23  Yavuz, p. 576.

24  Robins, "Avoiding the Question," p. 179.

25  Çağrı Erhan-Ömer Kürkçüoğlu, "1980–1990: Ortadoğu'yla İlişkiler," in *Türk Dış Politikası Kurtuluş Savaşından Bugüne Olgular, Belgeler, Yorumlar*, edited by Baskın Oran, vol. 1 (İstanbul: İletişim, 2002), p. 151.

26  Altunışık, "Soğuk Savaş Sonrası Dönemde Türkiye-İsrail İlişkileri," p. 190.

27  Ayşe Karabat, "Hayalet İttifak: Türkiye-İsrail İlişkileri," *Radikal*, 21 July 2001.

as more pro-Turkish than they actually are and Israel benefits from this perception in its relations with Turkey.[28]

## The End of the Cold War and Shifts in Foreign Policy

The post-Cold War period in Turkish foreign policy was characterized by several important changes. With the dissolution of the Soviet Union, the main threat to Turkey was over. After long period of time, Turkey no longer shared a border with Russia. This change had important effects on the Turkish security framework. Although Turkey was happy with these developments, some concerns about a decline in its geopolitical importance for its Western allies were raised.

The positive atmosphere in Turkey's relations with the Arab Middle Eastern countries were affected negatively by three important developments. These were the end of Iran-Iraq War, the Gulf War and the peace process.[29] Although Turkey was in favour of the end of the Iran-Iraq War, the military power of Iraq at the end of the war was a threat for Turkey. During the war, Arab countries and anti-Iran western countries contributed a lot to the military power of Iraq. The regional balance with the armistice changed in favour of Iraq and its neighbours were not happy with that. With the Saddam Hussein government in power, the danger for the stability in the region was imminent. The Gulf War and the destabilization of Iraq caused security and economic problems for Turkey and resulted in a change of Turkey's former policy. Similar to the support for the end of the Iran-Iraq War, Turkey was in favour of a peace process for the solution of the Palestinian problem. However, Turkey's increasing relations with Israel after the peace process was a blow for its relations with the Arab countries of the region.

With the end of bipolar rivalry, US was the dominant power in the Middle East. At that point, the Gulf War gave the opportunity to Turkey to show its continuing importance to the West. In the 1990s, there was an extensive foreign policy agenda for the policy makers beyond the questions of membership in the EU; problems with Greece, the Cyprus issue, and foreign policy and international issues were all debated in the public opinion.[30]

In the post-Cold War period, Turkey's relations with the countries in the Balkans, the Middle East and the Caucasus developed. Turkey's policymakers, however, argued that the relations with these countries would not supersede Turkey's relations with the West. An important shift occurred in Turkish foreign policy towards the Middle East. During the Cold War years Turkey generally preferred non-intervention into the Middle Eastern affairs, but this policy changed dramatically when Turkey assumed an important role in the Gulf War. In this region, another important change in Turkish foreign policy was forging close ties with Israel.[31]

---

28  Yavuz, p. 579.
29  Davutoğlu, *Stratejik Derinlik,* p. 412.
30  Kut, p. 46.
31  Yasemin Çelik, *Contemporary Turkish Foreign Policy* (NY: Preager, 1999), p. 147.

Chapter 7

# Turkish Foreign Policy towards the Middle East since the Cold War Era

## TFP towards the Middle East in the 1990s

The 1990s witnessed important changes in Turkish foreign policy behaviour in the Middle East. With the dissolution of the Soviet Union, the main threat to Turkey's security ended. The Soviet threat was the main motive behind Turkey's attachment to the Western alliance. The global changes of the time affected Turkish foreign policy. Just before the end of the Cold War, Turkish foreign policy towards the Middle East was described by Robins as "routine and well understood. In substance it was materially oriented and politically non-interventionist. In style it was low key and predominantly incremental. In essence it was intrinsically uninterested in and comparatively aloof from the Middle East, while studiously concerned not to appear to be projecting power beyond its borders."[1]

The end of the Cold War changed the parameters of foreign policy making in every part of the world. However, the changes in Turkey were dramatic. It was no longer possible to act along the stable, bipolar structure within the international system, since the nature of the system became chaotic. The end of ideological rivalry between the two camps resulted in the resurgence of historical and cultural factors in foreign policy in every part of the world. For the Turkish case, this was especially true with the instabilities in its environment like the Middle East, the Balkans and the Caucasus. Although it was not easy to adapt to the new reality of the international relations for any country, the simultaneous problems in the nearby environment made this issue more difficult for Turkey. The developments in domestic politics also had serious consequences for the making of foreign policy in this period.

During the Cold War period, Turkey evaluated the issues in the Middle East like the oil crisis, the water problems and the Israeli-Palestinian problems within the general framework of Eastern and Western blocs. During the economic crisis times and fluctuations with the West, Turkey increased its interest in the region. And during the times of Soviet threat and good relations with the western camp, the Turkish policy towards the region was in line with that of the US and western bloc.[2]

At the end of the Cold War, it was no longer possible to pursue such a policy. With the end of the bi-polar Cold War, Turkey began to follow a more diversified foreign policy in its neighbouring regions. The Middle East was no exception in this development and Turkey's active involvement in Middle Eastern affairs was

---

1    Robins, "Avoiding the Question," p. 180.
2    Davutoğlu, *Stratejik Derinlik*, p. 337.

labelled by some commentators and scholars as "new-Ottomanism" and "new Turkish imperialism."³ The Gulf War was an important turning point in Turkish foreign policy. The Gulf War and its aftermath left great policy dilemmas for Turkey. Turkey's active non-involvement policy during the Iran-Iraq war had turned into an active involvement policy with the interventions in northern Iraq, problems with Syria and strategic cooperation with Israel.⁴

We can argue that Turkish foreign policy toward the Middle East in the 1990s was dominated by security concerns. In this decade several factors limited the foreign policy options of Turkey in this region: Threats against its security, US policy in the Middle East, Turkey's relations with Israel and the problems with other countries caused by the Turkey's relations with Israel, and general instability in the region. The 1990s witnessed an increase in the role of the army in the foreign policy decisions in Turkey. Security concerns and policies related to Turkey's main security problems legitimized the role of the army and limited the initiatives of the governments to diversify the options. The political instabilities of weak coalition governments and the successive economic crises also prevented a stable policy during the decade. This political instability, besides the increasing threat perceptions, legitimized the role of the military in the formation of foreign policy. Ironically, the only continuity in the Turkish foreign policy in this era was the shuffling of the foreign ministers.⁵ Security concerns mostly dominated Turkish policy until the capture of Öcalan in 1999. There was a power vacuum in northern Iraq because of Iran-Iraq War and Iraq's invasion of Kuwait and the subsequent Gulf War. As the control of central Iraqi forces in northern Iraq decreased, the PKK used this region for its terrorist operations against Turkey.

In this part, by giving a short summary of Turkey's relations with its two Middle Eastern neighbours after the end of Cold War, namely Syria and Iran, I will focus on Turkish foreign policy towards Iraq and Israeli-Palestinian Conflict in that era.

**Relations with Syria**

During the 1990s Turkey's relations with Syria mainly were dominated by security and water issues. In this decade Turkey's most problematic relations in the region were with Syria. The Turkish authorities believed that contrary to the agreements signed in 1987 between Özal and Asad, Syria was supporting PKK terrorists and had increased its support in the second half of the 1990s. Turkey hardened its policy toward Syria in these years for several reasons. These can be summarized as Syria's increasing support of the PKK, especially in Hatay; Syria's attempts at the internationalization of water problem; and an agreement with Greece to permit Greek

---

3   Efraim Inbar, "Regional Implications of the Israeli-Turkish Strategic Partnership," *Middle East Review of International Affairs* 5, no. 2 (June 2001), p. 6, available [online]: http://meria.idc.ac.il/journal/2001/issue2/jvol5no2in.html [16 June 2006].

4   Davutoğlu, *Stratejik Derinlik*, p. 397.

5   Ibid., p. 47.

*Turkish Foreign Policy towards the Middle East since the Cold War Era*     117

war planes to use Syrian airspace in case of a problem with Turkey.[6] When Turkey signed agreements with Israel in 1996 on military training and defence cooperation, Syria perceived a great challenge from these agreements and tried to counterbalance these agreements by mobilizing the Arab and the Muslim world against this alliance and by increasing military cooperation with Greece and Armenia.

In order to balance this threat and press Syria to accept Turkish demands, agreements that were signed with Israel were used as leverage. However, Israel remained silent in the autumn of 1998 when Turkey threatened Syria and did not want to be dragged into this conflict. Despite some joint initiatives between Turkey, Iran and Syria in 1993–1994 to combat groups that were hostile to their security, these attempts were fruitless. The attempts to improve economic relations between Turkey and Syria also failed since core issues like the waters of the Euphrates and the PKK were not solved. Syria was not satisfied with the Economic Cooperation Protocol of July, 17, 1987, which committed Turkey to release at least 500 cubic meters of water per second to Syria.[7] Syria used the terrorist threat against Turkey in the issue of the water conflict and also in relation to the issue of Hatay. It also tried to get a favourable agreement with Turkey by using this threat in the distribution of the waters of the Euphrates. This condition continued until Turkey's demand from Syria to expel Öcalan and the end to the support of the PKK in autumn 1998. When Turkey threatened Syria with military action, Egypt and Iran started intense diplomatic activity in order to eliminate the possibility of direct armed clash. These initiatives also were supported by the US. Öcalan left Syria and the PKK camps in this country were closed. The two countries signed an agreement concerning security issues and Turkey came out of this crisis with its main objectives realized and without having had to make good its military threats.[8] With this agreement, the Syrian side for the first time acknowledged that the PKK is a terrorist organization and also agreed to do the following: Expel PKK leader from Syria, arrest PKK militants active in Syria and uproot the PKK camps there, cease providing support to PKK and forbid it to use Syrian soil against Turkey and extend cooperation with Turkey against PKK well into the future.[9] Turkish authorities were cautious in the implementation of this agreement.

Beside this political development, the economic relation between these two countries started to develop after this agreement. Syrian President Hafez Asad died in June 2000 and was replaced by his son, Beshar Asad. As a sign of improvement of relations between the two countries, the new Turkish President, Ahmet Necdet Sezer, went to Syria to attend the funeral of Hafez Asad. This was his first visit to a foreign country and Sezer was warmly welcomed by Beshar Asad.[10] The fruitful results of the improved relations between Turkey and Syria became obvious during the late Iraqi Crisis in 2003 and after the terrorist attacks in Istanbul in November 2003. The

---

6    Meliha B. Altunışık, "Güvenlik Kıskacında Türkiye-Ortadoğu İlişkileri," in *En Uzun Onyıl,* edited by Gencer Özcan and Şule Kut (İstanbul: Boyut, 1998), p. 338.

7    Mahmut Bali Aykan, "The Turkish-Syrian Crisis of October 1998: A Turkish View," *Middle East Policy* 6, no. 4, (June 1999), p. 175.

8    Hale, p. 305.

9    Aykan, "The Turkish-Syrian Crisis of October 1998: A Turkish View," p. 174.

10   Fırat and Kürkçüoğlu, p. 567.

problematic relations between Syria and the US led this country to improve relations with Turkey. Beshar Asad visited Turkey and this was the first visit of a Syrian president to Turkey. Not only did the contacts between the officials of the two countries increase, but the contacts among the people of these two neighbours developed and the trade levels increased. Turkey's exports to this country nearly tripled within a period of five years until 2005 from 184 million US dollars to 547 million US dollars.[11] The period after 1999 represented a new era in relations between Turkey and Syria and the relations between two countries developed in several ways to an unprecedented level in comparison with the years since the independence of Syria.

**Relations with Iran**

Turkey's relations with Iran in this decade were affected by issues related to ideological differences and Iran's support of the PKK. Iran started to follow a pragmatic foreign policy after the death of Khomeini. But there were also groups in Iran who favoured a more assertive foreign policy similar to the time of Khomeini. Turkey believed that moderates in Iran should be supported and tuned its policy against Iran not to alienate moderates. Problems emerged, however, between these two countries when Iran was accused of supporting some political suicides in Turkey in the early 1990s.[12] There was a short break in the relations between two countries after these allegations. When the new government under the premiership of Mesut Yılmaz came to power in 1997, however, the relations resumed.

Another problem between the two countries was related with the PKK issue. Although there were periodic security agreements, the Turkish side was suspicious about the application of these agreements. Similar to Syria and Turkey, Iran also was worried about the developments in northern Iraq. In this respect, these three countries tried to coordinate their efforts to eliminate the possibility of a Kurdish state there. Although Turkey's priorities in northern Iraq coincided with the Iran's, there was a rivalry between them in regard to Central Asia. In the first years of 1990s, there was an expectation that in the former Soviet territories of Central Asia, there would be a fierce competition between Turkey and Iran to export their styles of government to the newly independent states. Turkey was accepted as the western style and strongly supported by the US. The newly independent states of the Central Asia, however, continued their relations with Russia and followed a balanced approach in their foreign policies. They established good economic and political relations with Turkey and Iran. Also both Turkey and Iran had an interest in preventing the Central Asian states from reverting to the status of satellites of Russia.[13] In this respect, the long waited rivalry and conflict between Turkey and Iran in Central Asia did not materialize.

In terms of economic relations, the recent years have witnessed an increase in the amount of trade between the two countries. A natural gas pipeline agreement was signed in August 1996. The construction of this pipeline has materialized and

---

11  http://www.deik.org.tr/ikili/2006317113635suriye-ikili-Mart2006.pdf  [4  October 2006].

12  Fırat and Kürkçüoğlu, p. 580.

13  Hale, p. 313.

is providing Turkey with three billion cubic meters of natural gas annually. The amount of trade between the two countries has increased since the construction of this pipeline and so has the decline of the threat of the PKK. The volume of trade between Turkey and Iran has more than tripled since 2000 from 1,051 million US dollars to 4,368 million US dollars.[14]

The invasion of Iraq and the issues related with Iran's nuclear problems have been two important factors in the relations between Turkey and Iran in the last couple of years. Although Turkey is not happy with Iran's desire to have a nuclear program and a possible nuclear arsenal, it has followed a cautious policy and refrained from direct confrontation with Iran. Turkey also has played a facilitator role in the diplomatic efforts between Iran and the European countries to reach peaceful solution to the problems related to Iran's nuclear program. Besides the common interests towards a possible Kurdish state in northern Iraq, Iran has tried not to alienate Turkey on the nuclear issue. Iran has cooperated with Turkey in the struggle against the PKK for these two reasons.

## Relations with Israel and Palestine

Turkey was the first Muslim country to recognize Israel and have economic and cultural relations with this country. However, Turkey has always tried to follow a cautious policy and balanced its relations with Israel in order to eliminate the criticisms of Muslim and Arab countries. Beside this, Israel's occupation of Palestine has met with strong criticisms from Turkish public opinion. Israel tried to boost relations during the 1950s and 1960s as a part of the periphery strategy.[15] The relations between the two countries began to sour after the Sinai War of 1956. Turkey opted to develop her relations with the Arab world and this resulted in the decrease of the level of relations between Turkey and Israel. The early signs of the development of the relations came during the mid 1980s and the real changes occurred in this respect in the post-Cold War period.

### The Gulf War and the Peace Process

As said before, the end of the Cold War, the Gulf War and the peace process have affected Turkey's foreign policy towards the Middle East. In this atmosphere, Turkey's involvement in regional affairs increased. Relations between Turkey and Israel developed during the 1990s. Turkey was not happy with the invasion of Kuwait by Iraq. Although it did not deploy military force for the evacuation of Iraqi forces from Kuwait, Turkey was a member of the coalition. The Gulf War and the aftermath dramatically affected the Palestinian-Israeli conflict and Turkey's policy towards this issue. During the Gulf War, the PLO was in support of Iraq and its credibility shrank in the eyes of public opinion in several countries. Beside this, some

---

14  http://www.deik.org.tr/ikili/200623174833Iran-ikili-ocak2006.pdf [4 October 2006].

15  Alan Makovsky, "Israeli-Turkish Relations A Turkish 'Periphery Strategy'?" in *Reluctant Neighbor*, edited by Henri J. Barkey (Washington DC: US Institute of Peace Press, 1996), p. 150.

declarations of Arafat who was establishing similarities between Iraq's invasion of Kuwait and Turkey's intervention in Cyprus, negatively affected Turkey's relations with the PLO.[16]

Adaptation to the new world order after the end of the Cold War also played its part in forging closer ties between Turkey and Israel. The US was the only superpower in the world and both of the countries tried adapt themselves to its policies in the region. From the point of Turkey, the removal of the Soviet Union as an important player from Middle Eastern politics mean that Turkey's closer relations with Israel despite the criticisms of the Arab countries would not cause tensions with Moscow.[17]

The aim to eliminate the threat of the PKK was one of the motives of Turkey's increasing relations with Israel in the 1990s. Turkish army's huge modernization programs and the search for a new partnership in the region after the Gulf War also played their part. The positive atmosphere in the Middle East created by the Oslo Process coincided with PKK terror and this coincidence helped the justification of rapprochement between Turkey and Israel.[18]

The reasons for the increasing relations between Turkey and Israel are explained by some scholars as follows: The first is that the positive atmosphere created by the peace process gave the opportunity to Turkey to increase its relations with both of the sides in order to have strong friendships in the Middle East. Second, Turkey needed the support of the Jewish lobby in its relations with the United States and the European Union in order to balance the effects of the Armenian and Greek lobbies. Third, Turkey's neighbours, Iraq, Iran and Syria were supporting the PKK and Turkey was in search of friendship in the region. Turkey and Israel did not have direct problems, so they increased the level of their relations. Fourth, the demands by some parts of the public opinion in Turkey for the establishment of better economic and political relations with Arab countries were rejected by some others and they favoured the development of relations with Israel. Fifth, the US was in need of strong friends in the Middle East in its so called "new world order" and in this respect the US supported Turkey and Israel to increase the level of their relations.[19] US participation in military exercises with Turkey and Israel in the Mediterranean as in the case of the Reliant Mermaid in January 1998 is an example of this support.

Some scholars argue that the most significant gain from this cooperation for Turkey was cementing its relations with the US and securing the pro-Israel lobby in Washington.[20] Some others argued that Turkish security planners realized with the Gulf War that the Europeans saw NATO strictly as an organization for conflicts of within Europe and had no intention of sending soldiers to fend off a non-European attack on a peripheral state like Turkey.[21] Consequently, Turkish policymakers

---

16  Aras, "The Place of the Palestinian-Israeli Peace Process," p. 146.

17  Hale, p. 296.

18  Ofra Bengio and Gencer Özcan, "Changing Relations: Turkish-Israeli-Arab Triangle," *Perceptions* 5, no. 1 (March–May 2000), p. 4.

19  Çağrı Erhan-Ömer Kürkçüoğlu, "1990–2001 İsrail'le İlişkiler," in *Türk Dış Politikası, Kurtuluş Savaşı'ndan Bugüne Olgular, Belgeler, Yorumlar* edited by Baskın Oran, vol. 2 (İstanbul: İletişim,2001), pp. 568–9.

20  Hale, p. 300.

21  Makovsky, p. 153.

perceived Israel as an ally in the solution of the Middle Eastern problems. The basic advantages that can be derived from this rapprochement for Israel are creating a Turkish market for Israel's military industry, creating deterrence against Syria and breaking Israel's regional isolation.[22]

The Arab-Israeli peace process that began in Madrid on 30 October 1991 provided a space to manoeuvre for Turkey in its relations both with the Palestinians and Israel. This process enabled Turkey to increase its relations with Israel and the traditional policy of balance started to change in favour of Israel. Within the positive atmosphere of this period, Turkey decided to normalize relations with Israel and increase it to ambassadorial level and also re-open its Consulates General in East Jerusalem. According to this, Turkey simultaneously increased its relations with Israel and Palestine to the ambassadorial level on 19 December 1991. The Consulate General in East Jerusalem is linked directly to the Ministry, not to the Embassy in Israel, in order to make it clear to Israel and to the Arab world that Turkey accepts Jerusalem as a corpus seperatum.[23]

The change to have increasing relations with Israel did not happen rapidly and the Turkish authorities continued to follow a cautious stance in explaining the relations with Israel. For example, the Office of General Secretariat of General Staff replied to a question in 1992 about the level of relations between Turkey and Israel as "Muslim and secular Turkey pays greater attention to establish a balance in its relations with Israel and the Arab world under the light of the realities of the Middle East."[24]

The relations between Turkey and Israel in the 1990s started to develop first in areas like tourism, culture and education. Several agreements were signed between two countries during the visits of the Minister of Culture Abdülkadir Ateş and Minister of Foreign Affairs Hikmet Çetin to Israel in 1992 and 1993.[25] Later on, several high level visits reinforced the relations. In this respect, Israeli President Ezer Weizman visited Turkey in January 1994. This was Weizman's first visit to a foreign country and also the first official contact between two countries at the level of heads of states.[26]

The reciprocal visits between Turkey and Israel until 1996 reinforced the relations between these countries. Turkey also paid great attention to the Palestinians during this period and Turkish officials visited both Israel and Palestine when they are in the region. Turkey was one of the first states to recognize the state of Palestine following its declaration by the Palestinian National Council in November 1988. Turkish Prime Minister Tansu Çiller visited President Arafat in Gaza in November 1994 during her visit to Israel and she was the first head of government to do so.[27] Yaser Arafat also visited Turkey several times in this period and the agreement on

---

22  Anat Lewin, "Turkey and Israel: Reciprocal and Mutual Imagery in the Media, 1994–1999," *Journal of International Affairs* 54, no. 1(Fall 2000), p. 244.

23  Altunışık, "Güvenlik Kıskacında Türkiye-Ortadoğu İlişkileri," p. 192.

24  Ibid., p. 193.

25  Gencer Özcan, "Türkiye-İsrail İlişkileri 50. Yılına Girerken," in *Türk Dış Politikasının Analizi*, edited by Faruk Sönmezoğlu (İstanbul: Der Yayınları, 1998), p. 168.

26  Altunışık, "Güvenlik Kıskacında Türkiye-Ortadoğu İlişkileri," p. 192.

27  Makovsky, p. 160.

the Cooperation in Education and Cultural Affairs on 25 September 1993 was the first official document signed between Turkey and Palestine.[28] As can be seen from several examples, the general public opinion in Turkey was supportive of formation of Palestinian state. A significant portion of the public opinion in the country did not want Turkey to endanger the country's interest in the Palestinian issue in order to pursue ties with Israel.[29] None of the major political parties could ignore this reality and governments tried to balance their policies towards these two sides. The feelings of the public opinion and their reflections in the political parties had their impacts on Turkish diplomacy and the psychological hold of the Arab world on Turkish diplomacy towards Israel was not shattered until 1993.[30]

*Strategic Cooperation with Israel*

Agreements signed between Turkey and Israel in the first half of 1996 signified a turning point in these relations. On 23 February 1996 the Military Training and Cooperation Agreement, on 14 March 1996 the Free Trade Agreement and 28 August 1996 the Defence Industry Cooperation Agreements were signed between Turkey and Israel. These agreements showed in what areas the relations between these two countries would concentrate.[31] The military training and defence cooperation agreements provided mutual military visits, joint military exercises, and the acquisition of military know-how, cooperation in surface to air missiles and the exchange of intelligence. These agreements and increasing cooperation between Turkey and Israel caused a major uproar in the Arab public opinion and drew strong criticisms from governments, especially from Syria, Egypt and Iran. Especially Syria perceived a major strategic threat from this cooperation and the tension between these two countries led to troop build-ups along the frontier during the June 1996.[32]

This increasing cooperation between Turkey and Israel negatively affected Turkey's relations with its other neighbours. In 1996, President Süleyman Demirel left the OIC meeting in Tehran early because of the criticisms and the Arab League demanded Turkey to re-consider these agreements with Israel. Abdulhalim Haddam, Deputy President of Syria at the time, described this cooperation between Turkey and Israel as the biggest threat to the Arabs since 1948.[33] Arab regimes implied that as a Muslim country Turkey's strategic cooperation with Israel shows that the problems in the region were not problems of Muslims, but the problems of Arabs. Arab political elites tried to use Turkey's cooperation with Israel as a pretext for their Arab nationalist propaganda and to benefit from this situation to strengthen their

---

28  Işıl Anıl, "Soğuk Savaş Sonrasında Türkiye ve Arap-İsrail Barış Süreci," in *Türkiye ve Ortadoğu Tarih, Kimlik Güvenlik*, edited by Meliha Benli Altunışık (İstanbul: Boyut, 1999), p. 138.

29  Makovsky, p. 159.

30  Robins, *Suits and Uniforms*, p. 249.

31  Özcan, pp. 169–171.

32  28 Kemal Kirişçi, "Post Cold War Turkish Security and the Middle East," *Middle East Review of International Relations* 1, no. 2 (July 1997), p. 2, available [online]: http://meria. idc.ac.il/journal/1997/issue2/jv1n2a6.html [17 June 2006].

33  Inbar, p. 6.

shaky legitimacy.[34] In order to eliminate criticisms, Turkey several times declared that its cooperation with Israel was not against any third party.

Turkey continued its good relations with Israel despite the fluctuations in the Palestinian-Israeli Peace Process. The assassination of Rabin and the election of Netanyahu as the Prime Minister resulted in setbacks in the peace process. Despite several criticisms, Turkey continued to develop relations with Israel in this period. Some countries in the region argued that Turkey's cooperation with Israel encouraged Netanyahu in his acts that damaged the peace process and his uncompromising policy against Syria.[35] The US viewed this cooperation as the first example of the regional coalition of pro-American Middle Eastern states. Turkey was unenthusiastic about it and opposed some of the initiatives of Netanyahu. Netanyahu came to power in April 1996 in Israel and pressed for the conclusion of an outright military pact with Turkey as the main axis of a regional security framework. Turkey rejected this in the absence of a settlement of Arab-Israeli conflict.[36] This development shows the limits of this cooperation. Although Turkey continued its relations with Israel despite the fluctuations in the peace process, it refrained from a military pact, which was unnecessary from its point of view. At the end, this was cooperation, not an alliance, since there was no commitment by either side to wage a joint war on any third parties as seen during the tensions between Turkey and Syria prior to the expulsion of Öcalan from Damascus.

The reasons for change in Turkey's cooperation with Israel and the end of the balanced policy in Palestinian issue were several. Different from the economically driven policy towards the Middle East in the 1980s, Turkey's policy towards the region in the 1990s was determined by security concerns. Because of Syria's sheltering of the PKK and the power vacuum in northern Iraq after the Gulf War, there was a great danger against the territorial integrity of Turkey. Consequently, Turkey's primary aim in formulating its Middle East policy was the elimination of threat of terror.

The pioneering role of the military in the development of the relations with Israel was related with this reality. The military training agreement signed between Turkey and Israel in February 1996 remained confidential for some months. The civilian authorities also had limited information about the elements of this agreement. The Turkish side revealed the existence of the agreement in April 1996 and there it became evident that the Ministry of Foreign Affairs and the Minister of Defence were in the dark about some elements of the agreement.[37] It is argued by Robins that the reason of the leaking of the agreement to the public was to make a strong political statement. The statement had two components, one for the domestic audience and the other for the southern neighbour. Domestically, "the Turkish military was making it clear to all political parties, especially to Refah Partisi (Welfare Party), that they were sufficiently powerful to control the strategic direction of Turkish foreign policy, regardless of who formed the government or occupied the premiership. To

---

34  Davutoğlu, *Stratejik Derinlik*, p. 367.
35  Altunışık, "Güvenlik Kıskacında Türkiye-Ortadoğu İlişkileri," p. 199.
36  Hale, p. 299.
37  Robins, *Suits and Uniforms*, p. 260.

Syria the leak contained a warning to desist from its unacceptable international behaviour of supporting terrorism on pain of facing an alliance of superior military might operating on two fronts."[38] This development represented an example of the increasing role of the military in the Turkish foreign policy and the legitimization of this role by the security threat.

Turkey wanted to benefit from Israel's intelligence and technical capacities in fighting the PKK. Beside this, Turkey faced accusations of human rights abuses and had problems getting military technology from Europe because of these criticisms. Turkey wanted to get military technology from Israel without facing these criticisms. On the other side, this cooperation was also beneficial for Israel since it was trying to integrate itself into the region in the post-Cold War era.[39]

The cooperation between Turkey and Israel at that time was not a result of full approval of each other's policies, but because of the belief that cooperation was to the benefit of both sides. These benefits were related mostly to the issues of security. Israel had no problems with the Kurds and perceived them as a non-Arab ally in the region. Israel assisted the Kurds of Iraq during the 1960s and 1970s in their struggle against the central administration. Israel refused to condemn the PKK as a terrorist organization and refused to be drawn into the issue of the creation of a Kurdish state.[40] Although the policies of Syria and the Kurds of these two countries differed greatly, there was a bargain here. Accordingly, after the visit of the Turkish Defence Minister Turhan Tayan to the occupied Golan Heights in May 1997, Netanyahu for the first time criticized the PKK and the support of Syria for the PKK.[41] But when Turkey threatened Syria to expel Öcalan and had tense relations with Greece and Greek Cypriots about S-300 missiles, Israel distanced itself from Turkey and showed that its strategic relations with Turkey should not be dragged it into this conflict.[42]

In those years, the relations between Turkey and Israel continued independent of the developments in the Peace Process. During 1997, the Turkish Head of Staff İsmail Hakkı Karadayı and Defence Minister Turhan Tayan visited Israel separately and had high level contacts. Reciprocally Israel's Minister of Foreign Affairs David Levy and Defence Minister Izak Mordechai visited Turkey in that year. It is argued by some scholars that the coincidence of Mordechai's visit with the OIC meeting in Tehran is difficult to explain.[43] Despite these high level contacts independent of the negative developments in the peace process, Turkey did not completely ignore the Palestinian side. Turkey continued its support of Palestine on issues like Jerusalem, the Jewish settlers, and the protection of sacred places like the al Aqsa Mosque. For example, Turkey supported the Palestinian proposal in the General Assembly of the UN to stop new Israeli settlements in Jerusalem.[44]

---

38  Ibid.
39  Ahmet Davutoğlu, "Yahudi Meselesinin Dönüşümü ve İsrail'in Yeni Stratejisi," *Avrasya Dosyası* 1, no. 3 (Autumn 1994), p. 94.
40  Robins, *Suits and Uniforms*, p. 257.
41  Altunışık, "Güvenlik Kıskacında Türkiye-Ortadoğu İlişkileri," p. 199.
42  Lewin, p. 244.
43  Özcan, p. 174.
44  Anıl, p. 139.

By having relations both with Israel and the Palestinian Authority, Turkey is in a position to help in overcoming some of the problems between these two sides. The criticisms of the Palestinian Authority for Turkey's close relations with Israel were softer than those of some other countries in the region. The reason for this was Turkey's support for Palestinians on several platforms and the Palestinians' belief that they could affect Israel via Turkey. In this respect, the Palestinians demanded that Turkey be active in the efforts for the settlement of the problem and give priority to the peace process on the agenda of Turkish foreign policy.[45]

*The Decline of the Security Threat and the EU Candidature*

Turkey benefited from these relations with Israel in terms of military technology and creating a threat against Syria. In the case of the expulsion of Öcalan from Syria, although Israel declared that it would not support Turkey on this issue, Syria was under pressure from two sides and could not resist Turkey's threats. In the autumn of 1998, under the pressure of Turkey, Öcalan left Syria. After this and the signature of the Adana Protocol on 19–20 October 1998, Turkey's threat perceptions started to decline. Turkey began to show signals of a return to the former balanced foreign policy. In considering the negative memories of the 1950s and of the Baghdad Pact, Turkey tried to improve its relations with the Arab countries and created a dialog with Syria and established the "Bilateral Consultation Mechanism" with Egypt.[46] In this respect, Turkey's relations with Israel and the Arab countries were balanced. From the point of Israel, Turkey's policies during the S-300 crisis, Turkey's use of military pressure on Syria over Öcalan, and the attacks on Israel's missions in Europe after the capture of Öcalan in Kenya show the side effects of the relations with Turkey.[47]

Beside these factors, with the new government of Ehud Barak in Israel in July 1999 the peace process was revitalized. This new environment created room to manoeuvre for Turkey and with the continuous support of Turkey for the Palestinians, it become an important country in the peace process in the eyes of both sides. However, we should be aware that the role expected for Turkey by Israel and Palestine is different. Although the Palestinian side accepts Turkey's mediator role, the Israeli side expects Turkey to be a facilitator in the process. Israel wants to Turkey to help it in ameliorating its problematic relations with some states in the region and the Islamic world by using Turkey's experience and impact. But this is not a role of mediation. Israel is happy with the mediator role of the US and does not want any other state to pursue such a goal. The reasons for this are obvious. Israel is one of the strategic allies of the world's only superpower and is influential in US foreign policy decision making with the help of the Jewish lobbies there. Beside this, Turkey's economic, political and military power is limited to play such a role.

The government changes in Turkey and Israel in 1999 caused some minor changes in the general level of relations. In that year, President Demirel visited both

---

45  Ibid.
46  Özcan, p. 176.
47  Robins, *Suits and Uniforms*, p. 268.

Israel and Palestine and the new Ecevit government maintained the level of relations. However, because of the positive attitude of Ecevit towards the Palestinians in their struggle, there were some changes in the expectations of Israel and Turkey in their relations. Referring to the positive attitude of Ecevit towards the Palestinians, Israeli Public Security Minister Shlomo Ben Ami argued that Ecevit's approach towards Turkey' relations with Israel would change the context of these relations. Ben Ami argued that his country "will improve relations with Turkey not with the perspective of Peace Process, but in a larger vision of regional security."[48] This meant that Israel wanted to develop its relations with Turkey independent from the peace process. However, having recognized the alienation in the region when problems arose in the peace process, Turkey paid attention to the developments in the peace process in formulating its relations with Israel and Palestine.

Turkey welcomed the initiative of US President Bill Clinton in July 2000 at Camp David for the settlement of the Israeli-Palestinian problem. The success or failure of this initiative would affect Turkey's policies with these two sides. The developments after the failure of the talks were very negative for the peace in the region and Turkey continued its contacts with both parties in this atmosphere. The death of the peace process and the emergence of the second İntifada made Turkey's relations with Israel uneasy when Palestinians were suffering because of the policies of Israel.

*The Second Intifada*

One of the turning points in the Palestinian Question was 28 September 2000. On that day, Ariel Sharon visited Harem el Sherif along with 1,000 police and this visit caused protests among the Palestinians there. Sharon was trying to make a gesture to the Israeli right wing voters in the coming elections. This visit and the death of some protestors as a result of the attitude of the Israeli police resulted in the emergence of the Second Intifada.

The developments during the Second Intifada and after the election victory of Ariel Sharon will shed light on Turkey's position on the peace process. Israel's new Prime Minister Sharon was arguing that the resumption of the talks for a settlement would begin when the violence stopped. The Palestinian side was demanding that Turkey use its political and geographic influence to stop Israel's killing of Palestinians. Turkey's impact on both sides and its interest in the peace process became obvious when the UN formed a commission, known as the Mitchell Commission, to inspect the situation in the region in spring 2001. Among the five members of the commission, the only commissioner from a Muslim country was Süleyman Demirel, former president of Turkey.

When the Intifada continued and Sharon was in power, Turkey's relations with Israel and Palestine were affected by these two realities. Turkey could not play its role as it wished in the settlement of the problem because of Israel's insistence of the end of the violence before the start of the negotiations. In this period, Turkey's relations with Israel continued especially on military and strategic issues. The relations between

---

48  *Milliyet*, 3 March, 2000.

the two countries continued mostly independent of the developments in the peace process. However, the sensitivity of the public opinion towards the developments in Palestine was rising and the government took this into consideration. This fact became obvious when Sharon visited Turkey on 8 August 2001. The atmosphere between the Prime Ministers during this visit was not warm and there were protests in the streets against the visit. Israeli media interpreted Ecevit's attitude as an effort to overcome the domestic and foreign criticisms and to show that Turkey did not accepts whatever Israel did.[49]

When Sharon besieged Arafat in Ramallah, Arafat sent letters to French President Chirac, Turkish President Sezer and Prime Minister Ecevit to help in lifting the siege.[50] Here the role attached to Turkey by Arafat is important. France is generally pro-Palestinian in this conflict as a member of the UN Security Council and at that time French Foreign Minister Vedrine criticized the US for its support for Israel. The call for Turkey was the result of its relations with both of the parties as a regional country.

The impact of public opinion in Turkey's policy on this issue became obvious once again in the spring of 2002. Israel occupied some of the Palestinian cities with the argument of security threats. There were strong reactions to this development in Turkish public opinion. After strong reactions, Israel declared that it had decided not to participate a joint military manoeuvre of Turkey, the US and Israel in Turkey.[51] These developments showed that despite the real politic reasons of the Turkish governments continuing relations with Israel, public opinion was very much sensitive to the events in Palestine and any democratic government would take this sensitivity into consideration.

This sensitivity also was reflected in the attitude of the government. The criticisms of Prime Minister Ecevit towards Israel's policies in Palestine became harsh by the time. Ecevit argued that Israel had committed "genocide in front of the eyes of whole world." He said that the intention of Sharon was not good from the beginning and that the Israeli government was not complying with the UN resolutions and was committing genocide.[52] Ecevit's words were criticized by the Israeli government and by the members of the Jewish lobby in the US and they called attention to their support for Turkey against Armenian allegations. After these criticisms Ecevit said that his words were has been misunderstood.[53]

Turkey played a facilitator role in the Palestinian-Israeli conflict. The official position of the country was declared as such that Turkey continued its relations with both sides of the conflict even during the times of crises and continued its efforts for the settlement of the conflict by facilitating the contacts between the two sides.[54] In this respect, the Turkish Minister of Foreign Affairs, İsmail Cem, went to the region with the Greek Minister of Foreign Affairs, Yorgo Papandreu, on 25 April 2002 and

---

49 *Israelinsider*, 9 August 2001.

50 www.ntvmsnbc.com/news/132523.asp. [28 January 2002].

51 www.radikal.com.tr/haber/php?haberno=33756. [2 April 2002].

52 *Radikal*, 3 April 2002.

53 www.radikal.com.tr/veriler/2002/04/12/haber/_34613.php. [12 April 2002].

54 Declaration of Ministry of Foreign Affairs, www.mfa.gov.tr/cempalestine.htm. [26 April 2002].

visited both the Israeli Prime Minister Sharon and Minister of Foreign Affairs Peres and also Arafat, who was under siege. Cem argued that Turkey had responsibilities for the people of the region and declared Turkey's proposal for the settlement of the problem as "simultaneous withdrawal of from the occupied territories according to the resolutions of the UN Security Council and prevention of terrorist actions, end of siege of Arafat."[55] Turkey's joint initiative with Greece aimed to show that the two old foes could come together and become friends and also try to help to the solution of another problem in the region. Turkey signalled what kind of a role it would play in the region as a candidate country of the EU. Turkey could contribute to the peace in the region as a non-Arab Muslim country, a member of the NATO and a candidate to the EU. In this respect, the common forum of the OIC-EU, which was held in Istanbul in February 2002, represented an example of Turkey's constructive role. These two initiatives of Turkey, a joint mission with Greece and the OIC-EU forum, are given by scholars as examples of the Europeanization of Turkish foreign policy and a "Europeanized strategy" towards the Middle East.[56]

In the first half of 2003, Turkey welcomed the initiative of the Quartet for a settlement to the problem, since Turkey's contribution to the problem might be easier if a stable environment was secured in the area. Despite the hopes in the beginning, the situation got worse again with time and Turkey was upset by these developments. Foreign Minister Gül declared that developments in the region negatively affected Turkey's efforts for the improvement of the economic conditions of the Palestinians.[57] At the end of the year, on 24 December 2003, Turkey declared an action plan in order to help the implementation of the Road Map and to contribute to the peace process. Turkey's initiative aimed to provide some basic necessities of the Palestinians and also to contribute to the normalization of social life in the occupied territories. In order to make this aid effective, the government's initiative included NGOs and the private sector beside the state's support and the appointment of a special coordinator, former minister Vehbi Dinçerler, for the implementation of the initiative.[58] In this respect, in August 2004, Turkey sent urgent food and medicine equalling 1 million US dollars to Palestine as a part of this plan.[59] After the setbacks in the implementation of the Road Map, Israeli Prime Minister Sharon declared his own "Disengagement Plan" on 18 December 2003 which aimed to withdraw from some of the occupied territories and locate Israeli forces in more secure positions. Most of the countries and also several groups in Israel and all of the Palestinians opposed this plan and argued that such an initiative would not contribute to the peace process.[60]

---

55  www.ntvmsnbc.com/news/148415.asp. [25 April 2002].

56  Lecha, p. 53.

57  *Dışişleri Güncesi,* September 2003, p. 50, available [online]: http://www.mfa.gov.tr/ NR/rdonlyres/0CA1BE2A-8A8B-4D66-8E61-6255F637EDA4/0/Eylul2003.pdf [9 July 2006].

58  *Dışişleri Güncesi,* December 2003, p. 127, available [online]: http://www.mfa.gov.tr/ NR/rdonlyres/A245DF54-7640-4CB6-8CE5-62835C78204F/0/Aralık2003.pdf [9 July 2006].

59  *Dışişleri Güncesi,* August 2004, pp. 7–8, available [online]: http://www.mfa.gov.tr/NR/ rdonlyres/82A29624-469C-4B08-B2E3-EB46483E6351/0/AGUSTOS2004.pdf [10 July 2006].

60  *Dışişleri Güncesi,* December 2003, pp. 178–179, available [online]: http://www.mfa.gov. tr/NR/rdonlyres/A245DF54-7640-4CB6-8CE5-62835C78204F/0/Aralık2003.pdf [9 July 2006].

Turkey and the European Union have adopted a common attitude towards the US reform process in the region. The essence of their argument is that reform and change can not happen until a solution to the Israeli-Palestinian conflict is found.[61] Both Turkey and the EU are critical of the targeted killing policies of Israel in the occupied territories. Turkey and the EU reacted to the assassination of the Hamas leader Sheikh Yassin, and Turkish Prime Minister Erdoğan postponed his visit to Israel.[62] Turkish criticisms of Israel continued when Israel attacked the refugee camps in Rafah on the pretext of rooting out a tunnel used for the smuggling of weapons from Egypt. Israel demolished several houses and killed civilians during this operation and then attacked people protesting the action. Turkey strongly criticized the policies of Israel and Erdoğan said that these policies were reaching the level of state terror.[63] US President Bush declared his concerns, but argued that Israel had the right to defend itself.[64]

In addition the policies of the Israeli government against the Palestinians, developments in northern Iraq and the arguments for the activities of Israel in that region also were a point of difference between Turkey and Israel at that time. When the Turkish authorities' criticisms against the activities in Palestine combined with the criticisms against the activities of Israel in northern Iraq, Israeli Foreign Minister Shalom said, "I am not sure, how long we will keep our silence against the open criticisms of Turkey."[65]

These reciprocal declarations signify that the perceptions of Turkey and Israel against each other are very different from their perceptions during the late 1990s. Turkey no longer followed a policy of close cooperation with Israel without paying attention to the developments in the Palestinian-Israeli problem. The decline of the security threat against Turkey, the decline of the army in the decision making process, the changes of governments in both Israel and Turkey, the rise of the public opinion and the sensitivities of the public opinion towards the sufferings of the Palestinians all played parts in this change. However, despite these reciprocal criticisms, both parties refrained from breaking relations completely. Although Turkish Prime Minister Erdoğan cancelled his visit to Israel and criticized its policies against the Palestinians harshly, in order to keep the channels open, the deputy head and some MPs of the AKP went to Israel for damage control.[66]

The death of Yaser Arafat on 11 November 2004 was a turning point in the history of the Palestine. Arafat had been the leader of the PLO for nearly 40 years and his name was identified with the Palestinian struggle. Both Erdoğan and Gül attended his funeral. After the elections in January 2005, in which 15 Turkish academics and civil servants worked monitoring of elections, Mahmoud Abbas became the head of

61 Soner Çağaptay, "Where Goes the US-Turkish Relationship?" *Middle East Quarterly* 11, no. 4 (Fall 2004), p. 48.

62 *Hürriyet*, 25 March 2004.

63 *Hürriyet*, 20 May 2004.

64 *Yeni Şafak*, 20 May 2004.

65 *Dışişleri Güncesi*, June 2004, p. 70, available [online]: http://www.mfa.gov.tr/NR/rdonlyres/82D08FA5-E3E2-4566-A147-A2EDCB8CFB3C/0/Haziran2004.pdf [10 July 2006].

66 http://www.zaman.com.tr/?trh=20040902 [10 July 2006].

the Palestinian State and Turkey praised the democratic choices of the Palestinian people. On 4–5 January 2005, Gül visited Israel and Palestine. The timing of this visit is important. Israel was pursuing a policy to isolate Arafat by declaring him an unreliable partner for negotiations and alienating him from the international community by not allowing statesmen visiting Israel to visit Arafat. Such an action was very much contrary to Turkey's policy of simultaneous contacts with both of the parties and equal distance. Because of this policy, Turkish side had refrained from high level visits to Israel in order to keep the balance. When Arafat left the political scene as a result of natural reasons, this policy came to an end since Mahmoud Abbas was an acceptable figure for Israel. After the change in the stance of Israel on this issue, Gül visited both to Israel and Palestine. After Gül, Erdoğan visited Israel and Palestine on 1–2 May 2005 and opened an office of *Türk İşbirliği ve Kalkınma Ajansı* (the Turkish Cooperation and Development Agency, TİKA) in Ramallah.[67] This office of TİKA played a role afterwards in the distribution of the aid provided by Turkey. In relation with the action plan declared at the end of 2003, the Turkish Union of Chambers (TOBB) met with Israeli and Palestinian counterparts in East Jerusalem to discuss the joint use and development of the Erez Industrial Zone and to provide education for Palestinians.[68] In this way, Turkey wanted to include the contribution of NGOs and the business community as track two actors in its policy towards the region.

## Relations with Iraq

Historically Turkey's relations with Iraq have been peaceful. Turkey was on good terms with the monarchy in Baghdad until 1958 when it was overthrown by a coup and declared the republic. During the republican period, political instability in Iraqi politics was persistent. Successive coups and rivalries dominated the politics until 1968 when the Baath Party controlled the state. Although the Baath regime was assertive in its foreign policy and this caused problem with the country's neighbours, the relations between Turkey and Iraq were cooperative during this period. Both of the countries were against Kurdish aspirations of autonomy or independence. Also in the 1980s, the economic relations between Iraq and Turkey were at their peak point. Turkey's positive neutrality policy – in which Özal played an important role – towards Iran and Iraq during the war was successful in terms of economic and politics.[69] Turkey not only stabilized relations with these two countries during a time of great turbulence, but also its position became stronger in the western circles during the war with its policies.

Turkey's need of foreign markets for its new economic policy of export-oriented development coincided with Iraq's increasing needs after the economic development of this country with the high oil prices and during the war with Iran. Iraq was the

67 *Dışişleri Güncesi*, May 2005, p. 87, available [online]: http://www.mfa.gov.tr/NR/rdonlyres/E45BB9B0-C32A-43C4-8A0F-29F072F3808E/0/MAYIS2005.pdf [12 July 2006].

68 *Dışişleri Güncesi*, June 2005, p. 73, available [online]: http://www.mfa.gov.tr/NR/rdonlyres/A14685DE-9A36-41DD-B5E3-E9AD5DF2695C/0/HAZIRAN2005.pdf [12 July 2006].

69 Robins, *Suits and Uniforms*, p. 57.

main trade partner of Turkey at that time and the amount of trade between these two countries increased during the Iran-Iraq war and Turkey's exports to this country equalled 1 billion dollars in 1985.[70] This was due to the Iran-Iraq war and Iraq's dire need of foods and processed products. Turkey also provided an important outlet for Iraq during the war with Iran, since the limited access of Iraq to the Gulf was in danger because of the war. Iraq exported its oil via the Kirkuk-Yumurtalık pipeline and Turkey also provided a land route for Iraq to other parts of the world.

Contrary to their economic relations, security problems and water issues (the distribution of the sources of the Euphrates and the Tigris) were sources of conflict between the two countries. Iraq and also Syria complained increasingly about the amount and the quality of the waters of the Euphrates and the Tigris especially after Turkey's ambitious Southeast Anatolia Project (GAP). Turkey's southern neighbours established connections between the issues of water and security. Although a technical committee was established between the three states to review the situation in 1982, there was little agreement among them. Turkey unilaterally pledged in 1987 to ensure an annual average of 500 cubic meters per second of the Euphrates to flow across the Syrian border and remains committed to honouring this figure.[71]

Syria supported the PKK for several years to use it as leverage against Turkey on the issue of the distribution of water. Iraq pursued a tough policy on the issue of the distribution of the waters of the Euphrates after the end of the Iran-Iraq War and cancelled the agreements regarding Turkish hot pursuit operations into northern Iraq. When Turkey asked for the renewal of the 1984 security protocol, Iraq's First Deputy Prime Minister Taha Yassin Ramazan argued that, without a resolution of the Euphrates problem· it was difficult to maintain cordial relations between the two countries.[72]

Since Iraq had positioned most of its military forces on the Iranian border because of the war in the 1980s, Baghdad's control of the north of the country had diminished and Kurdish groups got the advantage of it. The PKK also used northern Iraq in its operations against Turkey. Turkey's concerns in this respect increased after the end of the Gulf War and the imposition of no-fly zones.

*The Gulf War and its Aftermath*

The Gulf War and Turkey's support of the coalition against Iraq during this War was a turning point. Turkey's policy was criticized severely by the Baghdad government after the imposition of no-fly zones. However, Turkey's interests coincided in many ways with the interests of the central government in Baghdad. Turkey was not happy with the formation of no fly zones; it accepted this operation to overcome the refugee problem and criticisms of the western countries. Turkey also did not have any interest

---

70  Henri J. Barkey, "Koşulların Zorladığı İlişki: Körfez Savaşı'ndan Bu Yana Türkiye ve Irak," *Avrasya Dosyası* 6, no. 3 (Fall 2000), p. 31.

71  Robins, *Suits and Uniforms*, p. 232.

72  Süha Bölükbaşı, *Türkiye ve Yakınındaki Ortadoğu*, (Ankara: Dış Politika Enstitüsü, n.d.), p. 92, quoted in Henri J. Barkey, "Turkey and the New Middle East: A Geopolitical Exploration," in *Reluctant Neighbor,* edited by Henri J. Barkey (Washington DC: US Institute of Peace Press, 1996), p. 36.

132                          *Harmonizing Foreign Policy*

in the continuation of the economic sanctions against Iraq, since sanctions were also contrary to its interests. In order not to break from the western alliance, Turkey tried to influence its allies in accordance with its own interests to change the policies towards Iraq.[73] The three challenges for Turkey in northern Iraq after the Gulf War are defined by Robins as follows: First, Turkey wanted the prevention of a refugee influx into its territory as had happened in 1987. Second, Turkey did not want to see the emergence of a separate Kurdish entity in northern Iraq, for fear that this would act as a model for the Kurds in Turkey. Third, Ankara did not want to see northern Iraq used by the PKK as a springboard for attacks into Turkey.[74]

Baghdad's control over northern parts of Iraq was limited severely after the imposition of no fly zones and there was a power vacuum there. Beside the Kurdish groups like the Kurdistan Democratic Party (KDP) and the Patriotic Union of Kurdistan (PUK), the PKK also used this power vacuum there in order to increase its capabilities. Turkey was conducting cross-border operations against the PKK and getting the support of the KDP and the PUK. Turkey especially cooperated with the KDP since this group controlled the area adjacent to the Turkish border. In March 1991, when the Kurdish rebellion against Saddam Hussein was still raging, President Turgut Özal secretly invited the head of the PUK, Talabani, and the representative of the KDP, Dizai, to Ankara. This represented an important shift in Turkish policy and domestically there were some criticisms of such a policy.[75] It is argued that the Turkish military appeared to be alienated when it was not briefed on talks with the Kurdish leaders and the military believed that after this contact with the Kurdish groups of northern Iraq, Turkey would not be in a position to expect Iraq not to interfere in its own Kurdish problem.[76] Turkey tried to use these Kurdish groups against the terrorist activities of the PKK. These groups, especially the KDP, were also ready to cooperate with Turkey because the PKK was their rival and relations with Turkey might have provided them some advantages. The rivalry between Kurdish groups in northern Iraq presented a dilemma to Turkey. On the one hand, this rivalry seriously undermined the possibility of a Kurdish state in northern Iraq; on the other hand, the chaos that arose from these clashes might have provided an opportunity to the PKK to increase its presence in northern Iraq.[77] Turkey cooperated with these groups in its struggle with the PKK especially in the early years of the 1990s. But Turkey was not satisfied with the attitude of these groups, especially the PUK, towards the PKK during the military campaigns and discussed the situation in northern Iraq with Syria and Iran as a series of consultations beginning with the end of 1992 until 1995.[78]

The developments in 1993 represented an important turn in Turkey's policy towards northern Iraq. In that year, at the end of March, the PKK declared cease-fire

---

73  Hale, p. 308.

74  Robins, *Suits and Uniforms*, pp. 313–14.

75  Fırat-Kürkçüoğlu, p. 556.

76  Mahmut Bali Aykan, "Turkey's Policy in Northern Iraq, 1991–95," *Middle Eastern Studies* 32, no. 4 (1996), p. 347.

77  Hale, p. 308.

78  Robins, *Suits and Uniforms*, p. 327.

but 33 soldiers in civilian clothes were killed in Bingöl by some groups within the PKK. The death of Özal from a heart attack in April also contributed to this change. With Özal's death, Demirel became the President and Çiller became the Prime Minister. The attitude of both of them towards the PKK and to the developments in the northern Iraq was different from Özal. Also the policies of the Kurdish groups in northern Iraq were not successful in curbing the activities of the PKK there. Turkish intervention into the northern Iraq and the clashes between the KDP and the PUK were other factors of great importance.

The activities of the PKK reached their peak in 1994–1995. During this period, Turkey increased its campaign against the PKK and the threat of the organization started to decline with 1997. In March 1995, the Turkish military moved into Iraq with a force of 35,000. The main aim was to crush the PKK presence there. However, this operation also sent some messages to the US and the warring Kurdish groups of the KDP and the PUK that Turkey was unhappy with the power vacuum in the region and the increasing activities of the PKK there.[79] This intervention came soon after the admitting of Turkey to a Customs Union with the EU. There were criticisms from European capitals and this development showed the connection between Turkey's Middle East policy and its relations with the EU.

In August 1996, the Baghdad regime attacked the PUK forces with the help of the KDP. Ankara was happy with this development since it signified the role of the central government in Iraq. But Washington was very upset with this development and pressured the KDP and the PUK to came together and reach an agreement. With the pressure of the US, these two groups promised to help to eliminate Turkey's security concerns and Turkey accepted the de facto situation in northern Iraq.[80] Thanks to its continued cooperation with the KDP, Turkey secured a significant decline in the activities of the PKK from northern Iraq by 1997–1998.[81] After these successful cross-border operations and the capture of Öcalan in 1999, the PKK's activities from northern Iraq diminished considerably. Consequently, Turkey's threat perceptions emanating from Iraq declined. It is generally accepted that the US contributed significantly to the capture of Abdullah Öcalan.

During most of the 1990s, the impact of the EU on Turkey and Turkish foreign policy was limited since Turkey was not a candidate country and also because of the differences of the two sides about security perceptions. Turkey's struggle with the PKK and the criticisms of European countries from the point of human rights was the main point of friction. The security threat against the territorial integrity of the state legitimized the role of army in the politics in the eyes of the public opinion and many Turks believed that European countries either do not understand Turkey's concerns or consciously opposed Turkey's policies. These differences between Turkey and the European countries limited the impact of the EU on Turkey and Turkey's policy in the Middle East was in line with the US and Israel.

---

79  Barkey, "Turkey and the New Middle East," p. 42.
80  Fırat-Kürkçüoğlu, p. 563.
81  Hale, p. 310.

*The Decline of Security Threats and the Issue of EU Candidature after 1999*

The year 1999 witnessed important developments that affected Turkish foreign policy towards the Middle East. The capture of Öcalan, the general elections and the new coalition government, the two earthquakes in the country and the candidacy of Turkey to the EU might be given as these factors. Among them, the capture of the head of the PKK Abdullah Öcalan and candidacy to the EU were most influential factors for the TFP.

Turkey gained the status of candidate country to the European Union at the Helsinki Summit of the Union in December 1999. The rapprochement with Greece after the earthquakes and the popular sympathy for the suffering of the Turkish people, the change of government in Germany and the positive attitude of the Schröder government towards Turkey are given as some reasons for the positive decision at Helsinki.[82] However, we should not forget the mistakes of Greek foreign policy during the Öcalan affair and the change of the foreign minister and the attitude of Greece towards Turkey as a result of these mistakes. And the negative atmosphere after the 1997 Luxemburg Summit of the EU also led the European countries to review their position towards Turkey.

Turkey always declared that it was in favour of the territorial integrity of Iraq. Turkey's opposition to the partition of Iraq and the establishment of a Kurdish state in northern Iraq remained as its basic premise of Iraq policy. Turkey wished to maintain economic and diplomatic contacts with the Baghdad government. In the diplomatic sphere, Iraq maintained its embassy in Ankara throughout the period and Turkey re-opened its embassy in Baghdad in 1993, at the level of charge d'affaires.[83] Turkey also opened the Habur gate in September 1994 primarily to facilitate cross border trade in diesel. The tax revenues from this gate constituted an important source for the KDP, since it was controlling the gate.

Turkey was affected negatively by the sanctions against Iraq. These economic sanctions had not only economic but also security related problems in the southeast of the country. In this respect, Turkey tried to convince Saddam Hussein's administration to comply with the UN resolutions in order to secure the end of sanctions. Turkey also pressed in the international arena for the end of the embargo. A step in this direction came at the end of 1996 with the UN Security Council Resolution 986, allowing Iraq to export oil to the value of 2 billion dollars in each six months. Turkey benefited from this small step, but pressed for the overall lifting of sanctions. There were some other countries, even some members of the UN Security Council like Russia and France that were also in favour of the end of sanctions. As an incentive to Saddam, Turkish Foreign Minister İsmail Cem visited Baghdad with concrete proposals to end the sanctions.[84] Although no serious results emerged from these initiatives, Turkey tried to decrease its costs of economic and security problems.

---

82  Philip Robins, "Confusion at home, confusion abroad: Turkey between Copenhagen and Iraq," *International Affairs* 79, no. 3 (2003), p. 548.

83  Hale, p. 311.

84  Fırat-Kürkçüoğlu, p. 567.

It is a reality that 1990s were problematic years for Turkey in its policy towards Iraq. Lack of control of central government in northern Iraq caused serious damages to Turkish security and Turkey devoted enormous amounts of resources to its campaign against the PKK terror. Turkey always regarded northern Iraq as an exclusive part of the country, but the developments after the Gulf War created problems for this policy. Turkey showed some kind of flexibility by cooperating with Kurdish groups in northern Iraq in its Iraq policy but also maintained powerful military presence in the struggle with the PKK. The fact that the US turned a blind eye to its military operations within the Iraqi territory also helped Turkey.[85] It is argued by some other scholars that the USA restrained in criticisms of Turkey's human rights record in dealing with the PKK out of fear of endangering Operation Provide Comfort.[86] But the US's tacit approval of Turkey's operations into the territory of Iraq came to an end with the invasion of Iraq by allied operation. After the veto of the Turkish Grand National Assembly of the transfer of the US soldiers to Iraq via Turkish territory, the attitude of the US on this issue started to change. The opposition of Kurdish groups to the military presence of Turkey in Iraq after the invasion also played its part in this development.

The political and economic problems during the 1990s negatively effected Turkey's policy towards Iraq. It also can be said that the developments in Iraq contributed to the political and economic instability of Turkey. In either way, when the instability reached the level of crisis in the country, there was the problem of direction in the policy towards Iraq. But the threats to the security of the country were so acute that the military took the lead in some cases. Some of the politicians also enabled the military to play an important role because of the security threat or because of some other domestic problems. The instabilities resulted in the decline of the influence of the country in the developments in Iraq. We should not forget that northern Iraq constituted the most important aspect of Turkey's policy towards this neighbour.

The end of the Baat'h rule in Iraq with allied operation changed the situation dramatically. This operation and the developments prior to it seriously affected the policies of Turkey and the US against Iraq. The differences between these two countries became obvious before and after the invasion of Iraq. The new Iraqi constitution and the policies of new the Iraqi regime will determine the future of Turkey's relations with Iraq.

Turkey's Iraq policy during the 1990s was generally not in conformity with that of the US in essence. Turkey was not happy with the activities of the Kurdish groups in northern Iraq. Turkish authorities believed that the containment of PKK activities in northern Iraq could best be secured by the accomplishment of the re-establishment of Iraqi sovereignty there. Turkey accepted the formation of no-fly zones in northern Iraq in order to eliminate the danger of refugees and also the criticisms of human rights. The extension of the duration of Operation Provide Comfort was always an issue of debate in Turkish politics during this era. Most of the parties in opposition criticized the continuation of this operation and Turkey's contribution to this, but they changed their minds when they came to power. This operation was transformed

---

85  Hale, p. 329.
86  Henri J. Barkey, "Turkey and the New Middle East," p. 35.

into Operation Northern Watch and came to an end with the invasion of Iraq by the allied operation.

Turkey also was not happy with the continuation of economic sanctions towards Iraq. Turkey's economy and security negatively affected by these sanctions. Turkey lost an important market and the worsening economic conditions contributed to the destabilization of security in the south-east of the country. Despite these differences, Turkey and the US cooperated in several ways. Turkey enabled the US to monitor the developments in Iraq with Operation Northern Watch and the US helped Turkey in its struggle with the PKK.

The capture of Öcalan provided an important stimulus for the success of the Democratic Left Party of Ecevit in the general elections of 1999. The coalition government afterwards was nationalist in essence, with the existence of right and left nationalist parties within it. The decline of the terrorist threat from northern Iraq and the personal affinities of Ecevit to the central administration in Iraq were important factors that affected policy towards this country. In this period Turkey pursued the traditional policy for the reinstitution of the authority of the central government in the north and for a complete end to the sanctions. The longevity of the position of foreign minister Cem and his active policy in the region were a positive side of the period. When the intentions of the US government for the invasion of Iraq and toppling of the regime there became obvious after the invasion of Afghanistan in the post-9/11 world, domestic problems dominated the policy agenda of Turkey. The elections in November 2002 resulted in a completely different picture.

*The Invasion of Iraq*

During the election campaign, the Justice and Development Party (AKP) promised a flexible foreign policy that would be defined democratically by the National Assembly and the visit of the leaders of the party and the Prime Minister after the election to several European capitals to press for the opening of accession negotiations signified the direction.[87]

With the candidature to the EU, Turkey began to modify its legal framework in order to meet the Copenhagen Criteria. The legal changes brought Turkey closer to the EU and the candidature made Turkey more open to the pressures of the Union. The National Security Council in its meeting on 30 May 2002 recommended that the government abolish the death penalty and end the state of emergency in Hakkari and Tunceli at the end of July and in Diyarbakır and Şırnak at the end of November.[88] These recommendations opened the way for an important reform package to meet the Copenhagen Criteria that was passed in the Assembly on 3 August. The most important aspects of these reforms were the abolition of the death penalty, and the rights to broadcast and to educate children in languages other than Turkish.

After the election victory of the Justice and Development Party, the new government had to deal with several difficult issues like Iraq, the relations with

---

87  Christopher Brewin. "A Changing Turkey: Europe's Dilemma," *Journal of Southern Europe and the Balkans* 5, no. 2 (August 2003), p. 137.

88  *Hurriyet*, 31 May 2002.

the EU and accession negotiations with the Union, the Cyprus problem and the economy. Each of these issues was very sensitive and critical for Turkey and the new government under the premiership of Abdullah Gül had to deal with very difficult foreign policy topics at the same time just after the formation of the government in November 2002. After the formation of the government, among the pressing issues of foreign policy, getting a date for the accession negotiations with the EU was the most urgent and the focus was on this issue until the Copenhagen Summit.

Within the global atmosphere of "war on terrorism" in the post-9/11 attacks, the invasion of Iraq and removal of the regime of the country were two of the priorities on the agenda of the US. As one of the most important allies of the US in the region, Turkey, as a neighbour of Iraq, constituted an important part in the plans for the invasion. Although public opinion was against the war and invasion, it is generally assumed that, given its economic conditions and the possible US aid and also the long standing strategic relations with the US, Turkey would join coalition. Traditionally the limited role of the public opinion in the formation of the foreign policy and the close contacts between the Turkish and the US military were other reasons for these expectations. In order to get the support of Turkey for the US plans regarding Iraq, US Vice President Dick Cheney visited Turkey in Spring 2002. With the approaching invasion, high level visits between the two parts increased. Deputy Defence Minister Paul Wolfowitz and Deputy Foreign Minister Marc Grossman visited Turkey at the beginning of December 2002 to discuss the conditions of cooperation. After that, Tayyip Erdoğan, as head of his party, visited Washington and met with Bush. Erdoğan also visited Russia and China to obtain first hand information about the positions of these powers. However, beside the general opposition of the public opinion about such an operation, the rhetoric of the Turkish authorities on such a move described the US attitude as "lacking international legitimacy." Especially President Sezer insisted on this issue and Turkey's policy in this respect was in line with the France-German stance.

US was asking Turkey to use its joint air bases, permission to deploy US soldiers and equipment and the transfer of these soldiers and equipment to Iraq to the northern front. In return for this help, the US was prepared to provide financial assistance for Turkey's fragile economy, allow Turkish troops to move 20 km into the Iraqi territory to prevent an influx of refugees and terrorist attacks and a package of military benefits. The negotiations between Turkish and US officials about the details of cooperation continued longer than the expected and a memorandum of understanding was signed on January 10, 2003 for the upgrading of ports and bases.[89]

Beside the negotiations with the US, Turkey also negotiated with the countries in the region and tried to coordinate the policies of the neighbours of Iraq. In this respect, Prime Minister Gül visited Syria, Jordan, Egypt and Saudi Arabia within a week in the first part of the January and hosted high level visits from the UK and Syria.[90] Turkey consulted not only with the neighbours of Iraq, but also with the officials in Iraq for the prevention of the war and for a peaceful solution. In this respect, Iraq's Deputy Head

---

89  http://arsiv3.hurriyet.com.tr/anasayfa/0,,tarih~2003-01-10-m,00.asp [8 July 2006].

90  *Dışişleri Güncesi*, January 2003, pp. 1–2, available [online]: http://www.mfa.gov.tr/NR/rdonlyres/0BF50F75-A50B-4A8D-981A-A4CB3C12BDB4/0/OCAK2003.pdf [8 July 2006].

of State Taha Yassin Ramazan came to Turkey and Turkey made its position clear to the Iraqi side. It also warned about the consequences if a peaceful solution was not secured.[91] Although the priority was the prevention of the war, Turkey also considered other options and made it clear to the neighbours that a move of the Turkish military in northern Iraq would be for the stabilization of the area.[92] The neighbours of Iraq were in agreement on the protection of the territorial integrity of the country and opposed to the emergence of a Kurdish state in the north of the country.

With these considerations, the first meeting of "Summit of Iraq's Neighbours" convened in Istanbul on 23 January 2003 with the participation of Egypt, Iran, Syria, Jordan and Saudi Arabia. Originally it had been intended to be held at the level of leaders, but it was convened at the level of foreign ministers. The joint declaration after the summit urged Iraq to comply fully with the UN Security Council Resolution of 1441 and continue its full cooperation with the UN arms inspectors and pursue an active policy to provide information about its arsenal. The declaration also stressed "the protection of international peace and security is the main responsibility of the UN Security Council, implying that the US was to refrain from unilateral actions."[93] The participants of the Summit decided to convene again in the future in case of necessity and these meetings became a regular forum among the participating countries to discuss the problems in Iraq and their effects in the region. This initiative of Turkey created a mechanism with which to increase contact among the countries in the region and prevent misunderstandings and reduce the problems that might arise in relation to the future of Iraq. Official sources describe one of the aims of the meeting and following gatherings as to have a consensus among the countries of the region on the fate of the region and maintain the contact among the countries and to prevent competition among the neighbours over Iraq.[94]

The US pressure on Turkey was intensifying with the end of January since the aim of the US was to start the operation before the onset on spring and the hot weather. Public opinion in Turkey and in the world was against the war in Iraq and the US was urged to seek UN authorization. In Turkey, the National Security Council (NSC) called upon the government to seek parliamentary authorization for military measures in accordance with the constitution. The negotiations with the US came to an end and the parties agreed on the conditions of the deal. Accordingly 62,000 Americans were be stationed to transfer to Iraq and US would provide 2 billion dollars in aid and 24 billion dollars worth of loan guarantees. Beside this, Turkey would deploy 40,000 troops in northern Iraq in coordination with the US and the US committed to protect the maintenance of the unitary state in Iraq.

A common point of several declarations of Turkish statesmen during this period was their stress on the Turkish experience in 1991 during and after the Gulf War. Given the political and economic problems created in the country, Turkish officials tried to act cautiously. The negative effects of the Gulf War were seen by many

---

91  http://arsiv3.hurriyet.com.tr/haber/0,,sid~1@w~356@tarih~2003-02-06-m@ nvid~228565,00.asp [8 July 2006].

92  Robins, "Confusion at home, confusion abroad," p. 562.

93  *Zaman*, 24 January 2003.

94  Davutoğlu, interview by author, Istanbul, 28 May 2006.

people as having been one of the main causes of the political and economic problems of the 1990s.

The government decided to send the proposal about the transfer of the US soldiers via Turkish territory to Iraq and sending Turkish soldiers to Iraq to the National Assembly for vote on March 1. The NSC did not make a declaration in open support of the proposal and the President Sezer stated before the vote that the international legitimacy (meaning a second Security Council Resolution for the invasion) should be secured for the authorization of accepting foreign troops to the country or for sending Turkish troops abroad.[95] There was a general expectation that the NSC would make a declaration in support of the proposal. Given the strong opposition of the public opinion to such a policy, it is argued that the military abstained from exercising pressure to allow transferring of the US soldiers, leaving the painful decision to the government and consequently undermining its credibility.[96] In relation to the same issue, just before the critical NSC meeting on the 28 February 2003, it is said that the Commander of the Turkish Land Forces General Aytaç Yalman leaked the information that the Turkish military was not satisfied with the negotiations with the US to open the second front.[97] After this development, the government postponed the decision on this motion after the NSC meeting on 28 February 2003.

*The March 1 Motion and its Aftermath*

Prime Minister Gül did not impose party discipline for the motion and some members of the governing party were openly against the motion. The reason behind the decision of Gül not to impose party discipline might have been the fear of a split within the party given the strong opposition of the public to the motion. Beside this, his party was still in the making. On March 1, the National Assembly voted on the motion with 264 in favour and 251 against. Despite the simple majority, the motion was vetoed because of the lack of a majority for the motion among the deputies present in the chamber on the day.

A second motion for the use of Turkish airspace by the US and the sending of Turkish soldiers to northern Iraq was authorized on 20 March, just before the beginning of the war. Despite this motion, Turkey's relations with the US deteriorated. Although the government received the permission of the Assembly to send soldiers to northern Iraq, the US and the Kurdish groups in the north opposed such an incursion. US President Bush warned Turkey not to intervene into northern Iraq.[98] German Foreign Minister Fischer even threatened to withdraw crew from the NATO Awacs surveillance in case of an incursion into northern Iraq.[99] The US credit for Turkey was made conditional to the non-intervention of Turkey to northern Iraq and the Kurdish leaders in northern Iraq also warned Turkey not to intervene. Turkey's

---

95  *Milliyet*, 28 February 2003.

96  Misrahi, p. 24.

97  Lale Sarıibrahimoğlu, "1 Mart Tezkeresinin Artçı Sarsıntıları Sürüyor," *Bugün*, 29 April 2006.

98  BBC 24 March 2003, http://news.bbc.co.uk/2/hi/europe/2879299.stm. [10 April 2006].

99  BBC 22 March 2003, http://news.bbc.co.uk/2/hi/europe/2874635.stm. [10 April 2006].

policy prior to the invasion of Iraq and veto of transfer of US soldiers to the Iraqi territory are explained by some scholars as a result of possible secret German and French threats to keep Turkey out of the EU if Ankara joined the coalition against Saddam Hussein.[100]

The relations between Turkey and the US were seriously damaged by the arrest of Turkish soldiers in Sulaymaniyah on 4 July 2003. The members of the Turkish Special Forces were disarmed, hooded and detained by US troops on charges of conspiring to assassinate local elected officials. Most of the people in Turkey saw this act as a clear sign that the US favoured the Iraqi Kurds over a NATO ally.[101] As the infrastructure for a future Kurdish state in northern Iraq increased, the negative attitude of the Turkish public opinion towards the US increased with the feeling that US was backing this development.

Turkey abstained from allowing the transfer of US troops via its territory and from intervention into the northern Iraq after the invasion and the developments in northern Iraq. Turkey ended the state of emergency in some parts of the southeast of the country only several months before the invasion of Iraq. The transfer of 62,000 US troops and military equipment from İskenderun to northern Iraq would require some military measures and possibility of the re-establishment of state of emergency in this area. Such a situation was very problematic from the perspective of relations with the EU. Turkey was trying to secure a date for accession talks with the EU and carrying out some reforms in this respect. The end of the state of emergency after several years was one of the important aspects of these reforms. The dilemma of allowing the transfer of soldiers and imposing state of emergency again on the one hand and alienating the US on the hand played an important role in the restraint of the government in not pressing for the proposal in the Assembly. The government had been planning to focus in the two years after the Copenhagen Summit in December 2002 on the beginning of accession negotiations with the EU on the reforms for democratization. In order to continue democratization Turkey had to be distanced from the war.[102] This point signified the impact of the EU candidature on the decisions regarding the foreign policy of Turkey.

When the occupation faced strong resistance, Turkey was asked by the coalition forces to send soldiers to help the stabilization of the situation in Iraq. During August and September there were discussions in Ankara on this issue and President Sezer stressed the importance of international law, meaning not supporting such a move, and also pointed out that the responsibility belonged to the parliament to decide on this issue.[103] There were also opposition from some groups within Iraq, especially from the Kurds, to the Turkish presence there. Prime Minister Erdoğan was in favour of sending soldiers to Iraq and supported his position with several arguments, like

---

100  Simon Baynham, "Eurasian Janus: Turkey's Security and Defense Dilemmas in the Aftermath of the Iraq War," *Defense and Security Analysis* 19, no. 3 (September 2003), pp. 283–4.

101  Çağaptay, p. 48.

102  Davutoğlu, interview by author, Istanbul, 28 May 2006.

103  *Dışişleri Güncesi, August 2003*, p. 15, available [online]: http://www.mfa.gov.tr/NR/ rdonlyres/3280C72E-1D17-4396-BDEC-7F42C6903B09/0/Agustos2003.pdf [9 July 2006].

the need to fight the PKK militants and to get the support of the US in this struggle, Turkey's contribution to Iraq's economy and infrastructure after the war and also the support of some of the groups in Iraq. Parliament gave the permission to the government to send soldiers to Iraq for a period of one year with a motion on 7 October 2003.[104] Turkey started to discuss the details of this operation with the USA. However, the developments within one month induced the Turkish government to declare, in consultation with the US that it would not use the authorization received from the parliament to participate in the Iraq Stability Force. During this period of time, Kurdish groups and also some other groups within Iraq voiced opposition to the participation of Turkish soldiers to this force. On 14 October there was a suicide bomb attack against the Turkish Embassy in Iraq and this attack is interpreted as having been a warning to Turkey not to send soldiers to Iraq.[105]

In addressing the Parliament, Foreign Minister Abdullah Gül described Turkish foreign policy towards Iraq at the end of 2003 as "in consultation with the USA, in conformity with the EU principles and very much popular in the Middle Eastern and Islamic countries. When there are strong disagreements among the international public opinion on Iraq, Turkey has continued her close and sincere relations with every party."[106]

In the early days of 2004, Turkey continued its contacts with Iran and Syria to coordinate the policy on Iraq. In January Syrian President Bashar Asad visited Turkey, the first Syrian president to do this. Foreign Minister Gül visited Tehran and confirmed the common policies for the territorial integrity of Iraq. At that time, Turkey was against the federal demands on Iraq and Prime Minister Erdoğan declared that the demands of the ethnic groups in Iraq for a federal structure were wrong and could not bring stability to the country.[107] During 2004, there were several attacks and kidnappings against Turkish businessmen and drivers in Iraq. Some of these events were related to the issue of lack of authority and looting, but some of them are interpreted as having been a message from different groups in Iraq to Turkey that Turkish involvement, whether for military or civilian purposes, was not welcome. Not only Turkish businessmen and drivers were attacked, but five members of special police forces also were killed in an attack in December 2004.[108] So, although Turkey did not take part in the invasion, the civilian casualties of Turkey were high after the invasion of the country.

When Turkey was trying to take some protective measures for its own citizens, the developments in the city of Talafar, where the Turcomans are the dominant group, created more tension with the US. US soldiers were carrying out military operations with the argument that were several militant groups in the city. The

---

104   http://arsiv3.hurriyet.com.tr/anasayfa/0,,tarih~2003-10-07-m,00.asp [9 July 2006].

105   *Dışişleri Güncesi*, October 2003, p. 105, available [online]: http://www.mfa.gov.tr/NR/ rdonlyres/C6F49A2A-0ABC-4810-8EBF-CBBFCACC7864/0/Ekim2003.pdf [9 July 2006].

106   *Dışişleri Güncesi*, December 2003, p. 119, available [online]: http://www.mfa.gov.tr/ NR/rdonlyres/A245DF54-7640-4CB6-8CE5-62835C78204F/0/Aralık2003.pdf [9 July 2006].

107   *Dışişleri Güncesi*, January 2004, p. 122, available [online]: http://www.mfa.gov.tr/NR/ rdonlyres/DCEE2866-64A3-4AC9-84C1-634949B1A2FE/0/Ocak2004.pdf [10 July 2006].

108   http://arsiv3.hurriyet.com.tr/haber/0,,sid~1@w~3@tarih~2004-12-17-m@ nvid~511783,00.asp [11 July 2006].

civilian population of the city suffered from the operation. Given the sensitivity of the public opinion on this issue, the government had to respond in a decisive manner. In this respect, Gül contacted his American counterpart Powell and warned him that Turkey might re-evaluate its cooperation with the US on Iraq.[109] The operations came to an end in Talafar in fall 2005. When these continued, Turkey urged the US forces to consider the protection of the civilians in the city when carrying out operations there and also sent humanitarian relief to the city several times. This event shows the limits of the Turkish involvement in Iraq and how Turkey depended on the goodwill of the US in Iraq. This fact surfaced again on the issue of the struggle with the PKK in Iraq. Despite several demands and warnings, the US did not act decisively against the PKK presence in Iraq with several different arguments.

After the invasion of Iraq without a northern front, the conditions in Iraq and the relations between Turkey and the US regarding Iraq dramatically differed from the conditions prior to the invasion. The situation had been comparatively calm after the capture of Öcalan at the beginning of 1999 until the end of the PKK's ceasefire in June 2004. Turkey's need for military operations in the pursuit of the PKK terrorists had been limited. However, after the invasion of Iraq and the change of the conditions there and re-launch of the PKK attacks, Turkey became unable to conduct hot pursuit operations into Iraqi territory. The presence of a small number of Turkish armed forces in Iraqi territory with the consent of the groups there also became an issue of contention. However, we can expect these armed presence remain there, until the decrease of the PKK presence to a minimum in northern Iraq or the strengthening of the position of the Kurdish groups in Iraq to ask Turkey to remove these soldiers. The presence of the PKK there and the limited cooperation of the Iraqi authorities and the US help to legitimize the presence of these soldiers there.

The problems related with the dealing with the PKK surfaced again when Prime Minister Erdoğan declared that Turkey might carry out cross border operations into Iraq in its struggle with the PKK, if needed. America urged Turkey to try to cooperate with the Iraqi officials and Iraq's Interior Minister argued that the approval of Iraqi the parliament was needed for such operations.[110] Similar discussions were on the agenda in the spring of 2006, when Turkey transferred an important number of soldiers along its border with Iraq to prevent the infiltration of PKK terrorists from northern Iraq. Turkish authorities were unable to get enough cooperation from the Iraqi side or from the American side in this respect. Trilateral meetings between Turkey, the US and Iraq were held to limit the activities of the PKK and especially to cut the financial resources of the terrorist organization. The internal instabilities and resistance and terrorist attacks were at the top of the agenda of the Iraqi government and the US. Consequently, Turkish demands that Iraq and the US officials keep their promises not to shelter the PKK in Iraq were at the lower levels of the agenda for them and Turkey's demands were met partially by the Iraqi authorities and the US.

---

109 *Dışişleri Güncesi*, September 2004, p. 37, available [online]: http://www.mfa.gov.tr/NR/rdonlyres/6EBBB859-D639-415D-B048-57EB17078D4C/0/EYLUL2004.pdf [10 July 2006].

110 *Disisleri Güncesi*, July 2005, p. 40, available [online]: http://www.mfa.gov.tr/NR/rdonlyres/6397723E-ADBC-4355-8A56-195ABDA0953F/0/TEMMUZ2005.pdf [13 July 2006].

Beside the issue of dealing with the PKK, Turkey also continued to raise its concerns related to the future of Kirkuk and the unity of the Iraqi state after the promulgation of the Iraqi constitution.[111] Upon the demands of the Turkey for a more concerted action against the terrorist organization, the US introduced the idea of having special representatives to coordinate actions against the PKK. In this respect, two retired generals, one from the US and one from Turkey, were appointed in September 2006 as the special representatives to deal with this issue. On the demand of the US, the Iraqi side also appointed a special representative to coordinate the efforts on this issue. However, the policy of special representatives did not bring the desired results and became ineffective in the fall of 2007.

When the Turkish authorities talked about a possible intervention into northern Iraq against the terrorist activities, it is argued that the officials of the EU advised the officials in the Turkish Ministry of Foreign Affairs that Turkey should refrain from a long standing intervention since this might be perceived as an occupation in the EU capitals.[112] The Turkish officials replied that if it were required, it would end within a short time. Although it is argued in the same newspaper that the concern of the Turkish officials was the US, not the EU, this issue represents the impact of the EU on Turkish foreign policy towards Iraq. Turkey had to consider not only the response of the US in relation to its policies towards Iraq, but also the EU, since it is a candidate country to the Union.

Beside the issues related to the fate of the Turcomans and the PKK activities in Iraq, US operation in some cities like Fellujah and the death of civilians also created tensions between Turkey and the US. During the fall of 2004, the clashes in Iraq intensified and the number of civilian causalities increased. The killing of an armless wounded person in a mosque in Fellujah created criticism in the world public opinion and in Turkey. Foreign Minister Gül said that "these kinds of events have deep impact on the psychology of the people of the region."[113] Mehmet Elkatmış, MP of the governing AKP and the head of the Human Rights Commission of the Parliament, declared that the US was carrying out genocide in Iraq.[114] The arguments that the there was a note verbal form the USA to Turkey in relation to this criticism have been falsified by the Ministry of Foreign Affairs.[115] Turkey sent urgent aid amounting to 500,000 dollars for the civilians living in Fellujah. Turkey continued to contribute to ease the humanitarian disaster in Iraq by treating several wounded people from different parts of Iraq in Turkish hospitals.

Although Turkey supported the democratic process and return to the control of Iraq by the Iraqis, it also raised its concerns about the legitimacy of the elections in Iraq

---

111 *Dışişleri Güncesi*, August 2005, p. 19, available [online]: http://www.mfa.gov.tr/ NR/rdonlyres/DD1EEA90-8C61-40E3-A400-DC399AC3E27A/0/AGUSTOS2005.pdf    [13 July 2006].

112 *Zaman*, 20 July 2006.

113 http://arsiv3.hurriyet.com.tr/haber/0,,sid~1@w~2@tarih~2004-11-17-m@ nvid~497526,00.asp [11 July 2006].

114 http://arsiv3.hurriyet.com.tr/haber/0,,sid~1@w~7@tarih~2004-11-25-m@ nvid~501358,00.asp [11 July 2006].

115 *Dışişleri Güncesi*, November 2004, p. 53, available [online]: http://www.mfa.gov.tr/ NR/rdonlyres/995B2FC8-9E37-4963-8173-FFD51241B2BC/0/Kasim2004.pdf [11 July 2006].

on 30 January, before and after the elections. Turkey's concerns were concentrated on the rights of the Turcomans and the fate of the city of Kirkuk. Turkish Ministry of Foreign Affairs declared that there was an illegal and superficial population transfer to Kirkuk and Minister Gül sent a letter to the UN Secretary General Kofi Annan in which he evaluated the possible negative results of efforts to change the demographic structure of the city of Kirkuk.[116] It seems that Turkey's declarations and the letter sent to Annan aimed to create pressure on the Kurds to limit the population transfer before the elections, since it was not possible to intervene directly. However, despite these warnings an important number of Kurds were transferred to Kirkuk and the Kurdish groups won the elections.

Turkey's position just after the declaration of the results of the elections remained the same. It was declared that the objections should be taken seriously. Unhappy with the performance of the Turcoman parties, Prime Minister Erdoğan said that Turkey would adjust its policy according to the new realities.[117] These election results led Turkey to re-evaluate its policy of Turcomans and northern Iraq. Although contacts with different ethnic and religious groups in Iraq had begun earlier, this process intensified afterwards and Turkey tried to establish good relations with every actor in Iraq. Beside the visits of different political parties and influential political and religious figures in Iraq to Turkey and Turkish diplomats' contacts with them in Iraq, Turkey also hosted representatives of different groups from Iraq for academic forums during the preparation of the constitution of Iraq. Turkey's contribution to the constitutional and political process in Iraq continued with courses in Ankara on the election systems and democratic institutions.[118] In relation with the re-structuring of the Iraqi Ministry of Foreign Affairs, with the request of Iraqi side, 20 young Iraqi diplomats attended courses related to their field at the Turkish Ministry of Foreign Affairs in November and December 2005.[119]

Until 1999, Turkey's relations with the EU were problematic despite the existence of a customs union and being an applicant to the Union. Many people in Turkey and in Europe believed that Turkey would never join the EU. This feeling continued even after the official candidature of Turkey in 1999. Even some EU bureaucrats argued that, although Turkey had become a candidate to the Union, Turkey most probably could not meet the criteria for membership and its candidature would be cancelled despite lack of precedence or a rule for such kind of a situation.[120] The security concerns of Turkey during the 1990s and struggle with terrorism, and the criticisms of European countries for Turkey's in terms of human rights made the relations

---

116  *Dışişleri Güncesi*, January 2005, pp. 25–26, available [online]: http://www.mfa.gov.tr/NR/rdonlyres/D2CB5AFF-B646-4E0F-8D13-6A3B357167EE/0/OCAK2005.pdf [12 July 2006].

117  http://arsiv3.hurriyet.com.tr/haber/0,,sid~1@w~1@tarih~2005-02-16-m@nvid~537750,00.asp [12 July 2006].

118  *Dışişleri Güncesi*, May 2005, p. 41, available [online]: http://www.mfa.gov.tr/NR/rdonlyres/E45BB9B0-C32A-43C4-8A0F-29F072F3808E/0/MAYIS2005.pdf [12 July 2006].

119  *Dışişleri Güncesi*, October 2005, p. 49, available [online]: http://www.mfa.gov.tr/NR/rdonlyres/4428A895-DD1B-4CD0-994D-6CF1EFB53F30/0/EKIM2005.pdf [13 July 2006].

120  Michael Leigh, "Alternative Scenarios for the Europe's Future," *7th Cervia Summer School of Bologna University*, Cervia, Italy, 14 September 2001.

tense. These reciprocal perceptions resulted in a feeling on both sides that Turkey would never become a member of the EU. Consequently, the impact of the EU on Turkey and Turkish foreign policy was limited.

Today Ankara's foreign policy is moving in the direction of alignment with the EU. The engagement of Turkey by the European Union and the principle of conditionality along with the legacy of Özal's policies of economic interdependence are given as the critical factors that have brought the emergence of a new foreign policy.[121] Turkey did not allow the transfer of the US troops via its territory to Iraq and sending Turkish troops, and criticized some actions of the allied forces in Iraq. The motion of 1 March 2003 was a signal that democratic legitimacy would be the principle of Ankara in its foreign policy. The makers of foreign policy argue that this democratic and independent attitude of Turkey in the last couple of years has contributed to the image of Turkey in the eyes of other countries like Russia.[122] Although Turkey supported the USA's Greater Middle East Initiative and became one of the democratic partners in this process, it also stressed that the reforms should come within the region and should not be imposed from outside. The impact of public opinion on the formation of foreign policy is increasing and current polls show that the Turkish public opinion is against the US policies in the region. This opposition is very much related to the support of the US to Kurdish groups in Iraq and also the failure of the US to help in the elimination of PKK activities in northern Iraq.

Turkey's transformation with the EU candidature and the stabilization of economy and politics of the country has changed the framework of foreign policy. After putting its own house in order, Turkey has felt more confident in regional policy and has pursued an active diplomacy in the Middle East. Turkish policy towards the region was a compartmentalized one beforehand. Currently Turkey tries to follow a more comprehensive policy in the region.[123] Today Turkey has a regional policy and is very active in the Middle East in comparison with the former governments.[124] It is argued that Turkey's foreign policy in relation with the EU and the Middle East can contribute to Middle Eastern security in two senses: as an emerging role model and through its constructive diplomatic engagement in the region.[125] Turkey's reform process and the attempts to reconcile freedom and security, Islam and democracy are examples for the possible reforms on the region. Turkey's attempts at stabilization in Iraq and Palestine represent the constructive diplomatic efforts of the country. The current condition of Turkey has shown that instability is not inevitable in the Middle East. Turkish reforms at home and the calls for reform in the region are taken into account by foreign observers. The British Ambassador to Saudi Arabia underscored that the calls for reform in the Gulf region are worthwhile and that Turkey is a good model.[126]

---

121  Kirişçi, "Turkey's Foreign Policy in Turbulent Times," p. 29.

122  Abdullah Gül, "New Horizons in Turkish Foreign Policy," 22 May 2004.

123  Aybet, "The Future of Trans-Atlantic Relations and the Place of Turkey," 15 June 2006.

124  Ibid.

125  Bülent Aras, "Turkey and GCC: An Emerging Relationship," *Middle East Policy* 12, no. 4 (Winter 2005), p. 90.

126  *Arab News*, October 6, 2004, quoted in Aras, "Turkey and GCC: An Emerging Relationship," p. 92.

Turkey's geopolitical location is vital for the transfer of the natural resources of the Middle East and Central Asia to Europe. Beside the pipeline of Kirkuk-Ceyhan, the Baku-Tbilisi-Ceyhan pipeline is important for the transfer of natural resources. Turkey's geo-strategic location as an important energy corridor for the vast oil and gas resources of the Caucasus and Central Asia is given another important dimension of Turkey's contribution to Europe.[127] The developments in the past several years have made the importance of energy security obvious. With the rising demand and prices, and the use of natural resources by Russia as a weapon as in the case of Ukraine, the security of a constant supply of natural resources for Europe has become one of the most important issues on the European agenda. The agreements and construction of a pipeline between Turkey and Greece for the transfer of oil and gas to Europe represents the new dynamic in this issue.

---

127   Philip Gordon and Ömer Taşpınar, "Turkey on the Brink," *The Washington Quarterly* 29, no. 3 (Summer 2006), p. 67.

# Chapter 8

# The Europeanization of
# Turkish Foreign Policy

The theoretical framework and the examples of the chapter on Europeanization will be applied to the Turkish case in this chapter. In considering the definitions and uses of the term *Europeanization*, I will refer to this term as the changes in Turkish foreign policy as a result of the EU candidature. In this respect, the second part of Featherstone and Kazamias's definition of Europeanization suits my analysis, which focuses on the changes in the member countries and also non-member states. In terms of Börzel's top-down and bottom-up dimensions of the definition of the Europeanization, the top-down dimension will be dominant in my analysis since I will focus on impact of membership and candidature of the EU on countries. In this respect, the changes in the perceptions of the decision makers in foreign policy, the changes in the process of policy making and the changes in the policy actions will be analyzed. Since the membership of the countries that have become part of the EU in the latest enlargement is too new to make a fair judgement, I will refer to their candidature to the EU. The different position of the candidate countries because of the power asymmetry and conditionality, which sometimes makes them more open to pressures to change their foreign policy should be kept in mind in analyzing the impact of Europeanization on these countries.

## Foreign Policy Change

The analytical framework developed by Manners and Whitman will constitute the base of my analysis of impact of the EU candidature on Turkish foreign policy. The comprehensive structure of their analysis in comparison with other approaches to Europeanization is the reason for my choice. The first part of their analysis looks to the foreign policy change with the help of conceptualizations of "adaptation through membership" and "socialization of foreign policy makers." Although these concepts might be more suitable for the analysis of the changes of the foreign policy in the member countries, the candidate countries also adapt their foreign policies as argued by Featherstone and Kazamias in the previous chapters.

### Foreign Policy Change through Adaptation

Under the heading "Adaptation through Membership," there were opposing examples of adaptation and resistance to Europeanization. Britain, France, Greece and Denmark are given as the countries in which there have been resistance to Europeanization.[1] The reasons for this resistance are generally related to the historical background and the geopolitical environment of the country. In the chapter on Europeanization, in the example of Greece, Christian Orthodox culture and high military expenditures as a result of the turbulent environment and the problems with Turkey are given as some of the reasons for delay of and resistance to Europeanization.[2] Although Turkey is not a member yet, we may expect that the different cultural background and also the geopolitical environment may also cause some delays in Europeanization. Weak economic structure and high military expenditures are also true for the Turkish case. However, from 1999 onwards, the tensions between Turkey and Greece have been in decline and the EU agenda of the Turkey is one of the reasons for this situation. This development has had a positive effect on the decrease of military expenditures.

From the opposite point of view, Europeanization has been embraced by some countries for different reasons. We can even say that some factors may cause resistance to the Europeanization of foreign policy of a given state, whereas some others lead to the acceptance of Europeanization to overcome negative factors. These negative factors might be a fascist or authoritarian past, and a history marked by economic problems or colonial past. Forgetting the fascist and authoritarian past can be valid for Italy, Spain, Portugal and for Greece.[3] Although Turkey has not experienced a fascist rule, the authoritarian nature of the state before the multi-party system and the successive coups afterwards had negative imprints on Turkish political life. Despite the fact that these coups did not change the direction of the Turkish foreign policy fundamentally, the period after the coups and the new constitutions promulgated after the coups had their impact on foreign policy. The introduction of the National Security Council as an important figure in Turkish political life with the 1961 constitution and the strengthening the position of this body, which includes high level military officers, with the 1982 constitution had their impact on foreign policy making. With the changes in the constitution and the laws to meet the Copenhagen Criteria to begin to accession negotiations; the composition, the power and responsibilities of the NSC changed and the role of armed forces here were curtailed. This change not only had impact for domestic politics, but also for foreign policy formation and actions.

Overcoming the past marked with economic problems is valid for the same countries like Italy, Spain, Greece, and Portugal, with the addition of Ireland.[4] With the EU membership, the performance of the economies of these countries was better in comparison with the past years and this economic development positively affected their foreign policy performances. As their dependency decreased in terms of economics, these countries felt more secure. If a country is unstable from the point of economics, its foreign policy is open to pressures. Stabilization of the economy of any country may contribute to the strengthening of the positions of this country in the foreign policy domain.

---

1   Manners and Whitman, "Conclusion," p. 246.
2   Kazakos and Ioakimidis, p. x.
3   Manners and Whitman, "Conclusion," p. 247.
4   Ibid.

The development of the economy of a country also might have results opposite to the results mentioned above. Economic developments also may have an effect of moderation on the foreign policies of countries.[5] This also might be true for Turkey since economic development will create many interests at stake that will prevent pursuing quick changes or risky policies. The EU membership or even prospect of membership positively has affected the economies of several countries. The same is also true for Turkey. The EU candidature has contributed to the economic performance of the country in the last couple of years. However, the differences in terms of economic development are huge between some regions of Turkey. It is not easy for the Turkish case to overcome the disparities of economic developments among the regions within the country after EU membership. The most underdeveloped part of the country is the south east and the economic development of this region along with the ethnic issue will continue to have impact on Turkish foreign policy in general, the Middle East and Iraq policy in particular.

The economic conditions of Turkey prior to the invasion of Iraq were not stable after the crisis in 2001 and the possible negative effects of the invasion and the economic compensation constituted an important part of the negotiations between Turkey and the US. Although the American side did not openly establish a link between US support of the IMF-backed program of Turkey and Turkey's permission for US soldiers to Iraq, during the negotiations they told the Turkish side that they were closely following the developments in the IMF backed economic program.[6] The Turkish side was fully aware of the implications of this sentence.

The impact of the EU membership in overcoming colonial experiences has had different results for several countries. For example, Commonwealth relations are becoming increasingly less important in comparison with the EU relations for Britain; whereas the EU has provided a crucial mechanism for Spain and Portugal to help them overcome the tragic legacy of their colonial experiences.[7] With some reservations, I argue that the possible membership may help Turkey overcome Sevres syndrome and the continuous retreat or defensive psychology arising from the last years of the Ottoman Empire.

Although Turkey fought its independence war against the Western countries, the new republic accelerated the westernization reforms. Beside this psychology, the general mistrust towards the Europeans at the elite and societal levels may begin to disappear since Turkey's possible membership will be interpreted by many people as confirmation of Turkey's European identity. However, there are also differences between Turkey and the examples like Spain, Portugal and Britain. Different from these examples, Turkey's imperial past (Ottoman past) is related to its geographical vicinity, not in overseas. In relation to this geographical contiguity, the population within the borders of the country has strong imprints from the Ottoman past. Despite the great changes at the composition of the population within the country during and after World War I and the Independence War, the diversity of the population from the point of ethnic background remains as a fact. The continuing relations between

---

5　Ibid. p. 248.

6　Ahmet Davutoğlu, interview by author, Istanbul, 28 May 2006.

7　Manners and Whitman, "Conclusion," p. 247.

local populations with their "relatives" in the vicinity of Turkey make it less likely to forget the imperial past as the developments in the first years of the post-Cold War era proved.

In the case of Spain, the Europeanization of foreign policy also contributed to overcoming the negative aspects of a past related to Spain's relations with the US. Especially, during the time of Franco, Spain's relations with the US were very important and the US had a determining effect on the policies of Spain. Europeanization was seen as an alternative to a dependent relationship with the US.[8] Given a similar kind of relationship with US there might be some clues for the Turkish case. After Turkey's participation in the Korean War on the side of the Western World and Turkey's membership in NATO after the war, the relations with the US were the cornerstone of Turkish foreign policy during the Cold War period. When Turkey's relations with Europe strained because of the coups and human rights violations, the US was the main source of relief. The agreements related to the use of the airbases in Turkey were renewed after the 1980 coup and later several other times. This special relationship continued after the Cold War period when Turkey emerged as a secure island in an environment with full of conflicts.

On several occasions, the interests of Turkey and the US coincided and the general expectation of the international community prior to the invasion of Iraq was that Turkey could not resist the demands of its most important ally. Although Turkish figures also accept the similarities between Spain and Turkey in terms of historical background and special relationships with the US, the EU or Europeanization are not seen by them as an alternative in this respect.[9] However, it is accepted by the same people that increasing relations with the EU strengthen Turkey's position in some cases in bargaining with the US.

*Foreign Policy Change through Socialization*

The socialization of foreign policy makers is the other aspect of foreign policy change. The idea here is to what extent EU membership can shape the thinking of the policy makers. Institutions of the CFSP like the Security Committee of ambassadors or the Military Committee or the meetings among the ministers in the Council create the opportunity for the member countries to have close contacts with other states and to understand their thinking and positions. As mentioned in the previous chapters, participation in foreign policy is different from legal integration and it creates continuous and intensifying interaction. It is argued that the socialization of foreign policy makers emerges around three concepts: common reflexes, norms of behaviour and thinking and identity.[10] Although Turkey is not a member yet, we can see that there have been some contacts between the Turkish officials and their European counterparts within the framework of the Troika meetings and summit diplomacy. In the regular summits and unofficial meetings of the foreign ministers in each term of presidency, the leaders and ministers of the countries have come together regularly

---

8    Barbe, "Spain," p. 119.
9    Davutoğlu, interview by author, Istanbul, 28 May 2006.
10   Manners and Whitman, "Conclusion," pp. 249–50.

to discuss common problems. These kinds of gatherings contribute to increasing socialization among the decision makers.

In relation to these contacts, the contacts between bureaucrats of Turkey beyond the military and the ministry of Foreign Affairs contributed to the socialization of decision makers around the concepts of common reflexes and norms of behaviour and thinking. Along with the rise of low politics issues in security perceptions like organized crime, illegal migration and human trafficking, NGOs also contributed to the policy making. The transnational nature of these threats led to involvement of bureaucrats of different countries and also representatives of NGOs multilateral cooperative schemes. Consequently, officials form state agencies became more and more exposed to the culture of their counterparts in other countries as well as NGOs.[11]

As a candidate country, Turkey also attends the summits and the decision makers have increased their contacts with their counterparts. These summits and troika meetings serve as a mechanism in harmonization of Turkish foreign policy with that of the EU. For example, in the case of Iran's nuclear program, troika meetings between Turkey and the EU have contributed to the harmonization of policies.[12] However, we should also point out that, since Turkey has not been able to participate directly in the formation of a policy as a candidate country, harmonization very much depends on the nature of the issue. If the policies of the EU and Turkey are close to each other, then there is more likelihood of harmonization and the support of Turkey the decisions of the EU, like supporting a common position of the EU on a given issue. The process here is as follows: the EU agrees on a common position, and then the Union asks Turkey for its opinion. Since these positions are on general terms not on details, it is not difficult for Turkey to support these positions. However, Turkey supports these positions if it is in conformity with the national interests; it means Turkey acts selectively as many European countries do, like Britain and Greece. The common positions on Iran's nuclear program and Turkey's support for these are given as the latest examples.[13]

On this issue of common policy in harmony with the EU, Ambassador Oğuz Demiralp argues that as a candidate country, Turkey attaches great importance to conducting a foreign policy that is compatible with its membership prospects and supports his arguments by the 2003 Progress Report of the Commission on Turkey, which says: "Turkey has continued to position its foreign and security policy in line with that of the European Union and it has played a constructive role within the framework of the CFSP."[14] The same report also notes that Turkey has associated itself as a candidate country with the EU common positions, sanctions and restrictive measures and declarations. According to the results of a study conducted by the Turkish Foreign Ministry, Turkey aligned itself with 87 percent of the EU statements, draft conclusions and declarations during the first half of 2003.[15] The harmonization

---

11 Kirişçi, "Turkey's Foreign Policy in Turbulent Times," p. 32.

12 Davutoğlu, interview by author, Istanbul, 28 May 2006.

13 Ambassador Oğuz Çelikkol, Turkey's Special Representative for Iraq, interview by author, Ankara, 22 May 2006.

14 Demiralp, p. 15.

15 Ibid.

of Turkish foreign policy with the EU in terms of the common positions and joint actions is increasing as the accession process continues. According to the progress report of 2006 for Turkey, the harmonization of Turkey with the EU in terms of foreign and security policy is around 96 percent. The report mentions Turkey's participation in the UN, NATO and EU-led operations and the harmonization in the policies towards Syria, Lebanon, Iraq, Iran and Afghanistan are given as positive developments.[16] Turkish officials report that the EU asks the Turkish opinion on several international issues like Iran, Iraq and the Middle East and the level of harmonization is a success. The divergences between Turkey and the EU are related mainly to the issues of Cyprus and Armenia. The same officials also stress that the differences between Turkey and the EU on some issues are natural since Turkey is not a member yet and even the members can not agree on every issue.[17] The report also stresses that in terms of administrative capacity, the organization of the Ministry of Foreign Affairs of Turkey is compatible with the EU CFSP structures.[18]

In another example related to the Palestinian issue, during the invitation of the Hamas members to Turkey, there were calls from the EU to Turkish governments that as a candidate country, Turkey should pursue a harmonized policy with the EU. In response to these calls, Turkish authorities argued that there was not enough consultation on the side of the EU with Turkey before framing a policy towards Hamas after the victory of Hamas in the elections and the developments in Palestine important for Turkey. Later on, officials of the Commission, which shares the right to initiative with the member states, started to consult with the Turkish officials in framing a policy on Iran and Palestine.[19] It is reported by the Turkish officials that the EU asks the opinion of Turkey generally after reaching a conclusion but before issuing it and that Turkey generally participates and supports these common positions, since these are generally vague without details.[20] Although Turkey tries to harmonize its policy along with that of the EU's, sometimes it acts selectively, like many of its European counterparts since there are some points of difference.

Manners and Whitman argue that the socialization process of foreign policy formation is less pronounced in big countries like Germany, France and Britain which have extended agendas of foreign policy.[21] The socialization is more noticeable in smaller states like Portugal, Netherlands, Finland, Sweden, Denmark and Ireland. Turkey is a big country in comparison with the countries above and there is an extensive agenda of foreign policy with several dimensions. Here the size of the country and the extensive agenda makes the Turkish case similar that of the big members of the EU. However, we should not forget that Turkey is a candidate yet, not a member, and therefore open to pressures for more Europeanization.

---

16  *Radikal*, 13 Kasım 2006.

17  Ibid.

18  http://www.deltur.cec.eu.int/_webpub/documents/TR2006ProgressReport.doc [13 November 2006].

19  Davutoğlu, interview by author, Istanbul, 28 May 2006.

20  Çelikkol, interview by author, Ankara, 22 May 2006.

21  Manners and Whitman, "Conclusion," p. 251.

**The Foreign Policy Process**

In analyzing the Europeanization of the foreign policy process, the domestic factors of the foreign policy process and the bureaucratic factors in the policy process are important issues. The second part of the framework of Manners and Whitman deals with the foreign policy process by looking at different aspects of it.

*Domestic Factors in the Foreign Policy Process*

Manners and Whitman pay attention to five elements in analyzing domestic factors: constitutional design, the role of sub-national units, the relationship between governments and parties, the role of interest groups and the breakdown of domestic-foreign distinction.[22]

The constitutional design has an important role in determining the role of the actors and the position of the parliamentary oversight in foreign policy process. The role of the other actors, in the Turkish case the NSC, also is defined by the constitution. As mentioned in the pages above, the constitutional and legal changes along with the reform packages to meet the Copenhagen criteria, the nature of the state system, parliamentary or presidential or semi-presidential, are also important in defining the leading actors. Along with most of the European examples, in parliamentary systems the responsibility for foreign policy belongs to the government. Here the roles of the Prime Minister and Foreign Minister are decisive. The nature of the government, one party or coalition, also greatly affects the functioning of the foreign policy and the role of the actors. With the changes mentioned in the chapter on the historical background of Turkish foreign policy and the decision making process, the composition and mandate of the NSC are re-arranged in a way to increase the role of the civilians. Beside this, the changes in the bureaucratic structure of the General Secretariat of the NSC and appointment of an ambassador to this position are milestones in the direction of Europeanization. Although the role of the President is generally symbolic in the parliamentary systems, Turkey's 1982 constitution strengthened the position of the President. The role of the powers of the President became obvious during weak governments, like during the Akbulut government, and also during coalition governments. Especially in times of coalition governments, the role of the President and his constitutional rights, and his position as the head of the NSC legitimized a high profile for the President in foreign policy.

In coalition governments, when the Prime Minister and Foreign Minister are from different parties, there might be some problems, despite the arguments for the consensual nature of European politics. During the latest coalition government of the Democratic Left Party, Nationalist Action Party and Motherland Party, although the Prime Minister and Foreign Minister are from the same party and there are not big differences among them, the differences among the parties regarding the European agenda and Europeanization have been the main source of break down of coalition.

Since Turkey is a unitary state, the responsibility for the foreign policy lies on the government and the local administrations do not have any say on this issue, unlike

---

22  Ibid., p. 252.

the cases of federal states. Another element in analyzing the impact of domestic politics is the role of the political parties. The research on Europeanization shows that the preferences of the party in government shaping the foreign policy appears decreasing relevance and the parties across the EU similar views on foreign policy as a result of three factors:[23] First, the increasing acceptance of neo-liberal principles after the 1970s minimized the differences between parties. Second, the collapse of the communist bloc led to a crisis in socialist alternative. Third, participation in the EU decision making procedures appears to have changed the views and expectations of the political parties on foreign policy issues. The first two of these arguments also are true mostly for Turkey, since most of the mainstream parties have similar views on foreign policy priorities of the country. Since Turkey can not participate in the decision making process of the CFSP discussions, the impact of this element is limited for Turkey as a candidate country. As I mentioned in the beginning of this chapter, Europeanization through socialization is limited for the candidate countries. The formal and informal contacts between Turkish officials during and after the EU decision making procedures contribute to the approximation of the views.

The roles of interest groups also have been increasing in the foreign policy making process. Several economic and non-economic interest groups can be included in this category. Employers groups, trade unions and think tanks that have connections with these institutions and also ethnic communities have their views on foreign policy. Even the Catholic Church in Italy and the Orthodox Church in Greece are mentioned as religious institutions that have powerful influence in this respect.[24] In Turkey the biggest employers group, TÜSİAD, has a foreign policy forum, makes its views on foreign policy public, and also works in relation with the universities in this respect.[25] MÜSİAD (Association of Independent Businessmen and Industrialists), which has more conservative roots in comparison to TÜSİAD; also publicizes its views not only on economic policy, but also on foreign policy through publications. Another economic organization TOBB, which represents the small business community, established a think tank, EPRI (Economic Policies Research Institute), and publishes reports on foreign policy issues. TESEV (Turkish Economic and Social Studies Foundation), the best known think tank of Turkey, also has a special branch for foreign policy and strongly supports the European agenda and describes one of aims of its foreign policy program as to "contribute to the harmonization of Turkey with the European Union."[26] Contrary to the views expressed on the side of Europeanization, ASAM[27] (Eurasia Strategic Research Centre) questions the changes in foreign policy in relation with the European agenda on the issues like Cyprus and Iraq. There also other new NGOs like TASAM (Turk-Asia Strategic Research Centre), SETA[28] (Foundation for Political, Economic and

---

23  Ibid., p. 255.
24  Ibid., p. 256.
25  http://www.dispolitikaforumu.com [20 July 2006].
26  http://www.tesev.org.tr/etkinlik/dis_politika.php [20 July 2006].
27  http://www.asam.org.tr/tr/index.asp [12 December 2006].
28  http://www.setav.org [12 December 2006].

Social Researches), and USAK[29] (International Strategic Research Institution) that also work on the foreign policy issues of Turkey and publicize their views.

The existence of think tanks is a new phenomenon for Turkey and the role and functions of these institutions are increasing. Although some of these institutions have proved their viability, time is needed for think tanks to mature in Turkey. The post-Cold War era and the EU candidature have provided fertile ground for the activities of these institutions. However, the criticisms of the Chief of Staff about one of the publications of TESEV and the discussions in the public opinion afterwards has signalled that the bureaucratic structures in Turkey do not welcome some of the work of the think tanks and do not want to include the ideas of these kinds of institutions in their policy making. This fact is true for domestic politics, but it is also partly true for foreign policy.

People from different ethnic groups also want to have their say in foreign policy, especially in terms of the fates of their relatives in the neighbouring countries of Turkey. This is especially true in relation to the developments in the Balkans and the Caucasus. Beside the ethnic linkages, religious affinities also have led to demonstrations on the developments in Iraq and Palestine in the past few years. For example, the Saadet Partisi (Felicity Party) organized meetings in different cities of Turkey to protest the policies of Israel during July 2006 and had an impact on the policy of the government given its popular base. The opposition of the public to US policies towards Iraq before and after the invasion also have played their part in the formation of policy. Although there was not a consensus in public opinion about the US policies towards Iraq before the invasion, the majority of the public was against the invasion and transfer of the US soldiers via Turkish territory. There were demonstrations just a few days before the motion in different cities around the country.[30] The strong opposition from several segments of society towards the transfer of the US soldiers to Iraqi territory affected the votes of the MPs and the decision of the AKP not to a have binding party policy on the vote on March 1, 2003.

The last element determining the relationship between domestic politics and foreign policy is the breakdown of distinction between domestic and foreign issues. With the Europeanization of most areas of economic and politics, the domestic-foreign border have become less clear-cut and formerly national spheres have become area of the EU domain. However, it is accepted by Manners and Whitman that the last three elements of adaptation in the domestic process are not related only to EU membership. The general trend of globalization has also impacts on these changes; it is not easy determine the level of the EU effect here. The EU agenda after the declaration of Turkey's candidature provided a new venue for the changes in this respect, especially in terms of the increasing role of the NGOs.

*Bureaucratic Factors in the Foreign Policy Process*

The other sub-title of the policy process of Whitman and Manners is the role of bureaucratic politics. In order to analyze this role they try to address three major

29  http://www.usak.org.tr/home.asp [12 December 2006].
30  http://webarsiv.hurriyet.com.tr/2003/02/27/254366.asp [13 December 2006].

questions: the questions of autonomy and command, the relationship between the foreign ministry and other ministries, and the question of who is responsible for coordinating foreign policy, especially in the European context.[31] The issues of autonomy and command deal with the relationship of the bureaucracy to the president, prime minister, foreign minister and the degree of centralization or autonomy of this bureaucracy. The relationship between the top decision making level of ministers and the ministries responsible for the implementation of the decisions is crucial in determining the efficiency and flexibility of foreign policy issues. The structure and the quality of the personnel play an important role in the results of the decisions. The structure and the nature of the governments led to varying degrees of autonomy for the foreign ministries and permanent representations across Europe. The Netherlands, Denmark, Spain, Portugal, Greece and Germany are given as the examples with greatest autonomy for the ministries of foreign affairs, whereas the French and British cases are given as examples with the least amount of autonomy.[32] In the British and French cases there are other institutions dealing with the EU and answerable to the Prime Minister. But this does not mean that there is not any change in the structure of the ministries after the membership. Although there have been re-structuring in most of the countries after membership, the ministries of Spain and Greece had departments within the ministry dealing with the EU with greater autonomy.[33]

Keeping in mind the candidate status of Turkey in comparison with the examples above, I tried to ascertain the changes and adjustments in the Ministry of Foreign Affairs of Turkey. The officials of the Ministry of Foreign Affairs informed me that there have been no structural changes within the ministry after the candidature, but there has been an increasing adjustment in terms of minds and perceptions.[34] The establishment of *Avrupa Birliği Genel Sekreterligi* (General Secretariat for the European Union) (ABGS) in 2000 was very much related to the candidature of Turkey to the EU. According to the law on the ABGS, it is functioning under the Prime Ministry and should contribute to the harmonization efforts to prepare Turkey for full membership in the EU.[35] The same law stipulates that the coordination of external relations and the accession negotiations are conducted by the Ministry of Foreign Affairs and the ABGS should help this harmonization process.[36] But the role of this institution is related mainly with accession negotiations and the main responsibility for the harmonization of foreign policy with the EU still belongs to the Ministry.[37] Some problems of the ABGS in terms of personal resources and infrastructure facilities still need to be addressed.[38] We may expect a re-arrangement within the Ministry in case of the membership of Turkey or re-adjustment of the role of the ABGS after the membership.

---

31 Manners and Whitman, "Conclusion", p. 258.
32 Ibid., p. 259.
33 Ibid.
34 Sadık Arslan, Turkish Diplomat, interview by the author, Oxford, 16 February 2006.
35 http://www.abgs.gov.tr/en/Laws.htm [21 July 2006].
36 Ibid.
37 Çelikkol, interview by author, Ankara, 22 May 2006.
38 http://www.hurriyet.com.tr/gundem/4190985.asp?gid=48 [23 July 2006].

In terms of coordinating foreign policy, Manners and Whitman detect two forces at work: consolidating the EU policy coordinating mechanisms in the office of prime minister after the success of the British and French systems and the expansion of the external relations of several ministries as they conduct their own foreign policies with other states ministries through the EU's technical councils and the Commission.[39] When we look at the Turkish case from the first point of view, we see that despite the increasing activity of the Prime Minister, there has been no structural change here. Instead of an institutional coordination of foreign policy under the Prime Minister's office similar to the cases in Europe, there is coordination depending on individuals.[40] Here some members of the government, high level officials of the Ministry of Foreign Affairs and some advisors play crucial roles, but this is not coordination.

From the perspective of the expansion of external relations of other ministries, the case of Turkey is different from that of member countries. With the accession negotiations, the contacts of the ministries with the EU bodies increased, but this is different from relations between ministries of different countries. Although the increasing contacts of the ministries with the EU bodies will have their impact on the relations of these ministries, real Europeanization in this respect will occur after membership when the officials of the ministries attend the Council meetings with their counterparts.

## Foreign Policy Actions

The third part of the framework looks to the foreign policy actions of the members and deals with the question of in which way the participation of the members in the CFSP alters the behaviours of the states and whether this participation creates opportunities or constrictions for the members.[41] Here the actions of the members are defined in two groups: actions within the EU: constriction or opportunity; and actions without the EU: special relationships and special interests.[42]

*Actions within the EU*

Use of Europeanization for the modernization of foreign policy outlook is given as an example for Italy, Ireland, Spain, Portugal and Greece.[43] The EU also provides a leadership role for some countries, especially during the six months presidency, and increasing their economic and diplomatic weight, as in the cases of Spain and Britain. The examples of these increasing weights can be found in the important role given to the British and Spanish diplomats as special representatives like Javier Solana (High Representative for CFSP), Felipe Gonzales (EU special representative

---

39  Manners and Whitman, "Conclusion," p. 260.
40  Davutoğlu, interview by author, Istanbul, 28 May 2006.
41  Manners and Whitman, "Introduction," p. 10.
42  Manners and Whitman, "Conclusion," pp. 261–6.
43  Ibid., p. 262.

for Yugoslavia), Miguel Moratinos (special envoy for Middle East Peace Process), Peter Carrington and Lord Owen (special representative to Yugoslavia).[44]

In explaining whether the EU membership is seen as a constriction or as an opportunity for foreign policy, the pre-existing foreign policy orientations represent the base point for discussion. In considering the danger of the acceptance of these orientations as overly deterministic, Manners and Whitman argue that it is possible to talk about three patterns of membership impacts on foreign policy actions: extensive foreign relations, European foreign relations and international foreign relations.[45]

Extensive foreign relations refer to the counties which have extensive foreign relations outside the EU and this reality affects the foreign policy behaviour of this country and its relations with the EU members. Britain and France are given as the examples of this category and here the EU is seen as a constriction for national foreign policy. I believe that the EU membership for these countries requires them to change their focus from other countries more towards Europe and this can be defined as a re-arrangement of priorities instead of a constriction. The international nature of the CFSP generally allows the states to continue their existing foreign policy agendas. Although Turkey's foreign policy agenda might not be as extensive as these two examples, the historical legacy and the geopolitical position of the country require Turkey to have an extensive agenda. I believe that Turkey's possible membership will require an adjustment to the EU in the foreign policy agenda. However, the changes in the pre-existing agenda very much depend on the issue at stake and also the capabilities and power of the member state. This is also true for Turkey. Since Turkey might be open to some pressures as a candidate country to adjust its foreign policy, I believe that the issue at stake will be the determining factor in this respect. When asked whether the EU candidature has constrained Turkish foreign policy actions in the Middle East, the officials argue that this fact has not created constraints on the general attitude of Turkish foreign policy in the region since the agreement among the member states is on general terms and there are differences among them.[46] For this reason, Turkey has not faced problems with the EU in the Middle East policy in general terms.

The second pattern of the membership impact on foreign relations refers to the countries with less extensive foreign policy agenda. Here the member countries prefer to work with the EU. It also is argued that the EU presents an opportunity to hide difficult decisions or the absence of any preconceived policy.[47] Smaller states with limited capacity and states which historical reasons wish to enmesh themselves in European policy making. For example, Germany's criticism of Israel in relation to its policies in Palestine for historical reasons is difficult. However, such criticisms might be made more easily within the EU framework.[48]

This pattern of European foreign relations also functions as a balance between "Europeanist" or "Atlanticist" foreign policy trends. In countries like Spain, Italy,

---

44  Ibid.
45  Ibid., pp. 262–3.
46  Çelikkol, interview by author, Ankara, 22 May 2006.
47  Manners and Whitman, "Conclusion," p. 263.
48  Ibid.

and Greece and to certain degree Denmark "this pattern of foreign policy can be viewed as a solution to the tensions between pro-European (read "EU" or "anti US") and pro-American (read "NATO" or "anti EU") forces within these countries."[49] Here, this pattern acted as an opportunity for foreign policy action. Within the EU, several countries have special relations with the US beside the countries mentioned above. Turkish officials believe that Turkey's case is not different from that of other examples and US not only supports Turkish membership in the EU, but also supports membership of East European countries.[50]

As a candidate country, this pattern of Atlanticist-Europeanist also has some relevance to Turkey. Turkey has had strong relations with the US beginning with the Cold War. Although there have been fluctuations in this relationship because of some issues like the Johnson Letter and the arms embargo after the 1974 intervention in Cyprus, mutual needs have contributed to the continuation of this relation. The close relationship between Turkey and the US is a source of concern for some countries within the EU and there is the fear that Turkey would be a second Trojan horse of the US, after the UK. The developments prior to the invasion of Iraq nullified these arguments since Turkey blocked the transfer of US soldiers to Iraq via its territory, whereas most of the new members of the EU supported the policy of the US in Iraq. US open support for the start of accession negotiations with Turkey in December 2002 back fired and countries like France made their discomfort on this support public.

Similar to several pro-American countries in Europe, the "Atlanticist"-"Europeanist" divide can be tested in the Turkish case. In terms of Turkey's Middle East policy, especially towards the Palestinian-Israeli conflict, the foreign policy decision makers believe that Turkey's candidature and acting together with the EU support the arguments of Turkey against the policies of the US in the region, without requiring fundamental changes in the general pattern of the policy.[51]

The third pattern of foreign policy actions is international foreign relations referring to the policies implemented through other international organizations like the UN, NATO or the OSCE. This pattern is related to the Cold War experience of the country or its neutral background. The examples of this type of action are found in the cases of Austria, Finland and Sweden and to some extent Germany.[52] This type of action neither creates obstacles nor opportunities for the members, but functions as another forum for foreign policy. Turkey followed a neutral policy after the establishment of the republic until WWII and became a member of the western alliance after the threats of the USSR against its territorial integrity. During the Cold War, Turkey acted as a dedicated ally of NATO and its policy towards the Middle East is framed within this general western orientation. This orientation had its effects in the post-Cold War era and Turkey placed great importance on the role of NATO in international security since it is not a member to the EU yet. The security threats around its vicinity will lead Turkey to emphasize the role of NATO in the near future.

---

49  Ibid.

50  Çelikkol, interview by author, Ankara, 22 May 2006.

51  Davutoğlu, interview by author, Istanbul, 28 May 2006.

52  Manners and Whitman, "Conclusion," p. 264.

*Actions without the EU*

The last part deals with foreign policy actions which are kept separate from the EU context. The intergovernmental nature of Europe's foreign policy allows member states to share some aspects of foreign policy and retain some part of it and it is argued that tacit understandings exist among the member states as regards special interests.[53] The relations that member states retain are related to the national security of the states. The examples of special relations of Britain and France as members of the UN Security Council and Finland, Austria, Sweden and Ireland as post-neutral states are not valid for the case of Turkey. However, the national issues of Greece also are given as special relations and this has relevance for Turkey. As mentioned in the chapter on Europeanization, national issues related to security in the near environment are immune from Europeanization.[54] On several issues, instead of adapting itself to the European frameworks of EPC/CFSP, Greece tried to use these frameworks to satisfy its own foreign policy objectives. Here, it is argued by Stavridis that in case of Macedonia, Greece's foreign policy Europeanized and Greece moved to the general position of the EU members, whereas on the issue of Cyprus (including Turkey) Europe moved closer to Greece's position.[55] As the examples in the chapter on Europeanization suggest in regard to Britain and Spain along with Greece, countries judge the issues case by case and we see Europeanization on foreign policy in some policies and the continuation of former policies in some others.

Issues related to the national security in Turkey also have similarities with the Greek example and these issues can be immune from Europeanization. However, Turkey's candidate status makes this issue more complicated. Especially some of these national security issues create tensions with the EU members, as in the examples of the Cyprus and Aegean problems. Beside these, the policy towards northern Iraq might be analyzed in this respect. Turkey's policy towards Iraq and especially northern Iraq is very much influenced by the EU candidature. Turkey should always consider the policies of the influential members of the EU in particular and the general attitude of the EU in general in its policy towards Iraq. For example, it will be very difficult for Turkey to oppose the policies of Germany during the process of integration. The official figures in Turkish foreign policy accept that similar to the case of Greece, the impact of Europeanization is limited on crucial national security interests, but they also admit that there have not been serious developments to test this argument.[56] In the past few years, Turkish national interests have been in conformity with the general attitude of the EU in several crisis situations.[57] We can say that if Turkey's national interest is neutral on an issue, it is easy for Turkey to harmonize with the EU. However, in the case of conflict of national interests with the EU, Turkey would pursue its own agenda.

---

53  Ibid., p. 266.
54  Kavakas, p. 159.
55  Stavridis, p. 21.
56  Davutoğlu, interview by author, Istanbul, 28 May 2006.
57  Ibid.

**Other Schemes of Europeanization and Turkish Foreign Policy**

Similar to the scheme of Manners and Whitman, the framework developed by Michael Smith analyzes how participation in the CFSP feeds back into EU member states. The main factors in Smith's analysis are: Elite socialization, bureaucratic reorganization, constitutional change and increase in the support for common policy.[58] From these factors, similar to the Manners and Whitman's socialization argument, we may conclude that elite socialization is limited for the Turkish case, since the participation of the Turkish officials in EU institutions that are deciding on common policies are limited in comparison with the member countries. Bureaucratic adaptation also is partially applicable since the changes in Turkey as a candidate country are not extensive as in the cases of members. From the point of constitutional changes, we can say that the impact of Europeanization is easy to detect here, since there are several constitutional and legal changes carried out in Turkey which have consequences for making and implementing foreign policy. From the point of increasing public awareness, the case of Turkey is similar to other examples since the awareness of the Turkish public on the issues of foreign policy in the post-Cold War period increased, especially with the developments in the Balkans.

Christopher Hill's analysis of the issue looks to the factors below: state's attitudes towards the CFSP, impact of the socialization effect, shifts in public and elites' opinion, states' attitudes towards countries other than the EU members and institutions other than the EU that complicate their participation in the CFSP, effects on the state of convergence between economic relations and the CFSP, administrative and domestic political factors that strain the cooperation with the EU members, states' response to the increasing importance of security issues within the CFSP, and states' views on the institutional changes regarding the CFSP; responsibility handling, especially that linked to the Presidency.[59]

Among these factors, as mentioned before, the socialization effect is limited in the Turkish case. Shifts in the public and elite's opinions are issues that have to be examined. The Turkish public and elite were very supportive of common actions in the Balkans similar to the Europeans. However, in cases where Turkish concerns are not shared by the Europeans, like the case of northern Iraq, I think the shifts towards convergence between European and Turkish public opinions are in danger. The administrative and domestic factors are not so much important after the changes to meet the accession negotiations criteria. The point of increasing importance of the security issues within the CFSP is not a serious problem for Turkey given Turkish participation in several international missions after the Cold War and the arguments that Turkey's contribution will be on security issues. The other aspects of this definition are related mostly to member countries and have a limited effect on Turkish foreign policy.

The approach of Featherstone and Kazamias to Europeanization gives six dimensions for a good analysis of Europeanization: institutional adaptation within government, transformation in the structural power of domestic actors, adjustment

---

58  Smith, "Conforming to Europe," p. 614.
59  Hill, "Preface," pp. xi–xii.

of domestic macroeconomic regime, new dynamic with the domestic party system, and pressure to redefine the national identity and a strategic tool in the pursuit of foreign policy interest.[60] Some aspects of this approach are applicable to Turkey. In terms of institutional adaptation within the government, there has been limited change yet. But there has been a structural transformation of domestic actors in terms of the foreign policy decision making process with the changes in the composition and mandate of the NSC and the NSC General Secretariat. The pressure for the redefinition of national identity is also valid for the Turkish case. After the EU candidature and reforms to meet the accession criteria, there has been a debate within Turkey about national identity and in relation to this, national interest. Ethnic and religious backgrounds and their expression, the citizenship and their reflections on the national interest to be pursued by the state are among the controversial topics of discussion in the society.

Using Europeanization as a strategic tool for pursuing foreign policy interest is not applicable for Turkey. This issue is valid for the members and especially for Cyprus and Greece. Although all of the members try to influence the agenda of European foreign policy, these two states represent the peak point in this respect. The case of Cyprus represents a good example here, since Cyprus's application for membership in the EU is not related to the aim of material benefits, but with the materialization of foreign policy objectives. Brian White's framework of analysis[61] contributed to the discussions in terms of the identity in foreign policy along with the arguments of Delanty and Rumford.[62] These two approaches tried to contribute to the discussions by bringing fresh ideas of critical theory and post-modernist approaches to the field.

**Europeanization in Candidate Countries**

Europeanization affects not only the member states but also candidates of the EU. However, there should be some adaptations in the framework developed for the member states. In the pages above, in applying the theoretical frameworks, I omitted some factors since they are not suitable for the analysis of Europeanization in candidate countries and Turkey. The two basic factors that make the candidate different from members are described as power asymmetry and conditionality. The asymmetric relationship between candidates and the EU provides the Union more routes to influence the candidates and pressures these countries to change and to adapt to Europe. Conditionality in the accession process requires the candidates to comply with the conditions.[63] Although the intergovernmental nature of the CFSP in the EU allows the member states' governments to pursue their own policies, it is difficult for the candidate countries because of the two factors mentioned above.

In considering the arguments mentioned here, some other scholars argue that the Europeanization effect is strong externally, until the accession of the states to the

---

60  Featherstone and Kazamias, pp. 15–16.
61  White, "The European Challenge to Foreign Policy Analysis," p. 39.
62  Delanty and Rumford, p. 2.
63  Grabbe, p. 303.

EU.[64] Here the policies of the Cyprus government can be a good example. Cyprus seemed to pursue a peaceful settlement of the dispute in the island before the accession and Greece prevented any concrete demand from other countries for the solution of the problem before the accession with the threat to veto eastern enlargement. Since the legislation in the field of the CFSP is limited and the nature of the process is intergovernmental, the Europeanization of foreign policy is more valid for candidate countries. Once the countries are in, the intergovernmental nature allows them to press for their foreign policy objectives in regard to the candidate countries. The creation of formal accession conditions provides EU member states more leverage against the applicants to comply with the demands in comparison with the former applicants since the institutionalization of the EU increased with time.

The general attitude of the countries in terms of foreign policy and Europeanization of their foreign policy can be analyzed in two phases: before accession and after accession. Before accession, when these countries are candidates, they try to adjust their policies to the general policy of the EU members. Here, the actions of foreign policy of the countries can be analyzed under two subtitles: legal and diplomatic. After the accession process, the countries are unable to change the legal agreements they have made. But their attitudes in the diplomatic field may change. After the accession, they may drag their feet on several issues and bring their foreign policy objectives to the top of the agenda of the EU.

In terms of legal actions they have to solve their border problems and have good neighbourly relations. This is the part where the candidates really have to do something. The application of this condition to Turkey's candidacy is very much related to the problems with Greece in the Aegean Sea. When Turkey was declared a candidate country at the Helsinki Summit in 1999, it was urged to make every effort to resolve any outstanding border disputes. The Presidency Conclusions of this summit also decided that failing to solve these disputes within a reasonable time (until the end of 2004 in this case) would lead to the bringing the dispute to the International Court of Justice.[65] In this respect, the officials of the Foreign Ministries of Turkey and Greece had preliminary talks for the bilateral solution of the problems. The content of these talks and the progress in the direction of the solution were kept secret. However, there is a general feeling that the positive developments made when the PASOK government was in power in Greece lost momentum with the New Democracy government in Greece.

During the accession period, on the diplomatic front, the candidates try to adjust their policies to the European policies and norms. Here the candidates generally promise not to do something, for example, refraining from attacking a neighbouring country. In this period, the candidates try to show that they are following peaceful relations with their neighbours and trying to solve the problems in a peaceful way, as can be seen in the attitude of the Greek Cypriots. Just before the accession to the membership in May 2004, the Greek Cypriots seemed to support the UN Plan

---

64  Bulmer and Radaelli, p. 2.

65  Presidency Conclusions of Helsinki European Council, 10–11 December 1999, available [online]: http://www.consilium.europa.eu/ueDocs/cms_Data/docs/pressData/en/ec/ACFA4C.htm [26 July 2006].

(Annan) for a peaceful settlement of problem in Cyprus. However, when they felt secure in their membership, the Greek Cypriot leadership opposed the plan and the EU Commissioner of enlargement Gunter Verheugen declared that he had been deceived and the attitude of the Cypriot administration was just opposite of its former stance.[66] This attitude of the Greek Cypriots supports the argument that Europeanization in foreign policy is strong externally.

---

66 *Sabah*, 22 April, 2004.

# Conclusion

In this conclusion, I will summarize findings in relation to the theoretical discussions about the changes in the foreign policies of the countries after the EU candidature and membership and the place of Turkey within this picture. Later on I will touch upon the similarities between Turkey and the EU towards the Middle East and the possible points of convergence and divergence in the foreign policy towards the region.

From the point of foreign policy change through candidature, resistance may dominate the adaptation dimension. We may say that the different cultural background and geographical environment, similar to the case of Greece, is an important factor for Turkey. The turbulent environment of the country, the role of the military which is legitimate in the eyes of many Turks given the terrorist threat and because of the traditional security culture, high military expenditures might be some reasons of resistance to the Europeanization of foreign policy and constitute a setback in the harmonization of Turkish foreign policy with the EU.

Overcoming the negative impacts of the coups in the Turkish political culture and limiting the role of the military in relation to the foreign policy with the EU candidature will not be easy. Although the reforms to meet the Copenhagen Criteria introduced some positive changes after 1999, it will take some time to reach the European standards given the terrorist threat and the current security culture and resistance of the military. This cultural difference and the legitimacy of the role of the military in the formation of policy may cause some hindrances in the process of harmonization.

Economic factors also should be considered in the analysis of the impact of the EU and harmonization of the foreign policy of Turkey with the EU. The EU candidature is affecting the Turkish economy positively and the stabilization of the economy strengthens Turkey's foreign policy priorities. However, the developments have proved that Turkey could pursue its objectives even during economically weak conditions, as in the case before the invasion of Iraq. Contrary to the strengthening of the former positions, economic stabilization as a result of EU candidature may lead to the moderation of foreign policy objectives. In the Turkish case, the business community, which has close connections with the European business circles, has advocate a more dovish position on several foreign policy issues like that of Cyprus and Iraq. Instead of security driven policies, the EU mentality prioritizes economics based options in the foreign policy of the country. Increasing economic interdependency with neighbours and with other countries also leads to moderation in the foreign policy of the country. In comparison with the 1990s, people do not stress the negative side of the relations with the Middle Eastern countries, but focus on the positive sides and stress the importance of economic relations with the Middle

Eastern neighbours. This development supports dovish policies and interdependence between Turkey and its Middle Eastern neighbours.

It is too early to evaluate the impact of the EU candidature on the foreign policy in terms of overcoming the negative aspects of the historical legacy. The relationship of the Turkish foreign policy elite and that of the common people with Europe has several dimensions. Despite the modernization attempts beginning from late Ottoman times to adopt the western standards, "Sevres Syndrome" has made an imprint in the minds of the elite and also the common people. Turkey's European identity is crucial for the elites of the country. Although the official candidature of Turkey to the Union is interpreted by several people in Turkey and in Europe as the confirmation of the European identity of Turkey, arguments questioning the eligibility of Turkey for EU membership because of cultural characteristics and special conditions have created some question marks in the minds of Turkish people about the future of this process. The reform process to meet the Copenhagen Criteria also have led to the emergence of nationalist coalitions of left and right and also the re-emergence of "Sevres Syndrome". Consequently, the impact of the EU on the overcoming the negative aspects of the historical legacy very much depends on the discourses of the Europeans and possible membership of the country. If Turkey becomes a member, then the "Sevres Syndrome" might be overcome.

The EU candidature and membership are seen in some European countries as alternatives to the dependent relations with the US. During the Cold War period the dominance of the security concerns legitimized special relations with the US for several countries. Turkey's special relations with the US developed in the post-Cold War period. The policies of Turkey and the US in the Middle East were in line with each other despite some differences in the priorities especially in relation to Iraq. The differences between Turkey and the US surfaced before the invasion of Iraq. I believe that EU candidature affected the decision of the country to not allow the transfer of US soldiers to Iraq and the policies of Turkey towards the Middle East afterwards. Just a couple of months before the invasion of Iraq, Turkey ended the emergency rule in the south-eastern parts of the country in relation to the reforms to meet the Copenhagen Criteria. The transfer of 62,000 US troops would require extra measures and the re-imposition of emergency rule in the south-east of the country, which was conflicting with the EU agenda of the country. And in order to continue with the process of democratization, Turkey needed to avoid war. There were demands on the side of the military to re-impose emergency rule in case of the transfer of those US soldiers. This factor was taken into consideration by the government during the negotiations with the US and the preparations for the motion.

The reforms that were carried out to meet the Copenhagen Criteria and the impact of the EU candidature in the democratization are obvious. The impact of democratization on Turkish foreign policy can be seen from the new attitude of Turkey in the current developments in Cyprus, Iraq and Palestine. Public opinion and NGOs have played an increasing role in the decisions. We see the increasing impact of public opinion on the foreign policy in the cases of Iraq and Palestine. The refusal of transfer of US soldiers to northern Iraq in the Grand National Assembly was to a certain degree related to the impact of public opinion. The issue of the transfer of US soldiers caused fierce domestic polemics in Turkey. Allowing the transfer of US soldiers via Turkish territory to attack Iraq would have been a big handicap for a country on the road to the European Union with a government which was claiming to introduce a new foreign policy to Turkey. The Turkish public was opposing to such an action and the government did not press hard for the acceptance of the motion. There was a general belief that the Turkish state would cooperate with the US, especially given the special relationship between the Turkish military and the US official circles. But these expectations did not come true with the decision of the Turkish Parliament on 1 March 2003.

A similar impact of democratization also can be seen in the change on the policy of Israeli-Palestinian conflict. The sensitivities of the public are much more reflected on the policies of the Ecevit (1999–2002) and Erdoğan (2003– ) governments on their policies towards this issue. Despite the negative memories towards Arabs because of the developments during World War I, the Turkish public is very sensitive to the sufferings of the Palestinian people. During the 1990s when the security concerns of Turkey were high and Turkey was not a candidate for the EU, the governments and makers of foreign policy were able to ignore the criticisms of the public in its relations with Israel. The security concerns and the influential role of the military bureaucracy in the relations with Israel played the crucial role here and Turkey developed its relations with Israel despite the negative developments in the peace process and the deterioration of the situation in Palestine. The democratization process with the EU and the decline of security threats led to the diminishing the role of the military and this led to a change in the policy of Turkey in the Palestinian-Israeli problem.

The socialization of foreign policy makers is the other aspect of the foreign policy change. The idea here is to what extent EU membership can shape the thinking of the policy makers. Although Turkey is not a member yet, there are some contacts between the Turkish officials and their European counterparts within the framework of troika meetings and summit diplomacy. These kinds of gatherings contribute to increasing socialization among the decision makers. These summits and troika meetings serve as mechanisms in the harmonization of Turkish foreign policy with that of the EU by affecting the minds of policy makers reciprocally. For example, in the case of Iran's nuclear program, troika meetings between Turkey and the EU contributed to the harmonization of policies. However, we should also point out that since Turkey could not participate directly in the formation of a policy at the EU level as a candidate country, harmonization very much depends on the nature of the issue. If the policies of the EU and Turkey are close to each other, then there is greater likelihood of the harmonization and support of Turkey for the decisions of the EU, like supporting a common position of the EU on a given issue.

In another example related to the Palestinian issue, during the invitation of Hamas members to Turkey, there were calls from the EU to Turkish governments that as a candidate country, Turkey should pursue a harmonized policy with the EU. In response to these calls, the Turkish authorities argued that there was not enough consultation on the side of the EU with Turkey before framing a policy towards Hamas after the victory of Hamas in the elections and the developments in Palestine important for Turkey. These two cases show that, although Turkey tries to harmonize its policy along with that of the EU's, sometimes it acts selectively, like many of its European counterparts, since there are some points of differences among the countries.

The changes in the domestic factors and bureaucratic factors of the foreign policy process in the harmonization of foreign policies of Turkey and the EU is also analyzed in the book. The constitutional design, the relationship between the government and the parties and the role of the interest groups are analyzed in order to understand the changes after the EU candidature.

In parliamentary systems the responsibility for foreign policy belongs to the government. Here the roles of the Prime Minister and Foreign Minister are decisive. However, there are also other actors that are influential in the making of foreign policy, for example, the President and the NSC in the case of Turkey. The composition and mandate of the NSC were re-arranged in a way to increase the role of civilians. From the point of constitutional design, the changes in the composition and mandate of the NSC as a result of the EU reform agenda have their impacts on the harmonization process. The role of the president as the head of the NSC is important and becomes crucial especially in times of crisis situations and coalition governments. The differences among the parties of the coalition on the EU agenda led to the break up of the latest coalition government in Turkey. Although the EU agenda is supported by every actor of this process, there are differences between the government and the president and the military wing of the NSC in relation to some foreign policy areas like Cyprus and Iraq. The government takes the views of other actors in relation to foreign policy but the changes in the composition and mandate of the NSC and the re-structuring the Secretariat of the NSC's increased the power of the government.

The roles of the interest groups and the changes in this respect are other points of analysis in the evaluation of the impact of the EU candidature on foreign policy. The EU candidature and membership have positively affected the roles of the NGOs in the foreign policy making process in several countries. In Turkey different interest groups have wanted to have their say in foreign policy either by their publications and activities, or by the think tanks they have established. I gave some examples of the think tanks in the chapter on the Europeanization of Turkish foreign policy. The existence of think tanks is a new phenomenon for Turkey and the role and functions of these institutions are increasing. Although some of these institutions proved their maturity, there is still long way to go for the think tanks in Turkey. The post-Cold War era and the EU candidature have provided fertile ground for the activities of these institutions. However, the criticisms of the Chief of Staff about one of the publications of TESEV and the discussions in the public opinion afterwards signal that the bureaucratic structures in Turkey are not welcoming some of the work of the think tanks and do not want to include the ideas of these kinds of institutions in their policy making. This fact is true for domestic politics, but it is also partly true for foreign policy. Also the contacts and flow of information between the Ministry of Foreign Affairs and the academics and institutions working on foreign policy are not strong enough or systematic. With the help of EU candidature, the think tanks in Turkey are working with the Ministry on some projects and regularly following developments in the EU integration process. The EU agenda has led to the establishment of separate sections for foreign policy in some think tanks like in TESEV and EPRI and has enabled several groups to publicize their views.

The role and functioning of the bureaucratic structures is another important point in the analysis of the impact of the EU candidature on Turkish foreign policy and the harmonization of the policy with the EU foreign policy. The questions of command and control, the relations between the Ministry of Foreign Affairs and other ministries and the issue of the coordination of foreign policy are three important points in the analysis. There are different examples in several European countries in terms of the autonomy of the Ministry of Foreign Affairs and re-structuring the ministries after the EU candidature and membership. In the case of Turkey, there has been no structural change within the ministry since the candidature of the country, but there has been an increasing adjustment in terms of minds and perceptions. The role of the ABGS has been limited with the accession negotiations and the main responsibility for the harmonization of foreign policy with the EU still belongs to the MFA.

Similar to the changes in the cases of Britain and France, there has been increasing activity on the part of the Prime Minister and the Office of the Prime Minister in Turkey in terms of coordinating the foreign policy. However, in the Turkish case, despite the increasing activity of the Prime Minister and its office, there has been no structural change. Instead of an institutional coordination of foreign policy under the Prime Minister's office similar to the cases in Europe, there has been coordination depending on individuals. Any change of individuals in this office, may result in the end of this reality.

The changes in the foreign policies of the members and the candidates with the effect of the EU can be analyzed under two headings: actions within the EU and actions without the EU. In the first case, the question is whether the EU has created opportunities or constrictions for the countries. The second case deals with the special interests of the countries and their special relations with some other states and institutions despite the EU membership.

In explaining whether EU membership is seen as a constriction or as an opportunity for foreign policy, the pre-existing foreign policy orientations represent the base point for discussion. Three patterns of membership impacts on foreign policy actions are discussed in the chapter on Europeanization: extensive foreign relations, European foreign relations and international foreign relations.

Extensive foreign relations refer to the countries which have extensive foreign relations outside the EU and here the EU is seen as a constriction for national foreign policy. I believe that EU membership for these countries requires them to change their focus from other countries more towards Europe and this can be defined as a re-arrangement of priorities instead of a constriction. Although Turkey's foreign policy agenda might not be as extensive as the examples of Britain and France, the historical legacy and the geopolitical position of the country require Turkey to have an extensive agenda in comparison to its economic power. I believe that Turkey's possible membership will require an adjustment to the EU in the foreign policy agenda. Since Turkey might be open to some pressures as a candidate country to adjust its foreign policy, I think that the issue at stake will be the determining factor in this respect. For example, the candidate status of Turkey and the pressures on the country from the EU have led to some change in the policy towards Iraq and Cyprus.

It can be said that the candidature has created some constrictions for Turkey in its policy towards Iraq, especially in terms of military operations. Also there have been several calls from Europe for Turkey to improve relations with Armenia.

In terms of the actions within the EU, the term European foreign relations is given as an opportunity for countries to hide difficult decisions and to balance the "Europeanist-Atlanticist" divide. It is a fact that some countries on the European continent have special relations with the US. The Cold War realities strengthened these relations and some of these relations continued after the EU membership of these countries. Turkey is generally accepted as a country which has close relations with the US and this relationship is a source of concern for some countries within the EU. There is the fear that Turkey will turnout to be the second Trojan horse of the US within the EU. The developments prior to the invasion of Iraq nullified these arguments when Turkey blocked the transfer of the US soldiers via its territory to Iraq, whereas most of the new members of the EU supported the policy of the US in Iraq. Also the open support of the US for the start of accession negotiations with Turkey in December 2002 back fired and countries like France made their discomfort public on this issue.

Similar to several pro-American countries in Europe, the "Atlanticist"-"Europeanist" divide can be tested in the Turkish case. In terms of Turkey's Middle East policy, especially towards the Palestinian-Israeli conflict, the foreign policy decision makers believe that Turkey's candidature and acting together with the EU support the arguments of Turkey against the policies of the US in the region, without requiring fundamental changes in the general pattern of the policy. We can say that the Europeanization has created constraints for Turkey in its policy towards Iraq, whereas it has created some opportunities in its policy towards the Israeli-Palestinian conflict.

The intergovernmental nature of Europe's foreign policy allows member states to share some aspects of foreign policy and retain some part of it as their own. National issues related to security in the near environment are immune from Europeanization. This might be true for the case of Turkey. However, Turkey's candidate status makes this issue more complicated. Since Turkey strives to be a member, it is open to pressures from the current member states in some foreign policy issues like Cyprus and the Aegean. Turkey's policy towards Iraq and especially northern Iraq are very much influenced by the EU candidature. Turkey is forced to consider the policies of the influential members of the EU in particular and the general attitude of the EU in general in its policy towards Iraq. If Turkey's national interest is neutral on an issue; it is easy for Turkey to harmonize with the EU. However, in case of conflict of national interests with the EU, Turkey would most probably pursue its own agenda given the discussions related with the Cyprus issue and the negative attitude of the some member states against the membership of Turkey.

Shifts in the public and elite's opinion are issues that have to be examined in the analysis of the impact of the EU and the harmonization of foreign policies. The Turkish public and elite were very supportive of common actions in the Balkans similar to the Europeans. However, in cases where Turkish concerns are not shared by the Europeans, like the case of northern Iraq, I think the shifts towards convergence between European and Turkish public opinions are in danger. The decline for the support of the EU membership among the Turkish public opinion during 2005 and 2006 in comparison with the past is very much related to the developments related to Cyprus and Iraq. The international nature of the CFSP allows the nation states to pursue their own agenda and Turkey, as a candidate country, is open to pressures in these foreign policy areas. The sensitivities of the public on these foreign policy topics is one the important reasons for the decline of the support for the EU membership.

The pressure for the redefinition of national identity in relation to the EU candidature and membership is also valid for the Turkish case. The EU candidature leaves Turkey open to pressures from several countries on some foreign policy issues like Cyprus and northern Iraq, which are perceived as the cornerstones of the definitions of the national interests of Turkey in foreign policy. After EU candidature and reforms to meet the accession criteria, there is a debate within Turkey about national identity and, in relation to this, the national interest to be pursued in foreign policy. Ethnic and religious backgrounds and their expressions, the citizenship and their reflections on the national interest to be pursued by the state have been among the controversial topics of discussions in society. These discussions also have led to the questioning of the EU agenda by some segments of society who fear that the EU agenda is undermining the current national identity and foreign policy objectives in relation to this identity.

In the theoretical discussions about the impact of EU membership and candidature on the foreign policies of countries, two basic factors that make the candidates different from members are described as power asymmetry and conditionality. Although the intergovernmental nature of the CFSP in the EU allows member states' governments to pursue their own policies, this is difficult for the candidate countries because of the two factors mentioned above. Since the legislations in the field of CFSP are limited and the nature of the process is intergovernmental, the Europeanization of foreign policy is more obvious in the candidate countries. Instead of advising some kinds of legislative changes for candidates, current members try to apply pressure on the candidates in the area of foreign policy according to their own national interests. The intergovernmental nature of the CFSP allows them to press for their foreign policy objectives in relation to the candidate countries. The demands on the side of the some the EU members for Turkey in pursuing a more harmonized policy with them in the Middle East should be seen from this perspective.

The general attitude of the countries in terms of foreign policy and the Europeanization of their foreign policy can be analyzed in two phases: before accession and after accession. Before the accession, when these countries are candidates, they try to adjust their policies towards the general policy of the EU members. Here, the actions of foreign policy of the countries can be analyzed under two subtitles: legal and diplomatic. After the accession process, the countries are unable to change the legal agreements they made during the accession process. But their attitude in the diplomatic field may change. After the accession, they may drag their feet on issues and bring their foreign policy objectives to the top of the agenda of the EU.

In terms of legal actions, the candidates are required to solve their border problems and have good neighbourly relations. This is the part that candidates have to really have done something. Turkey's cautious policies towards the developments in northern Iraq have been influenced by this reality. Although Turkey's non-intervention into northern Iraq is mostly the result of the opposition of the US and Kurdish groups, it is a fact that an interventionist policy would conflict with the general attitude of the EU and problems with a neighbour is a source of concern for the EU agenda of Turkey. Given the opposition to the membership of Turkey form some European countries, the relationship between candidature and the reasons for the cautious attitude of Turkey become easy to understand.

During the accession period, on the diplomatic front, the candidate countries try to adjust their policies to the European policies and norms. Here the candidates generally promise not to do something, for example, refraining form attacking a neighbouring country. In this period, the candidates try to show that they are following peaceful relations with their neighbours and trying to solve the problems in a peaceful way, as can be seen in the attitude of the Greek Cypriots.

Turkey's foreign policy towards the Middle East in the post-Cold War era witnessed important changes from the traditional trend. Security concerns dominated Turkey's policy towards the region and Turkey was involved actively in Middle Eastern politics. The security threat to the integrity of the country and the negative atmosphere with the neighbouring countries paved the way to the increasing cooperation between Turkey and Israel. The US supported this rapprochement and the conditions of the peace process made this cooperation easy. In the same period, the EU was also satisfied with the peace process and financially contributed to this atmosphere. But Turkey's struggle with the PKK and human rights violations during this struggle, the role of army in Turkish politics, close cooperation between Turkey and the US, and Turkey's problems with Greece helped in the perpetuation of a negative atmosphere between Turkey and the EU. This situation grew worse when the EU declined Turkey's candidacy for membership in 1997. This decision limited Turkey's options and increased Turkey's dependency on the US and Israel in the Middle East. Until 1999, Turkey's relations with the EU were problematic despite having a customs union and being an applicant to the Union. Many people in Turkey and in Europe believed that Turkey would never join the EU. This feeling continued even after the official candidature of Turkey in 1999. The attitude of the politicians and the bureaucrats on the side of the EU reinforced these negative perceptions. Consequently, the impact of the EU on Turkey and Turkish foreign policy were limited in the period before the candidature.

In the last couple of years, however, the situation has started to change and Turkey's Middle East policy has come closer to that of Europe. Beside the candidature of Turkey, the end of support from some European countries of the PKK, the effects of September 11 and the general opposition to terrorist activities in the world, the government change in Israel and the policies of Israeli governments in Palestine, and the differences between the US and Turkey over the future of Iraq also have made the Turkish foreign policy towards the Middle East closer to that of Europe.

Until the late 1990s Turkey's policies regarding the Middle East had very much common with those of the US and Israel. Both the US and Israel were in favour of a weak and de-centralized Iraq. This was, however, contrary to the security interests of Turkey. This difference surfaced before the US-led coalition's invasion of Iraq. The decision of the US-led coalition to intervene to Iraq also showed the challenges to establish a common foreign and security policy within the EU. Some of the new members of the EU acted along with the US despite the opposition from Germany and France. On 30 January 2003 UK, Spain, Denmark, Portugal, Italy, the Czech Republic, Hungary and Poland declared that Europe should act along with the US. A similar declaration came from the ten NATO candidate countries. Here the case of Turkey, however, was unique. Turkey had been an ally of the US for years and there was a general belief that Turkey could not oppose the demands of the US in considering the military, economic and political conditions of the country. The Turkish parliament, however, did not allow the transfer of the US troops to northern Iraq via Turkish territory and sending Turkish troops there on March 1, 2003. This decision seriously effected Turkey's relations with the US and also is accepted as the manifestation of greater democracy and the weakening of pro-US military's power in the country. This development was a signal for the countries within the EU that are opposed to the membership of Turkey that Turkey will not always act with the US.

This decision of the parliament also nullified the arguments that in case of membership, Turkey would act as the Trojan horse of the US within the EU. Turkey's current policy in the Cyprus issue also helped to change the negative attitude of some of the EU member countries against Turkey and prevented the description of Turkey as a troublemaker. The divisions among the members and the candidates of the European Union during the Iraqi crisis induced the Greek presidency of the time to convene a special summit on Iraq and the Middle East on 17–18 February 2003. In this respect, the Turkish Prime Minister declared that Turkey saw its benefit in contributing to the EU's Middle East and Iraq policy. The members of the EU tried to agree on a common position in this crisis and as the only candidate country bordering Iraq, Turkey's efforts at a peaceful solution to the problem were acknowledged by the Union with a declaration after the Summit.

Ankara's foreign policy today is moving in the direction of alignment with the EU. The motion of 1 March 2003 was a signal that democratic legitimacy will be the principle in its foreign policy. The makers of foreign policy argue that this democratic and independent attitude of Turkey in the last couple of years has contributed to the image of Turkey in the eyes of other countries like Russia. Although Turkey supported USA's Greater Middle East Initiative and became one of the democratic partners in this process, it also stressed that the reforms should come from within the region and should not be imposed from outside. This stance is very much in line with the attitude of the Europeans. The impact of public opinion on the formation of foreign policy is increasing and current polls show that Turkish public opinion is against the US policies in the region. This opposition is very much related to the support of the US to the Kurdish groups in Iraq and also the failure of the US to help to the elimination of PKK activities in northern Iraq.

Turkey's transformation with EU candidature and the stabilization of the economy and politics of the country have changed the framework of foreign policy. After putting its own house in order, Turkey has felt more confident in regional policy and pursued an active diplomacy in the Middle East. The arguments on the contribution of Turkey's foreign policy to the EU and to the Middle Eastern security stress two points: Turkey's position as an emerging role model and its constructive diplomatic engagement in the region. Turkey's efforts at stabilization in Iraq and Palestine represent the constructive diplomatic efforts of the country.

Turkey's geopolitical location is vital for the transfer of the natural resources of the Middle East and the Central Asia to Europe. In addition to the pipeline of Kirkuk-Ceyhan, the Baku-Tbilisi-Ceyhan pipeline is important for the transfer of natural resources. The developments in the past several years have made the importance of energy security obvious. With the rising demand and prices, and the use of natural resources by Russia as a weapon in foreign policy, as in the case of Ukraine, the security of a constant supply of natural resources for Europe has become one of the most important issues on the European agenda. The agreements and construction of a pipeline between Turkey and Greece for the transfer of oil and gas to Europe represent the new dynamic on this issue. Turkey's candidature to and the possible membership in the EU are positive factors in the improvement of the relations in terms of energy security and the projects for the future. The importance of the security of the energy supplies for Europe and the position of Turkey here have been stressed by several politicians and academics in relation to the possible contribution of Turkish membership to the Union.

The decrease of the threat to Turkey's security and the EU's acceptance of Turkey in 1999 as a candidate country opened a new phase in Turkey's relations with the EU. Turkey's candidature coincided with the increasing initiatives of the European Union to form a CFSP. Given the deficiency of military capabilities on the side of the EU, Turkey's possible role in this structure increased. The latest developments during the Iraqi invasion showed the EU what kind of an asset Turkey could be in its policy towards the region. Prior to the invasion of Iraq, Turkey as a key neighbour deployed serious efforts at a peaceful solution to the problem. Turkey followed a policy similar to that of the core countries of the EU, contrary to that of some of the new members of the Union. Turkey's positive and peaceful approach also continued after the invasion. This policy is consistent with the realities of the region and the general attitude of the European countries.

In addition to the similarities in Iraqi policy, Turkey's policy in the Palestinian-Israeli conflict has much common with that of the EU. Both Turkey and the EU stress the importance of international law in the solution of the problem and pay attention to the sufferings of the Palestinian people. Given the open support of the US to Israel and the differences of capacity between the US and other big actors in world politics, the EU's role in the peace process should be within the framework designed by the Americans. The limited capabilities of the EU in comparison with the US have led to the inactivity of the Union during the times of crisis. The diverging opinions among members prevent the EU from responding quickly to crisis situations. The EU contributed to the construction of infrastructure of a future Palestinian state within the peace process and accepted Israeli membership to some European platforms to break its isolation. Turkey's and the EU's contributions to the efforts of peace in this problem have mainly been on the fronts of diplomacy and economics in comparison with the military and strategic capabilities of the US and Israel.

Different from the approach of the US, Turkey and the EU have stressed the need to find a solution to the Palestinian-Israeli problem for a general reform process in the region in the direction of democracy. Both Turkey and the EU favour the revitalization of the peace process since the EU's and Turkey's capacities enable them operate in times of peace and stability. But the latest Sharon government and the governments since have destroyed the infrastructure of the Palestinian Authority. Since the EU paid most of the costs for this infrastructure, European countries have criticized these actions strongly. Also the atmosphere in Palestine and the differences between several groups limits the manoeuvring capability of the EU. Turkey, with its long history of relationships with both Palestinians and Israel and also as a candidate of the EU would contribute to the peace process in the diplomatic and economic aspects. Turkey enjoys the confidence of both sides and could contribute to search for mutually acceptable solutions to the problem.

The possible convergence of Turkey's Middle Eastern policy with that of European is related, beside its candidature or membership to the union, to the future policies of the big powers, especially those of the US. The unilateral attitude of the US after 9/11 and its ignoring criticisms of bypassing the United Nations and international law alienated some of its allies, like Turkey, in the Middle East. This unilateral approach also alarmed other big actors like the EU and caused them to reconsider their relationship with the US. Consequently, the stability of transatlantic relations has come under question and the Europeans have tried to limit their dependency on the US in security issues. The capabilities of the EU are not adequate to deal with the problems of the unipolar world unilaterally. Besides this fact, the weak position of the European countries has induced the countries on the continent to look for common solutions to common problems. The EU itself is a result of this development. Although there were some examples of unilateral approach in Turkish foreign policy in the post-Cold War era, the general tendency of the Turkish foreign policy has been to work with the international institutions and pursue a multilateral approach. The use of a multilateral approach is another point in the harmonization of foreign policies.

Different from the Clinton administration, the Bush administration has followed a unilateral approach in foreign policy and the attacks of the 9/11 were used as a legitimating tool in this manner. This unilateral attitude of the US in world politics and the discomfort of the some of the European countries have had consequences for Turkey's relations with the EU in terms of its foreign policy towards the Middle East. This situation has increased the status of Turkey in the security framework of Europe. The unilateral approach of the US has brought Turkey and the EU closer to each other.

Turkey's possible membership and role within the CFSP is becoming more important in the current threat perceptions of the EU. Although the history of the relationship between the EU and the Middle Eastern countries relation is a long one, there is no possibility for membership for these countries. The EU's attitude towards the Middle Eastern and Mediterranean countries has been very different from its policies towards East European countries. The EU has been criticized for its policies regarding the Mediterranean and Middle Eastern countries. The current threats to the EU, like illegal immigration, are mainly originated from these countries. Turkey constitutes the border between Europe and some Middle Eastern countries. A healthy relationship between Turkey and the EU may constitute an example for future relationships within the region.

Turkey's proximity to the region and the impact of this location to its membership and the contribution to the EU are also issues of contention. EU members debate whether the inclusion of Turkey to the EU means the inclusion of the Middle Eastern problems into the Union or Turkey neighbouring the Middle East will help the EU play a more active role there. Whereas the groups in the EU that oppose the membership of Turkey support the former argument, Turkish officials and academics and the supporters of Turkey within the EU favour the latter. Turkey's efforts at the peaceful solution to the problem in Iraq before the invasion and the initiatives of the democratic rehabilitation of the country afterwards are in line with the EU stance. The leading role of Turkey in creating consultation mechanisms among the neighbours of Iraq before the invasion and the continuation of this mechanism after the war is an example of Turkey's diplomatic influence in the region. Turkey's active and positive role during the elections in Iraq and convincing the Sunni groups to participate in the elections, and Turkey's facilitator role during the negotiations with Iran on the nuclear issue are given as examples of Turkey's possible contribution to the EU's foreign policy. The demands on the side of the Europeans to Turkey to contribute to the peace building activities in Lebanon after the Israeli invasion and bombings and Turkey's contribution to UNIFIL (the United Nations Implementation Force in Lebanon) mission along with other European countries is another example of the role of Turkey in this respect. The contribution of Turkey to the peace mission in Lebanon is helpful in overcoming the negative image of the EU in the Middle East, especially given its performance during the crisis.

The countries in the region also support Turkey's joining the Union and believe that this membership will contribute to the stability in the region. The Syrian President noted that with the membership of Turkey, their country would border the EU and would be happy with this development. Another example that shows the importance attached to the joining of Turkey to the Union by the Middle Eastern and Muslim countries is the outnumbering of Turkish journalists by journalists from these countries at the declaration of the opening negotiations with Turkey. Given the international atmosphere after 9/11 and the 7/7 London bombings, there was an increasing fear of a clash of civilizations in academic and political circles in the world. Turkey's path to modernization and entrance into the EU are given as answers to these kinds of arguments. The possible contribution of Turkey's membership in the EU against such a clash scenario has been raised by Turkish officials and academics and also by the supporters of Turkey's membership in Europe. Turkey's leading role along with that of Spain in the initiative of the Alliance of Civilizations, which was initiated by the efforts of the UN Secretary General Kofi Annan in July 2005, also is presented as another example of Turkey's possible role. Currently there are serious efforts for the institutionalization of this initiative.

Despite the existence of several common points, I also mentioned some differences between Turkey and the EU in the Middle East. In the Caucasus and the Balkans, other neighbouring regions of Turkey which are also important for Europe, harmonization between the interests and policies of Turkey and the EU might be more than the one in the Middle East. In considering the development of a neighbourhood policy of the EU, we may say that the stability in the Balkans and the Caucasus is in the interest of both the EU and Turkey. Both Turkey and the EU support the democratic and liberal transition in these regions. In the case of Balkans, the enlargement of the EU towards the region and attempts for the stabilization of this part of the continent is in the interest of both Turkey and the EU. In Caucasus, the increasing European attachment of Georgia and Azerbaijan is supported by Turkey and the EU.

Developments in the Middle East in general and in Iraq and in Palestine are high on the agendas of the foreign policies of many countries and international institutions. As a neighbouring country and also as a candidate for the EU, these issues have crucial importance for Turkey. In the post-Cold War period, these two cases are the cornerstones of the Turkish policy towards the Middle East. The importance of these issues also has been reflected in the attempts of Europe to have a common foreign policy, since the first signals of a common approach emerged in relation to the Palestinian problem.

Given the above factors, 1999 can be accepted as a turning point because of Turkey's candidature to the EU and the EU's attempt to strengthen the CFSP after the failures in the Balkans. From Turkey's point of view, the capture of Öcalan had consequences for the policies towards the Palestinian-Israeli conflict and Iraq. These factors and the EU candidature led to changes in Turkish policy towards these two cases.

# Bibliography

Albright, Madeleine K. "The Right Balance Will Secure NATO's Future," *Financial Times*, 7 December 1998.

Allen, David. "The European Rescue of National Foreign Policy," in *Actors in Europe's Foreign Policy*, edited by Christopher Hill (London: Routledge, 1996).

Altunışık, Meliha Benli. "Soğuk Savaş Sonrası Dönemde Türkiye-İsrail İlişkileri," In *Türkiye ve Ortadoğu: Tarih Kimlik Güvenlik*, edited by Meliha Benli Altunışık (İstanbul: Boyut, 1999).

Altunışık, Meliha Benli. "Güvenlik Kıskacında Türkiye-Ortadoğu İlişkileri," in *En Uzun Onyıl*, edited by Gencer Özcan and Şule Kut (İstanbul: Boyut, 1998).

Andersen, Svein S, and Kjell A. Eliassen. "Introduction: The EU As a New Political System," in *Making Policy in Europe*, edited by Svein S. Andersen and Kjell A. Eliassen (London: Sage, 2001).

Anıl, Işıl. "Soğuk Savaş Sonrasında Türkiye ve Arap-İsrail Barış Süreci," in *Türkiye ve Ortadoğu Tarih, Kimlik Güvenlik*, edited by Meliha Benli Altunışık (Istanbul: Boyut, 1999).

Aras, Bülent. "The Place of the Palestinian-Israeli Peace Process in Turkish Foreign Policy," *Journal of South Asian and Middle Eastern Studies* 21, no. 2 (Jan 1997): 49–72.

Aras, Bülent. "Turkey and GCC: An Emerging Relationship," *Middle East Policy* 12, no. 4 (Winter 2005): 89–97.

Aras, Bülent. *Turkey and the Greater Middle East* (Istanbul: Tasam, 2004).

Arslan, Sadık, Turkish Diplomat. Interview by the Author, Oxford, 16 February 2006.

Ash, Timothy Garton. "Why Britain is in Europe." Speech at St. Antony's College, Oxford, 1 June 2006.

Aybet, Gülnur. "The Future of Trans-Atlantic Relations and the Place of Turkey", Paper presented at the European Studies Centre, University of Oxford, 15 June 2006.

Aydın, Mustafa. *Turkish Foreign Policy Framework and Analysis* (Ankara: SAM, 2004).

Aydın, Mustafa. "Twenty Years before, Twenty Years after: Turkish Foreign Policy at the Threshold of the 21st Century," in *Turkey's Foreign Policy in the 21st Century*, edited by Tareq Y. Ismael and Mustafa Aydın (Aldershot: Ashgate, 2003).

Aykan, Mahmut Bali. "The Turkish-Syrian Crisis of October 1998: A Turkish View," *Middle East Policy* 6, no. 4, (June 1999): 174–189.

Aykan, Mahmut Bali. "Turkey's Policy in Northern Iraq, 1991–95," *Middle Eastern Studies* 32, no. 4, (1996): 343–366.

Aykan, Mahmut Bali. "The Palestinian Question in Turkish Foreign Policy from the 1950s to the 1990s," *International Journal of Middle East Studies* 25, no. 1, (February 1993): 91–110.

Bağcı, Hüseyin. "Demokrat Partinin Ortadoğu Politikası," in *Türk Dış Politikasının Analizi*, edited by Faruk Sönmezoğlu (İstanbul: Der, 1998).

Barbe, Esther. "Balancing Europe's Eastern and Southern Dimension," in *Paradoxes of European Foreign Policy*, edited by Jan Zielonka (London: Kluwer Law, 1998).

Barbe, Esther. "Spain, the Uses of Foreign Policy Cooperation," in *The Actors in Europe's Foreign Policy*, edited by Christopher Hill (London: Routledge, 1996).

Barkey, Henri J. "Koşulların Zorladığı İlişki: Körfez Savaşı'ndan Bu Yana Türkiye ve Irak." *Avrasya Dosyası* 6, no. 3 (Fall 2000): 29–49.

Barkey, Henri J. "Turkey and the New Middle East: A Geopolitical Exploration," in *Reluctant Neighbor*, edited by Henri J. Barkey (Washington DC: US Institute of Peace Press, 1996).

Baynham, Simon. "Eurasian Janus: Turkey's Security and Defense Dilemmas in the Aftermath of the Iraq War." *Defense and Security Analysis* 19, no. 3 (September 2003): 281–285.

Bengio, Ofra, and Gencer Özcan. "Changing Relations: Turkish-Israeli-Arab Triangle," *Perceptions* 5, no. 1 (March–May 2000): 1–8.

Bonvicini, Gianni. "Regional Assertion, the Dilemmas of Italy," in *The Actors in Europe's Foreign Policy*, edited by Christopher Hill (London: Routledge, 1996).

Börzel, Tanja A. "Pace-Setting, Foot-Dragging, and Fence-Sitting: Member State Responses to Europeanization," *Journal of Common Market Studies* 40, no. 2 (2002): 193–214.

Branch Ann P. and Jacob C. Ohrgaard. "Trapped in the Supranational-Intergovernmental Dichotomy: A Response to Stone Sweet and Sandholtz," *Journal of European Public Policy* 6, no. 1 (March 1999): 123–143.

Bretherton, Charlotte, and John Vogler. *The European Union As a Global Actor* (London and New York: Routledge, 2002).

Brewin, Christopher. "A Changing Turkey: Europe's Dilemma." *Journal of Southern Europe and the Balkans* 5, no. 2 (August 2003): 137–145.

Bulmer, Simon J. and Claudio M. Radaelli. "The Europeanization of National Policy?" *Queen's Papers on Europeanization*, no. 1, (2004), p. 1–22. http://www. qub.ac.uk/schools/SchoolofPoliticsInternationalStudiesandPhilosophy/FileStore/ EuropeanisationFiles/Filetoupload,5182,en.pdf [28 December 2005].

Burgess, Michael. "Federalism and Federation," in *European Union Politics*, edited by Michelle Cini (Oxford: Oxford University Press, 2003).

Cem, İsmail. *Türkiye Avrupa Avrasya* (İstanbul: İstanbul Bilgi Üniversitesi Yayınları, 2004).

Checkel, Jeffrey T. "Social Construction and Integration." *Journal of European Public Policy* 6, no. 4 (1999): 545–560.

Christiansen, Thomas, Knud Erik Jorgensen and Antje Wiener. "The Social Construction of Europe." *Journal of European Public Policy* 6, no. 4 (1999): 528–544.

Chryssochoou, Dimitris N. *Theorizing European Integration* (London: Sage, 2001).

Chryssochoou, Dimitris N., Michael J. Tsinisizelis, Stelios Stavridis and Kostad Ifantis. *Theory and Reform in the European Union* (Manchester: Manchester University Press, 2003).

Cini, Michelle. "Intergovernmentalism," in *European Union Politics*, edited by Michelle Cini (Oxford: Oxford University Press, 2003).

Cohn-Bendit, Daniel. "Europe's Crisis: What Is To Be Done?" Speech at St. Antony's College, Oxford, 2 November 2005.

Couloumbis, Theodor. "The Impact of EC (EU) Membership on Greece's Foreign Policy Profile," in *Greece and EC Membership Evaluated*, edited by Panos Kazakos and Panayotis Ioakimidis (London: Pinter, 1994).

Cowles, Maria Green, James Caporaso, and Thomas Risse. "Europeanization and Domestic Change: Introduction," in *Transforming Europe: Europeanization and Domestic Change*, edited by Maria Green Cowles, James Caporaso, and Thomas Risse (London: Cornell University Press, 2001).

Criss, Bilge, and Pınar Bilgin. "Turkish Foreign Policy toward the Middle East," *Middle East Review of International Affairs* 1, no.1 (January 1997): 1–10. http://meria.idc.ac.il/journal/1997/issue1/jv1n1a3.html [16 July 2006].

Çağaptay, Soner. "Where Goes the U.S.-Turkish Relationship?" *Middle East Quarterly* 11, no. 4 (Fall 2004): 43–52.

Çayhan, Esra. "Towards a European Security and Defense Policy: With or Without Turkey?" *Turkish Studies* 4, no. 1 (Spring 2003): 35–55.

Çelik, Yasemin. *Contemporary Turkish Foreign Policy* (New York: Preager, 1999).

Çelikkol, Oğuz. Ambassador. Turkey's Special Representative for Iraq. Interview by author, Ankara, 22 May 2006.

Dağı, Zeynep. "Ulusal Kimliğin İnşası ve Dış Politika," *Demokrasi Platformu* 2, no. 5 (Winter 2005): 57–71.

Davidson, Ian, and Philip H. Gordon. "Assessing European Foreign Policy," *International Security* 23, no. 2 (Fall 1998): 183–188.

Davutoğlu, Ahmet. "Yahudi Meselesinin Dönüşümü ve İsrail'in Yeni Stratejisi." *Avrasya Dosyası* 1, no. 3 (Autumn 1994): 94–104.

Davutoğlu, Ahmet. *Stratejik Derinlik Turkiye'nin Uluslararası Konumu.* Istanbul. Küre, 2003.

Davutoğlu, Ahmet. "The Intercivilizational and Interreligious Interaction in the Global Era: The Case of Turkey-EU Relations," Paper presented at the Halki Seminar *Mediterranean Crossroads: Culture, Religion and Security*, Halki Greece, (8–12 September 2002): 1–12.

Davutoğlu, Ahmet. "Türkiye Merkez Ülke Olmalı," *Radikal*, 26 February 2006.

Davutoğlu, Ahmet. Chief Advisor to the Prime Minister. Interview by author. Istanbul, 28 May 2006.

Delanty, Gerard and Chris Rumford. *Rethinking Europe: Social Theory and the Implications of Europeanization* (London: Routledge, 2005).

Demiralp, Oğuz. "The Added Value of Turkish Membership to European Foreign Policy," *Turkish Policy Quarterly* 2, no. 4 (Winter 2004): 13–19.

Dosenrode, Soren, and Anders Stubkjaer. *The European Union and the Middle East* (London: Sheffield Academic Press, 2002).

Elekdağ, Şükrü. "İki Buçuk Savaş Stratejisi," *Yeni Turkiye*, no. 3 (March–April 1995): 516–522.

Erhan, Çağrı, and Ömer Kürkçüoğlu. "1990–2001 İsrail'le İlişkiler," in *Türk Dış Politikası, Kurtuluş Savaşı'ndan Bugüne Olgular, Belgeler, Yorumlar*, edited by Baskın Oran. Vol. 2 (İstanbul: İletişim, 2001).

Featherstone, Kevin. "In The Name of Europe," in *The Politics of Europeanization*, edited by Kevin Featherstone and Claudio M. Radaelli (Oxford: Oxford University Press, 2003).

Featherstone, Kevin, and George Kazamias. *Europeanization and the Southern Periphery* (London: Frank Cass, 2001).

Ferreira-Pereira, Laura C. "The Military Non-Allied States in the CFSP of the 1990s". *European Integration online Papers* 7, no. 3 (2004): 1–14. http://eiop.or.at/eiop/texte/2004–003.htm [14 December 2005].

Fırat, Melek, and Ömer Kürkçüoğlu. "1945–1960 Ortadoğu'yla İlişkiler," in *Türk Dış Politikası Kurtuluş Savaşından Bugüne Olgular, Belgeler, Yorumlar*, edited by Baskın Oran. Vol. 1 (İstanbul: İletişim. 2002).

Fırat, Melek and Ömer Kürkçüoğlu, "1980–1990 Ortadoğu'yla İlişkiler," in *Türk Dış Politikası, Kurtuluş Savaşı'ndan Bugüne Olgular, Belgeler, Yorumlar*, edited by Baskın Oran, Vol. 1 (İstanbul: İletişim, 2002).

Gad, Emad. "The EU and the Middle East: An Egyptian View." *Perceptions* 8, no. 2 (June–August 2003): 1–12.

Glarbo, Kenneth. "Wide-awake Diplomacy: Reconstructing the Common Foreign and Security Policy of the European Union." *Journal of European Public Policy* 6, no. 4, (1999): 634–651.

Gordon, H. Philip. "Europe's Uncommon Foreign Policy." *International Security* 23, no. 3 (Winter 1997): 74–100.

Gordon, Philip, and Ömer Taşpınar, "Turkey on the Brink," *The Washington Quarterly* 29, no. 3 (Summer 2006): 57–70.

Grabbe, Heather. "Europeanization Goes East: Power and Uncertainty in the EU Accession Process," in *The Politics of Europeanization*, edited by Kevin Featherstone and Claudio M. Radaelli (Oxford: Oxford University Press, 2003).

Gül, Abdullah. "New Horizons in Turkish Foreign Policy," Boğaziçi Yöneticiler Vakfı, Dedeman Hotel, İstanbul, 22 May 2004.

Hale, William. *Turkish Foreign Policy 1774–2000* (London: Frank Cass, 2000).

Héritier, Adrienne, Christoph Knill, Susanne Mingers. *Ringing the changes in Europe: Regulatory Competition and the Transformation of the State. Britain, France, Germany* (Berlin: De Gruyter, 1996).

Hill, Christopher. "United Kingdom, Sharpening Contradictions," in *The Actors in Europe's Foreign Policy*, edited by Christopher Hill (London: Routledge, 1996).

Hill, Christopher. "Actors and Actions," in *The Actors in Europe's Foreign Policy*, edited by Christopher Hill (London: Routledge, 1996).

Hill, Christopher. "Preface," in *The Actors in Europe's Foreign Policy*, edited by Christopher Hill (London: Routledge, 1996).

Hill, Christopher. *Convergence, Divergence and Dialectics, National Foreign Policies and CFSP*, EUI Working Papers, RSC no. 97/66 (December 1997).

Hollis Rosemary. "Europe and the Middle East: Power by Stealth." *International Affairs* 73, no.1 (January 1997): 15–30.

Inbar, Efraim. "Regional Implications of the Israeli-Turkish Strategic Partnership." *Middle East Review of International Affairs* 5, no. 2 (June 2001): 1–18. http:// meria.idc.ac.il/journal/2001/issue2/jv5n2a5.html [16 June 2006].

Irondelle, Bastien. "Europeanization without the European Union? French Military Reforms 1991–1996." *Journal of European Public Policy* 10, no. 2 (April 2003): 208–226.

Jensen, Carsten Stroby. "Neo-functonalism," in *European Union Politics*, edited by Michelle Cini (Oxford: Oxford University Press, 2003).

Karabat, Ayşe. "Hayalet İttifak: Türkiye-İsrail İlişkileri," *Radikal*, 21 July 2001.

Kassim, Hussein. "Conclusion," in *The National Coordination of EU Policy, The Domestic Level*, edited by Hussein Kassim, Guy Peters and Vincent Wright (Oxford: Oxford University Press, 2000).

Kavakas, Dimitris. "Greece," in *The Foreign Policies of European Union Member States*, edited by Ian Manners and Richard Whitman (Manchester: Manchester University Press, 2000).

Kazakos, Panos, and Panayotis Ioakimidis. "Introduction," in *Greece and EC Membership Evaluated*, edited by Panos Kazakos and Panayotis Ioakimidis (London: Pinter, 1994).

Keyman, Fuat. "Yapıcı aktif- çok boyutlu dış politika," *Zaman*, 21 February 2006.

Kirişçi, Kemal. "Post Cold War Turkish Security and the Middle East," *Middle East Review of International Relations* 1, no. 2 (July 1997): 1–10. http://meria.idc. ac.il/journal/1997/issue2/jv1n2a6.html [17 June 2006].

Kirişçi, Kemal. "Uluslararası Sistemdeki Değişmeler ve Türk Dış Politikasının Yeni Yönelimleri," in *Türk Dış Politikasının Analizi*, edited by Faruk Sönmezoğlu (İstanbul: Der Yayınları, 1998).

Kirişçi, Kemal. "Between Europe and the Middle East: The Transformation of Turkish Policy, *Middle East Review of International Affairs* 8, no. 1 (March 2004): 1–13. http://meria.idc.ac.il/journal/2004/issue1/kirisci.pdf [17 July 2006].

Kirişçi, Kemal. "Turkey's Foreign Policy in Turbulent Times," *Chaillot Paper*, no. 92, (September 2006): 1–109.

Kosnikowski, Andzej. "EU-Israeli Relations," Carol Cosgrove-Sacks, in *The European Union and Developing Countries* (London: Macmillan Press, 1999).

Köni, Hasan. "Mısır-Türkiye-İsrail Üçgeni." *Avrasya Dosyası* 1, no. 3 (Autumn 1994): 45–53.

Krasner, Stephen D. "Structural Causes and Regime Consequences: Regimes As Intervening Variables," in *International Regimes*, edited by Stephen D. Krasner (Ithaca, London: Cornell University Press, 1983).

Kut, Şule. "Türkiye'nin Soğuk Savaş Sonrası Dış Politikasının Ana Hatları," in *En Uzun Onyıl*, edited by Gencer Özcan and Şule Kut (İstanbul: Boyut, 1998).

Larrabee, F. Stephen. and Ian O. Lesser. *Turkish Foreign Policy in an Age of Uncertainty*, Rand Corporation, 2003. http://www.rand.org/publications/MR/ MR1612/ [18 January 2004].

Lecha, Eduard Soler i. "Turkey and the EU: Bringing Together a Regional Power and a Global Actor," *Turkish Policy Quarterly* 2, no. 4 (Winter 2003): 47–55.

Leigh, Michael. "Alternative Scenarios for the Europe's Future." *7th Cervia Summer School of Bologna University*, Cervia, Italy, 14 September 2001.

Lewin, Anat. "Turkey and Israel: Reciprocal and Mutual Imagery in the Media, 1994–1999". *Journal of International Affairs* 54, no. 1 (Fall 2000): 239–262.

Major, Claudia. "Europeanization and Foreign and Security Policy, Undermining or Rescuing the Nation State." *Politics 25*, no. 3 (2005): 175–190.

Makovsky, Alan. "Israeli-Turkish Relations a Turkish "Periphery Strategy?" in *Reluctant Neighbor*, edited by Henri J. Barkey (Washington DC: US Institute of Peace Press, 1996).

Manners, Ian and Richard Whitman. "Introduction," in *The Foreign Policies of European Union Member States*, edited by Ian Manners and Richard Whitman (Manchester: Manchester University Press, 2000).

Manners, Ian and Richard Whitman. "Conclusion," in *The Foreign Policies of European Union Member States*, edited by Ian Manners and Richard Whitman (Manchester: Manchester University Press, 2000).

Manners, Ian and Richard G. Whitman. "The 'Difference Engine': Constructing and Representing the International Identity of the European Union." *European Journal of Public Policy* 10, no. 3 (June 2003): 380–404.

Marr, Phebe. "The United States, Europe and the Middle East, Cooperation, Co-optation or Confrontation?" in *The Middle East and Europe*, edited by B.A. Roberson (London: Routledge, 1998).

Ministry of Foreign Affairs, Synopsis of the Turkish Foreign Policy, available [online]: http://www.mfa.gov.tr/MFA/ForeignPolicy/Synopsis/ [8 July 2005].

Misrahi, Frederic. "The EU and the Civil Control of Armed Forces: An Analysis of Recent Developments in Turkey." *Perspectives* 22 (2004): 22–42.

Missiroli, Antonio. "The European Union: Just a Regional Peacekeeper?" *European Foreign Affairs Review*, no. 8 (2003): 493–503.

Moravcsik, Andrew. "Is Something Rotten in the State of Denmark? Constructivism and European Integration." *Journal of European Public Policy* 6, no. 4 (1999): 669–681.

Musu, Costanza. "European Foreign Policy: A Collective Policy or a Policy of Converging Parallels?" *European Foreign Affairs Review* 8, no. 1 (2003): 35–49.

Nicolaidis, Calypso. "Europe as a Normative Power: Why is the Euro-Med Partnership in Crisis and What Should Be Done About It?" European Studies Centre, University of Oxford, 16 January 2006.

Nuttal, Simon J. *European Foreign Policy* (New York: Oxford University Press, 2000).

Oran, Baskın. "Türk Dış Politikasının Teori ve Pratiği," in *Türk Dış Politikası Kurtuluş Savaşından Bugüne Olgular, Belgeler, Yorumlar*, edited by Baskın Oran (İstanbul: İletişim, 2002).

Özcan, Gencer. "Türkiye-İsrail İlişkileri 50. Yılına Girerken," in *Türk Dış Politikasının Analizi*, edited by Faruk Sönmezoğlu (İstanbul: Der Yayınları, 1998).

Paasivirta, Esa. "EU Trading with Israel and Palestine: Parallel Legal Frameworks and Triangular Issues," *European Foreign Affairs Review* 4, no. 3 (Fall 1999): 300–318.

Pernice, Ingolf, and Daniel Thym. "A New Institutional Balance for European Foreign Policy?" *European Foreign Affairs Review* 7 (2002): 369–400.

Perthes, Volker. "Points of Difference, Cases for Cooperation: European Critics of US Middle East Policy." *Middle East Report*, no. 208 (Autumn 1998): 30–32.

Puchala, Donald J. "Of Blind Men, Elephants and International Integration." *Journal of Common Market Studies 11*, no. 2 (December 1972): 267–284.

Puchala, Donald J. "The Integration Theorists and the Study of International Relations," in *The Global Agenda: Issues and Perspectives*, edited by Charles W. Kegley and Eugene R. Wittkopf (New York: Random House, 1984).

Quadras, Alejo Vidal. "EU-Turkey: A Good Match?" *Turkish Policy Quarterly* 2, no. 4 (Winter 2004): 21–27.

Republic of Turkey T.C. Resmi Gazete (Mukerrer), no. 24556, 17 October 2001.

Roberson, B.A. "Introduction," in *The Middle East and Europe*, edited by B.A. Roberson (London: Routledge, 1998).

Robins, Philip J. "Avoiding the Question," edited by Henry J. Barkey, in *Reluctant Neighbor* (Washington DC: US Institute of Peace Press, 1996).

Robins, Philip. *Suits and Uniforms: Turkish Foreign Policy since the Cold War.* London: Hurst, 2003.

Robins, Philip. "Confusion at Home, Confusion Abroad: Turkey between Copenhagen and Iraq." *International Affairs* 79, no. 3 (2003): 547–566.

Rodman, Robert W. "Middle East Diplomacy after the Gulf War," *Foreign Affairs* 70, no. 2 (Spring 1991): 1–18.

Rosamond, Ben. *Theories of European Integration* (Basingstoke: Macmillan, 2000).

Rosamond, Ben. "New Theories of European Integration," in *European Union Politics*, edited by Michelle Cini (Oxford: Oxford University Press, 2003).

Salame, Ghassan. "Torn Between the Atlantic and the Mediterranean, Europe and the Middle East in the Post-Cold War Era," in *The Middle East and Europe*, edited by B.A. Roberson (London: Routledge, 1998).

Saleh, Nivien. "The European Union and the Gulf States: A Growing Partnership," *Middle East Policy* 7, no. 1 (October 1999): 50–71.

Sarıibrahimoğlu, Lale. "1 Mart Tezkeresinin Aıtçı Sarsıntıları Sürüyor,' *Bugun*, 29 April 2006.

Schimmelfennig, Frank, and Wolfgang Wagner. "Preface: External Governance in the European Union," *Journal of European Public Policy* 11, no. 4 (August 2004): 657–660.

Şenel, Muzaffer. "Avrupa Birliği'nin Ortadoğu Barış Sürecine Etkileri," in *Filistin Çıkmazdan Çözüme*, edited by Ibrahim Turhan (İstanbul: Küre, 2003).

Sjursen, Helene. "The Common Foreign and Security Policy: Limits of Intergovernmentalism and The Search for a Global Role," in *Making Policy in Europe*, edited by Svein S. Andersen and Kjell A. Eliassen (London: Sage, 2001).

Smith, Karen E. "EU External Relations," in *European Union Politics*, edited by Michelle Cini (Oxford: Oxford University Press, 2003).

Smith, Michael. "Conforming to Europe: The Domestic Impact of EU Foreign Policy Co-operation." *Journal of European Public Policy* 7, no. 4 (October 2000): 613–631.

Smith, Michael. "The Framing of European Foreign and Security Policy: Towards a post-Modern Policy Framework?" *Journal of European Public Policy* 10, no. 4 (August 2003): 556–575.

Smith, Michael E. *Europe's Foreign and Security Policy, the Institutionalization of Cooperation* (Cambridge: Cambridge University Press, 2004).

Smith, Michael E. "Rules, Transgovernmentalism, and the Expansion of European Political Cooperation," in *European Integration and Supranational Governance*, edited by Wayne Sandholtz and Alec Stone Sweet (Oxford: Oxford University Press, 1998).

Stavridis, Stelios. "The Europeanization of Greek Foreign Policy: A Literature Review": 1–27. http://www.lse.ac.uk/collections/hellenicObservatory/pdf/Stavridis-10.pdf [10 July 2006].

Tavlaş, Nezih. "Türk-İsrail Güvenlik ve İstihbarat İlişkileri," *Avrasya Dosyası* 1, no. 3 (Autumn 1994): 5–31.

Tsakaloyannis, Panos. "The Limits to Convergence," in *The Actors in Europe's Foreign Policy*, edited by Christopher Hill (London: Routledge, 1996).

Tonra, Ben. *The Europeanization of National Foreign Policy: Dutch, Danish and Irish Foreign Policy in the European Union* (Aldershot: Ashgate, 2001).

"Turkey Accepts EU Military Force," *Facts on File World's News Digest*, 3 December 2001.

Ülgen, Sinan. "Of Chaos and Power: Will Europe Become a Strategic Community?" *Turkish Policy Quarterly* 2, no. 4 (Winter 2004): 39–46.

Uzgel, İlhan. "TDP'nin Oluşturulması," in *Türk Dış Politikası Kurtuluş Savaşından Bugüne Olgular, Belgeler, Yorumlar*, edited by Baskın Oran (İstanbul: İletişim Yayınları, 2002).

Wagner, Wolfgang. "Why the EU's Common Foreign and Security Policy Will Remain Intergovernmental: A Rationalist Institutional Choice Analysis of European Crisis Management Policy" *Journal of European Public Policy* 10, no. 4 (August 2003): 576–595.

Wiener, Antje and Thomas Diez. *European Integration Theory* (Oxford: Oxford University Press, 2004).

White, Brian. "The European Challenge to Foreign Policy Analysis," *European Journal of International Relations* 5, no. 1 (1999): 37–66.

White, Brian. *Understanding European Foreign Policy* (London: Palgrave, 2001).

Yavuz, Hakan. "İkicilik (Duality): Türk– Arap İlişkileri ve Filistin Sorunu," in *Türk Dış Politikasının Analizi*, edited by Faruk Sönmezoğlu (İstanbul: Der, 1998).

Yurdusev, Nuri. "Perceptions and Images in Turkish (Otoman)-European Relations," in *Turkey's Foreign Policy in the 21st Century*, edited by Tareq Y. Ismael and Mustafa Aydın (Aldershot: Ashgate, 2003).

**DIŞİŞLERİ GÜNCESİ ( MFA Press Releases)**

*Dışişleri Güncesi*, January 2003. http://www.mfa.gov.tr/NR/rdonlyres/0BF50F75-A50B-4A8D-981A-A4CB3C12BDB4/0/OCAK2003.pdf [8 July 2006].

*Dışişleri Güncesi*, February 2003. http://www.mfa.gov.tr/NR/rdonlyres/4DC42D46-4F41-4959-990C-AC6CBF6BE9CB/0/SUBAT2003.pdf [8 July 2006].

*Dışişleri Güncesi*, June 2003. http://www.mfa.gov.tr/NR/rdonlyres/AB5F397B-1E53-4A45-AE52-89BC9CA80E49/0/Haziran2003.pdf [9 July 2006].

*Dışişleri Güncesi*, July 2003. http://www.mfa.gov.tr/NR/rdonlyres/2F815293-BCB4-4638-8AD4-8A8B250D38A9/0/temmuz2003.pdf [9 July 2006].

*Dışişleri Güncesi*, August *2003*. http://www.mfa.gov.tr/NR/rdonlyres/3280C72E-1D17-4396-BDEC-7F42C6903B09/0/Agustos2003.pdf [9 July 2006].

*Dışişleri Güncesi*, September 2003. http://www.mfa.gov.tr/NR/rdonlyres/0CA1BE2A-8A8B-4D66-8E61-6255F637EDA4/0/Eylul2003.pdf [9 July 2006].

*Dışişleri Güncesi*, October 2003. http://www.mfa.gov.tr/NR/rdonlyres/C6F49A2A-0ABC-4810-8EBF-CBBFCACC7864/0/Ekim2003.pdf [9 July 2006].

*Dışişleri Güncesi*, December 2003. http://www.mfa.gov.tr/NR/rdonlyres/A245DF54-7640-4CB6-8CE5-62835C78204F/0/Aralık2003.pdf [9 July 2006].

*Dışişleri Güncesi*, January 2004. http://www.mfa.gov.tr/NR/rdonlyres/DCEE2866-64A3-4AC9-84C1-634949B1A2FE/0/Ocak2004.pdf [10 July 2006].

*Dışişleri Güncesi*, February 2004. http://www.mfa.gov.tr/NR/rdonlyres/A6A242D1-417F-4B4C-8EFA-890880A6DD1C/0/Şubat2004.pdf [10 July 2006].

*Dışişleri Güncesi*, June 2004. http://www.mfa.gov.tr/NR/rdonlyres/82D08FA5-E3E2-4566-A147-A2EDCB8CFB3C/0/Haziran2004.pdf [10 July 2006].

*Dışişleri Güncesi*, August 2004. http://www.mfa.gov.tr/NR/rdonlyres/82A29624-469C-4B08-B2E3-EB46483E6351/0/AGUSTOS2004.pdf [10 July 2006].

*Dışişleri Güncesi*, September 2004. http://www.mfa.gov.tr/NR/rdonlyres/6EBBB859-D639-415D-B048-57EB17078D4C/0/EYLUL2004.pdf [10 July 2006].

*Dışişleri Güncesi*, November 2004. http://www.mfa.gov.tr/NR/rdonlyres/995B2FC8-9E37-4963-8173-FFD51241B2BC/0/Kasim2004.pdf [11 July 2006].

*Dışişleri Güncesi*, January 2005. http://www.mfa.gov.tr/NR/rdonlyres/D2CB5AFF-B646-4E0F-8D13-6A3B357167EE/0/OCAK2005.pdf [12 July 2006].

*Dışişleri Güncesi*, March 2005. http://www.mfa.gov.tr/NR/rdonlyres/82D08FA5-E3E2-4566-A147-A2EDCB8CFB3C/0/Mart2005.pdf [10 July 2006].

*Dışişleri Güncesi*, May 2005. http://www.mfa.gov.tr/NR/rdonlyrcs/E45BB9B0-C32A-43C4-8A0F-29F072F3808E/0/MAYIS2005.pdf [12 July 2006].

*Dışişleri Güncesi*, June 2005. http://www.mfa.gov.tr/NR/rdonlyres/A14685DE-9A36-41DD-B5E3-E9AD5DF2695C/0/HAZIRAN2005.pdf [12 July 2006].

*Dışişleri Güncesi*, July 2005. http://www.mfa.gov.tr/NR/rdonlyres/6397723E-ADBC-4355-8A56-195ABDA0953F/0/TEMMUZ2005.pdf [13 July 2006].

*Dışişleri Güncesi*, August 2005. http://www.mfa.gov.tr/NR/rdonlyres/DD1EEA90-8C61-40E3-A400-DC399AC3E27A/0/AGUSTOS2005.pdf [13 July 2006].

*Dışişleri Güncesi*, October 2005. http://www.mfa.gov.tr/NR/rdonlyres/4428A895-DD1B-4CD0-994D-6CF1EFB53F30/0/EKIM2005.pdf [13 July 2006].

## Newspapers

*Milliyet*, 3 March 2000.
*Radikal*, 7 July 2001.

*Israelinsider*, 9 August 2001.
"İsrail Tatbikata Gelmiyor", *Radikal* 3 April 2002.
*Radikal*, 23 April 2002.
*Hürriyet*, 31 May 2002.
*Zaman*, 24 January 2003.
*Milliyet*, 30 January 2003.
*Milliyet*, 28 February 2003.
*Hürriyet*, 25 March 2004.
*Yeni Şafak*, 20 May 2004.
*Hürriyet*, 20 May 2004.
*Sabah*, 22 April 2004.
*The Guardian*, 6 July 2006.
*Hürriyet*, 18 July 2006
*Zaman*, 20 July 2006.


**Web Sources**

Ntvmsnbc www.ntvmsnbc.com/news/132523.asp. [28 January 2002].
Radikal www.radikal.com.tr/haber/php?haberno=33756. [2 April 2002].
Radikal    www.radikal.com.tr/veriler/2002/04/12/haber/_34613.php.    [12    April
     2002].
Ntvmsnbc www.ntvmsnbc.com/news/148415.asp. [25 April 2002].
Ministry of Foreign Affairs, Declaration of Ministry of Foreign Affairs on Palestine,
     www.mfa.gov.tr/cempalestine.htm. [26 April 2002].
Western European Union's Petersbeg Declaration, http://www.weu.int/documents/
     920619peten.pdf [24 December 2005].
BBC, 22 March 2003, http://news.bbc.co.uk/2/hi/europe/2874635.stm. [10 April
     2006].
BBC, 24 March 2003, http://news.bbc.co.uk/2/hi/europe/2879299.stm. [10 April
     2006].
http://daccessdds.un.org/doc/RESOLUTION/GEN/NR0/738/38/IMG/NR073838.
     pdf?OpenElement [8 May 2006].
http://www.deltur.cec.eu.int/!PublishDocs/tr/2004Recommendation.doc    [9    May
     2006].
http://europa.eu.int/council/off/conclu/june99/annexe_en.htm [10 June 2006].
European Security Strategy, A Secure Europe in a Better World http://www.iss-
     eu.org/solana/solanae.pdf [10 June 2006].
http://arsiv3.hurriyet.com.tr/anasayfa/0,,tarih~2003-01-10-m,00.asp [8 July 2006].
http://arsiv3.hurriyet.com.tr/haber/0,,sid~1@w~356@tarih~2003-02-06-m@
     nvid~228565,00.asp [8 July 2006].
http://arsiv3.hurriyet.com.tr/anasayfa/0,,tarih~2003-10-07-m,00.asp [9 July 2006].
Press Statement of the US Department of State http://www.state.gov/r/pa/prs/
     ps/2003/20062.htm [9 July 2006].
http://www.zaman.com.tr/?trh=20040902 [10 July 2006].

http://arsiv3.hurriyet.com.tr/haber/0,,sid~1@w~3@tarih~2004-12-17-m@
nvid~511783,00.asp [11 July 2006].

http://arsiv3.hurriyet.com.tr/haber/0,,sid~1@w~2@tarih~2004-11-17-m@
nvid~497526,00.asp [11 July 2006].

http://arsiv3.hurriyet.com.tr/haber/0,,sid~1@w~7@tarih~2004-11-25-m@
nvid~501358,00.asp [11 July 2006].

http://arsiv3.hurriyet.com.tr/haber/0,,sid~1@w~1@tarih~2005-02-16-m@
nvid~537750,00.asp [12 July 2006].

http://www.consilium.europa.eu/cms3_Applications/applications/search/
metaDoSearch.asp [24 July 2006].

http://www.consilium.europa.eu/ueDocs/cms_Data/docs/pressdata/en/misc/78358.
pdf [24 July 2006].

http://www.mfa.gov.tr/MFA_tr/DisPolitika/AnaKonular/Turkiye_AB/trab.htm
[26 July 2006].

http://www.mhp.org.tr/basinaciklamalari/basin2006/index.php?page=bsaciklama04
092006 [14 September 2006].

"How Europeans see themselves", Report of European Commission, p. 10, available
[online]:    http://ec.europa.eu./publications/booklets/eu_documentation/05/txt_
en.pdf [18 September 2006].

http://www.zaman.com.tr/?bl=dishaberler&alt=&trh=20060926&hn=352994
[26 September 2006].

http://www.zaman.com.tr/?bl=sondakika&alt=dis&trh=20060924&hn=352395
[26 September 2006].

Standard Eurobarometer, Public Opinion in the European Union, (Spring 2004),
available [online]: http://ec.europa.eu./public_opinion/archives/cceb/2004/cceb_
2004.1_highlights.pdf. [22 September 2006].

Standard Eurobarometer 65, Public Opinion in the European Union, (Spring 2006),
available  [online]:  http://ec.europa.eu/public_opinion/archives/eb/eb65/eb65_
first_en.pdf [22 September 2006].

http://ec.europe.eu/public_opinion/archives/notes/csf_pesc_papr03_en-pdf.    [22
September 2006].

http://www.deik.org.tr/ikili/2006317113635suriye-ikili-Mart2006.pdf  [4  October
2006].

http://www.deik.org.tr/ikili/200623174833Iran-ikili-ocak2006.pdf   [4    October
2006].

http://www.deltur.cec.eu.int/_webpub/documents/TR2006ProgressReport.doc
[13 November 2006].

http://www.chp.org.tr/index.php?module=news&page=readmore&news_id=319
[24 November 2006]

http://www.mhp.org.tr/raporlar/kibris/kibrisraporu.pdf [24 November 2006].

http://www.ikv.org.tr/ikv.php [24 November 2006].

Common Strategy of the European Council of 19 June 2000 on the Mediterranean
region, Official Journal of European Communities, 22 July 2000, available
[online:]        http://www.consilium.europa.eu/uedocs/cmsUpload/mediEN.pdf
[2 December 2006].

European Union Factsheet, The Euro-Mediterranean Partneship, available [online]: http://www.consilium.europa.eu/uedocs/cmsUpload/MEDIT.pdf [2 December 2006].

European Union Factsheet, EU-US Cooperation in Iraq, available [online]: http://www.consilium.europa.eu/uedocs/cmsUpload/1Iraq_final_150605.pdf [2 December ].

http://domino.un.org/UNISPAL.nsf/2ee9468747556b2d85256cf60060d2a6/fef015e 8b1a1e5a685256d810059d922!OpenDocument [4 December 2006].

http://www.mideastweb.org/mitchell_report.htm [4 December 2006].

http://ec.europa.eu/comm/external_relations/gulf_cooperation/intro/index.htm [4 December 2006].

Draft Final Report on an EU Strategic Partnership with the Mediterranean and the Middle East, available [online]: http://register.consilium.eu.int/pdf/en/04/st10/ st10246.en04.pdf [4 December 2006].

http://www.asam.org.tr/tr/index.asp [12 December 2006].

http://www.setav.org [12 December 2006].

http://www.usak.org.tr/home.asp [12 December 2006].

http://webarsiv.hurriyet.com.tr/2003/02/27/254366.asp [13 December 2006].

http://www.hazine.gov.tr/stat/yabser/ybs_bulten_ekim2006.pdf [30 January 2007].

# Index

1975 Helsinki Act 65

ABGS 156, 169
Aegean 160, 163, 170
Afghanistan 56, 94, 104, 112, 136, 152
Alliance of Civilizations 79, 103, 176
Annan 30, 79, 99, 144, 164, 176
Arafat 66–8, 120–21, 127–30
Asad 116–18, 141
Atatürk 92

Baghdad Pact 92, 107, 109–10, 125
Balkans 26, 33, 39, 43, 47, 56, 64, 82, 87–8, 104–5, 114–15, 155, 161, 170, 176–7
Barak 66–7, 125
Barcelona Process 60, 65, 70
Barroso 90–91
Belgium 33, 35, 37, 67
Black Sea 82, 95
Blair 49, 69
Bush 69, 75, 95, 129, 137, 139, 175

Caucasia 82, 87
Cem 83, 85–6, 97, 109, 127–8, 134, 136
Central Asia 86, 102, 105, 118, 146, 174
CFSP 20, 23, 25–9, 31–2, 34, 39, 40, 43–53, 55–7, 65, 67, 69, 75, 77–9, 150–52, 154, 157–8, 160–63, 171, 174–5, 177
Chirac 127
Clinton 66, 72, 126, 175
Cold War 1, 18–19, 32–3, 37, 43–4, 46, 55, 59, 61–5, 71–4, 76, 81–2, 85, 87–8, 92–6, 101–2, 104, 107–17, 119–21, 123–5, 127, 129, 131, 133, 135, 137, 139, 141, 143, 145, 150, 155, 159, 161, 166, 168, 170, 172, 175, 177
Commission 8, 12, 20, 45, 47–8, 52, 57, 90, 98, 108, 126, 143, 151–2, 157
Committee of Union and Progress 84
Common positions 28, 31, 47–8, 51–2, 57, 151–2

Copenhagen Criteria 90, 97–8, 136, 148, 165–6
Council 12, 20, 34, 39, 47–52, 61, 63–4, 69, 86–7, 92–3, 98–9, 103, 121, 127–8, 134, 136, 138–9, 148, 150, 157, 160
Crimean War 84
Cyprus 1, 30, 39, 70, 76, 78, 82–3, 88, 90, 92–4, 97, 99, 101–2, 104, 107, 110–12, 114, 120, 137, 152, 154, 159, 160, 162–6, 168–71, 173
Çiller 121, 133

Demirel 67, 96, 122, 125–6, 133
Democrat Party 89, 92
Denmark 29, 32, 35–7, 39, 75, 103, 147, 152, 156, 159, 173

Eastern Question, 88
Ecevit 98, 126, 127
Egypt 67, 69, 109, 111–12, 117, 122, 125, 129, 137, 138
EPC 26, 28, 34, 37, 38, 39, 40, 45, 46, 52, 61, 160
Erdoğan 100, 102, 104, 129–30, 137, 140–2, 144, 167
ESDI 48–9
Euphrates 117, 131
Europeanization 1, 11, 21–7, 29, 30–41, 54, 84, 128, 147–55, 157, 159–65, 168–71

Fellujah 143
France 29, 32–3, 35, 37, 39, 40, 43–4, 48, 66, 69, 72–5, 109, 127, 134, 137, 147, 152, 158–60, 169–70, 173

GCC 69–70
Germany 29, 33, 35–7, 44, 66, 72–5, 134, 152, 156, 158–60, 173
Golan Heights 113, 124
Greece 29, 32–4, 36–9, 54, 76, 97, 102, 114, 116–17, 124, 128, 134, 146–8, 151, 154, 156–7, 159–60, 162–3, 165, 172, 174

Gulf War  60, 65, 68, 72, 95–6, 107, 114,
       116, 119–20, 123, 131–2, 135, 138
Gül  100, 102–3, 128–30, 137, 139, 141–4

Haas  7
Habur  134
Hamas  69, 129, 152, 167
Hungary  75, 173

IMF  97, 102, 149
Iran  72–4, 79, 81, 105, 111–14, 116–20,
       122, 130–2, 138, 141, 151–2, 167, 176
Iraq  1, 32, 34, 43, 51, 55–6, 60, 68, 71–9,
       88, 90, 99–101, 104, 107, 109–10,
       113–14, 116, 118–20, 123–4, 129–45,
       149–50, 152, 1545, 159–61, 165–74,
       176–7
Ireland  29, 33, 35–7, 39, 46, 148, 152, 157,
       160
Israel  34, 37, 60–61, 63–4, 66–71, 74–8,
       94, 97, 108–14, 116–17, 119–30, 133,
       155, 158, 167, 172, 174–5
Italy  29, 33–4, 37, 74–5, 148, 154, 157–8,
       173
İncirlik  110–11
İnönü  92, 108

Javier Solana  49, 67, 157
Jerusalem  112, 121, 124, 130
Johnson Letter  93, 111, 159
joint actions  31, 39, 47–8

KDP  132–4
Khomeini  118
Kosovo  50–51, 73, 104

Laeken  50
Lebanon  63, 69, 79, 110–11, 113, 152, 176

Maastricht  23, 25, 44, 46, 56
Macedonia  39, 49, 51–2, 105, 160
Madrid Peace Conference  64
Mahmoud Abbas  129–30
Mediterranean  30, 39, 47, 60, 63–5, 70, 72,
       79, 82, 105, 120, 175
Menderes  92, 109–10
MFA  36, 169
Middle East  1–2, 34, 39, 43, 46–7, 49, 51,
       59–69, 71–9, 82–4, 86–8, 96, 100, 102,
       105, 107–17, 119–21, 123, 125, 127–9,
       131, 133–5, 137, 139, 141, 143, 145–6,
       149, 152, 158–9, 165–6, 170–7

Mitchell Committee  67
Monnet  6
Morocco  39
MÜSİAD  154

NATO  34, 43–4, 46, 48–52, 64, 73–6, 81–2,
       92, 96, 108, 111, 120, 128, 139–40,
       150, 152, 159, 173, 176
Netanyahu  66, 123–4
NSC  99, 153

OMC  32
Operation Northern Watch  136
Operation Provide Comfort  135
Osama bin Laden  68
OsCE  65–6, 81, 159
OsloAgreement  64
Ottoman  81–7, 92, 107, 149, 166
Öcalan  1, 38, 97, 111, 116–17, 123–5,
       133–4, 136, 142, 177
Özal  94–6, 100, 113, 116, 130, 132–3, 145

Palestine  37, 43, 67, 69–70, 75, 77–8, 101,
       108, 113, 119, 121–2, 124–30, 145,
       152, 155, 158, 166–7, 172, 174–5, 177
Palestinian Authority  62, 66, 69, 71, 77,
       125, 175
Palestinian-Israeli Conflict  74
Papandreou  38
PASOK  38
PKK  1, 38, 75–6, 88, 90, 96, 102, 116–20,
       123–4, 131–6, 141–3, 145, 172–3
PLO  63, 112–13, 119–20, 129
Poland  75, 173
Portugal  29, 33, 35–7, 75, 148–9, 152,
       156–7, 173
PUK  132–3

Road Map  68–9, 128
Russia  47, 68, 72, 74, 84, 102, 114, 118,
       134, 137, 145–6, 173–4

Saddam  61, 71, 114, 132, 134, 140
Saudi Arabia  112, 138, 145
Sevres syndrome  86, 149, 166
Sharon  67–8, 75, 77, 126–8, 175
Simitis  38
Soviet Union  43, 61, 84, 88, 93–4, 96,
       111–12, 114–15, 120
Spain  29, 33–7, 39, 74–5, 79, 103, 148–50,
       156–58, 160, 173, 176
St Malo  49

Sweden 29, 33, 35, 38, 54, 152, 159–60
Syria 102, 116–17, 124, 137

Taha Yassin Ramazan 131, 138
TESEV 154–5, 168–9
TFP 1–2, 81, 107, 115, 134
Thatcher 37
Tigris 131
TİKA 89, 130
TOBB 103, 130, 154
Turcomans 141, 143–4
TÜSİAD 103, 154

UK 29, 34, 37, 44, 54–55, 66, 75, 109, 137, 159, 173

UN 34, 37, 39, 51, 63–4, 68, 72, 79, 93, 96, 103–4, 108–9, 111–13, 124, 126–8, 134, 138, 144, 152, 159–60, 163, 176
UNIFIL 79, 176
UNMIK 104
USA 1, 33–4, 39, 55, 61, 63–4, 67–71, 73, 83, 94, 99, 100, 135, 141, 143, 145, 173
USSR 38, 59, 62, 73, 83, 95, 108–9, 159

WEU 38, 46, 48
World War I 92, 109, 149, 167
Wye River Memorandum 66

Yugoslavia 32, 38, 48, 73, 88, 95, 104, 158